Praise for

red helicopter

a parable for our times

"*red helicopter* is a transformative experience. James Rhee's story is a must read for anyone, of any age, who wishes to think, act, and lead with balance, agility, and wisdom."

—Jay Shetty, #1 *New York Times* bestselling author of *Think Like a Monk* and *8 Rules of Love*

"*red helicopter* is a breath of fresh air in a cluttered world of self-improvement and business literature. For anyone looking to find purpose in the chaos and to embrace life's deeper connections, *red helicopter* is a guiding light. I enthusiastically endorse this book for anyone eager to elevate their life and career with heartfelt authenticity and clear-eyed vision."

—Marshall Goldsmith, *New York Times* bestselling author of *The Earned Life, Triggers,* and *What Got You Here Won't Get You There*

"*red helicopter* is both a GPS for your soul and a superpower to fuel your journey to purpose. In a hustle-bent world, it stops time and takes you from where you are to where you aim to go. If you're ready to evolve, own your life, and excel in possibility, this is the book you've been waiting for."

—Mikki Taylor, award-winning journalist, former editor-at-large for *Essence* magazine, and author of *Force of Beauty: A Newark Family Memoir*

"Imagine if your habits were infused with meaning. This parable for our times will inspire you to transform yourself and your teams as they lead with integrity, agility, and courage."

—Charles Duhigg, *New York Times* bestselling author of *The Power of Habit, Smarter Faster Better,* and *Supercommunicators*

"*red helicopter* captures the essence of the human condition and the role it must play in success. James Rhee has captured the core of a curriculum that all schools teaching the principles of business—and life—should implement as we prepare for the future."

—Dr. Wayne A. I. Frederick, President Emeritus and Charles R. Drew Professor of Surgery, Howard University

"With experience and deep insight, James Rhee redefines the path toward success. Through masterful storytelling and experience, *red helicopter* elevates kindness, joy, and goodwill to their rightful place. Rhee shows us a better way to strive, one with our deep values at the center. A wonderful book that all of us who are driven and strivers desperately need to read."

—Steve Magness, *New York Times* bestselling author of *Do Hard Things*

red
helicopter

a parable for our times

a parable for our times

red
helicopter

lead change with kindness
(plus a little math)

James Rhee

HarperOne
An Imprint of HarperCollins*Publishers*

HarperCollins books may be purchased for educational, business, or sales promotional use. For information, please email the Special Markets Department at SPsales@harpercollins.com.

FIRST EDITION

Designed by Janet Evans-Scanlon
Illustrations by Heyon Cho

Library of Congress Cataloging-in-Publication Data has been applied for.

ISBN 978-0-06-331714-7

24 25 26 27 28 LBC 5 4 3 2 1

For Mom and Dad.
To the child inside each of us.

The voice of your conscience can always be singled out above the noise of your other wishes, because it always wants something seemingly useless, seemingly senseless, seemingly incomprehensible, but at the same time something actually beautiful and good, which can be achieved only through effort.

—LEO TOLSTOY

contents

red
helicopter

a parable for our times

Prelude

We all have a special story from childhood—one that can serve as both a beacon during times of darkness and a reminder of hardship and suffering during times of joy. Our perspective on the story's meaning can change with age, and also depending on the context. The reasons *why* we cling to a particular childhood story can remain elusive. Mine were, for almost forty years. But when its meaning finally emerged, my little childhood story helped change the course not only of *my* life, but of countless other lives around the world. All it took was kindness, a little math, and the unexpected friendship of a group of women who gave me permission to rediscover myself, and the courage to sing our collective song aloud.

My story happened when I was five years old and in kindergarten. One morning during drop-off, an unannounced visitor showed up in my classroom. It was the father of one of my good friends. The face of my all-time favorite teacher, Mrs. Griffith, was alight with anticipation as she called my name. Time felt like it stood still for that one moment. The sounds of happy chaos faded, and I felt the weight of many curious eyes watching me on a makeshift stage. Then my friend's dad handed me a small white bag containing a wrapped present. Inside was a toy red helicopter.

In that moment, I didn't fully understand why he was giving it to me, but I could sense that he was happy and sad at the same time. I remember feeling uncomfortable under the intense spotlight and the emotion filling the air. How did I respond? Well, I ran around in a fit of frenzied excitement, clutching my new toy, with my friend in close pursuit. In retrospect, I am quite certain that I never said "thank you" to my friend's dad.

Did I show the toy to my parents when I got home, or did they notice it first? My memories are fuzzy. I was five, after all.

"Why did they give you this red helicopter, James?" they asked.

I was nervous. I answered honestly. "I'm not sure."

There was a long, confused pause. My mom and dad looked like they were worried I had done something wrong. Maybe I had taken it from my classroom without asking. Or maybe they thought *they* had done something wrong. The United States was often a baffling place for my mom and dad, who were first-generation Korean immigrants. They didn't always have a handle on local customs. To put it in musical terms, they were understandably sometimes a beat or two behind, a half measure off. Maybe children in this country exchanged gifts during the holiday season? Maybe every five-year-old had received a red helicopter that day?

There were twenty or so kids in my kindergarten class at Minnesauke Elementary School. Every morning until the day I left for college, my mom packed me a lunch in a brown paper bag, usually deli meats on a kaiser roll with lots of mayonnaise, a snack, and a fruity drink. I was a friendly kid, an equal-opportunity liker, and I generally got along well with all my classmates. This particular friend often came to school without any lunch, so I would share mine with him. Why wouldn't I? I had enough, and he didn't. It wasn't a big deal.

Don't ask me how, but my parents soon got to the root of the red helicopter mystery (I am pretty sure Mrs. Griffith had something to do with it). One day, they called me into our tiny family room, where they were sitting, and gestured to me to stand in front of them. I did as I was told. My stomach hurt. I didn't know whether I was in trouble or where this might be going. My dad could be very Socratic—one syncopated question after the next, giving me space to think about and come up with an answer, right or wrong. Excellent preparation, it turned out, for law school. But a little stressful for a five-year-old.

"Why did you share your food with your friend?" my dad asked. So I explained, worried now that I was in trouble for somehow creating unnecessary financial pressure on my family or displaying ingratitude toward my mom, who always woke up early to prepare lunch for *her* son.

It turns out I wasn't in trouble at all. Just the opposite. My parents told me that my friend had lost his mom before the start of the school year. Overnight, his dad had become a single parent, responsible for four young children, with my friend being the youngest. He didn't have the wherewithal, financial or otherwise, to pack *his* son lunch every day. My friend must have told his family that his friend James sometimes shared his lunch with him on the days he came to school without one. Wanting to thank me, his dad had invested the time to buy a toy red helicopter and to show up to give it to me in person.

When my parents told me all this, I was confused. I felt sad for my friend. I couldn't imagine what it would be like to lose a mom. I also felt good about what I'd done. It appeared as a warm, good ache spreading deeply inside my chest. You know the feeling I'm talking about, right? But I was a little surprised at my dad's emotional reaction to what I'd done. Why *wouldn't* I share my lunch with my friend?

Part of my confusion stemmed from my dad's inability, or reluctance, to verbalize complex emotions, especially those relating to matters of the heart. Yes, there was an English-Korean language barrier. But I think the real driving force was my dad's discomfort with showing much emotion around his two sons. Maybe that explained the whole Socratic methodology. To put a finer point on it, one of my prized possessions to this day is a copy of *Aesop's Fables* he bought me when I was little. In the stories, animals talk to one another while playing out morality tales. My dad's intent was for me to learn and then apply to my own life the metaphors I read about in those stories. He and I never read those stories aloud together.

More than using words, then, my dad generally communicated matters of the heart nonverbally. As a result, as I got older and after I moved away, there were times when we had a difficult time communicating at all. Maybe that's why the look in his eyes in our family room that day is one I will never forget. A few years later, he and I were at my school bus stop when he pulled out a letter that had come in the mail that day. I had just been accepted into the gifted and talented program in our public school district, the letter said. He didn't congratulate me, but I remember the skip in my dad's step, the strong smell of his cologne, and the pride in his eyes.

But even that didn't compare to how proud he was when he

asked me about the red helicopter. My dad was a pediatrician. My mom was a nurse. Good grades and test results mattered, but not as much as how we behaved. Kindness, caring about others, and doing what was right were expected. But so were achievement and success, as the world conventionally defines them—money, titles, credentials, status. It was an apparent contradiction I would spend the next four decades struggling to reconcile during an era when money and power flexed their dominance over humanity.

Where is the red helicopter now? I don't know. It met the fate of most childhood toys—lost, given away, thrown out. When high school ended, I went off to Harvard College. After college, I taught high school for two years and then enrolled at Harvard Law School, thinking that I might become a public defender. Suffocating under a mountain of student debt, and with *high school teacher* and *law school graduate* on my résumé, I made an unlikely and somewhat improbable pivot into investment banking and private equity. I flew in private planes, helped manage billions of dollars, and grew and fed that résumé until it gleamed and would have made any set of parents, particularly ones who were immigrants, proud.

During those years, in my late twenties and thirties, I forgot all about the red helicopter. Or maybe more accurately, I buried that part of me. I will go so far as to say that the red helicopter, and everything it symbolized about my immigrant parents, my upbringing, and their value system, felt like a burden, a constraint. Sometimes even an embarrassment. Sure, I thought about it now and again, but in general there was no room for it in my life and career. Or so I thought.

Then, at a crucial time in my early forties, the red helicopter reappeared. It served as a signal fire for me when I was literally and figuratively in the darkness and feeling alone, and the entire world was telling me I had lost my mind—all while my dad was taking his last breaths. Over the next few years, the true meaning and lesson of the red helicopter unfolded and unfurled. I had resisted it on many occasions—too childish—but at the right moment, after I had walked away from my professional life in Boston and my identity as a "private equity guy" to help lead a broken, shell-shocked clothing company for plus-size, moderate-income Black women living in urban neighborhoods across the United States, the red helicopter resurfaced, and with it all the childhood experiences, values, and beliefs my parents had embedded in me. The red helicopter, and what it stood for, revealed itself gradually at first, and finally, triumphantly. It was at the heart of an unprecedented transformation of a business that on the surface couldn't have been an unlikelier fit for me—an improbable reinvention that both shocked and inspired the global investment and retail-consumer worlds.

You read that right. Seven years later, this story landed me on a TED conference stage, the covers of leading publications, and the podiums of the world's most prestigious industry conferences. It also generated laughably high, triple-digit financial returns for investors of FirePine Group, the impact investment platform I had founded several years earlier. Though many years have passed since I left the company, the ripple effects of the positive impact we created are still expanding and now reverberating in circles well beyond just the business community.

The real impact wasn't the *what*—the result, or the outcome; it was the *how*—the process itself. It was the *how* that ultimately changed people's minds and made a frenzied world pause, pay close attention, think, and *feel*. It was the *how* that linked together the lives of my parents with countless people, of all races and ethnicities, across the United States and the globe. It was the *how* that gently pushed me to acknowledge that so much of what I thought was truth wasn't truth, at least not exactly. Especially with regard to my mom, whose courage and leadership I had underestimated and taken for granted. It is this *how* that I am sharing with you.

The red helicopter is my story, but I'm guessing that you have your own red helicopter story. My story, and this book, is about how the pure, commonsense things we intuitively knew to be true as children are central to understanding who we are and how we should treat one another as human beings. It's about finding the courage to face down a world that would prefer we *forget* these truths and blur them with new rules and norms of behavior contrary to the ones we all know deep down are *right*. It's about challenging the powers-that-be (even if you are, like me, a card-carrying member of that power structure) and redefining words and concepts like *success*, *kindness, balance, growth, leadership,* and *goodwill* so that they better reflect our shared humanity. But, at its core, this is a story of how the simplest truths that we knew as children can change the trajectory of our lives and, yes, even our businesses. And how, for maybe both life and business, true success centers around balancing life, money, and joy through the creation and measurement of goodwill, and all of the connectedness that comes with it.

So take a walk with me. This book is designed for families, parents, and their children, as well as for any leader accountable for the livelihood and well-being of others. Although the narrative of this book tracks the arc of a gritty business transformation, the story and its teachings are about human beings working hard to make better lives for themselves and their loved ones. For some of you, this might be your first glimpse into the mysterious inner workings of private equity, big law, and other power centers. For all of you, my hope is that you learn, or relearn, a few valuable lessons about how to create a more sustainable balance between life, money, and joy for both yourself and others.

This is not a book of lists. There is no magic formula or elixir that gives you the three or five remedies for all that might ail you. The answers are embedded in the story, in the chorus of different voices and emotions (and a few formulas and frameworks). I'm not going to tell you how to feel, but I will at times pause and tell you what you need to know. I will introduce you to key principles underlying subjects like accounting, finance, behavioral science, economics, and corporate law (trust me, you need to know this stuff, and so do your children—and for some reason, these subjects are generally not taught in school—well before they enter the workforce as adults). But, more importantly, by weaving them into a simple story, I will show you how they all interact with one another in very human terms. Feel free to make the connections to your own life—or not—in whichever ways suit you best. Think of this book as a fable of sorts, though there are no talking horses or sheep. Given that people are involved, the word "parable" is a more fitting description. As hard as it will be to believe, however, everything in this story happened on the biggest stages of capitalism and society.

This book proceeds in a purposeful order, an arc of discovery, perspective change, and emergence. Of the ten chapters, nine are arranged in three distinct triplets (if this were a musical, or a song, chapter 7 is the "bridge"). Each triplet is a mini-book or, if you're a fan of theatrical musicals, an act in a much bigger show.

In "Act I: Life" (chapters 1–3), we set the stage by introducing a diverse group of actors and the challenges they faced as individuals and as a collective across a broad span of time. It is a convergence of seemingly disconnected experiences. There are glimmers of hope and strands of truth in a sea of chaos and hardship.

In "Act II: Money" (chapters 4–6), you learn alongside the undersized and underresourced cast as they join together to make sense of the systems undergirding capital-*L* Life and apply a few integrated basics of bankruptcy law, accounting, finance, and operations, on their way to accomplishing something astonishing. There were subtle and yet profound changes in perspective and behavior made possible by kindness plus a little math—just some simple addition, subtraction, and multiplication.

In the "Bridge" (chapter 7), we immerse ourselves in the emotions and feelings of the concepts we learned about in Act II. We do so by sharing in the bittersweetness of that intangible and shared asset we call goodwill.

In "Act III: Joy" (chapters 8–10), we use what we have learned together to celebrate the true value of friendship and human connectedness by exploring alternative ways to measure the success of a person, an organization, and even a society. If this sounds too complicated and difficult, the goal, weirdly enough, is to get you to focus on what you already know to be true. I believe that much of this wisdom is already inside you. In the end, I hope that you feel that this book provides you the space and the tools to rediscover these truths on your own terms, at your own pace.

The triplet design is there for a reason. In this sequence, a creative-minded person might note the act of creation itself. A spiritually minded reader might recognize the stages of an awakening. A teacher or parent might see the makings of a next-generation curriculum. A business-minded reader might glimpse a reinvention or turnaround process. No matter what your lens is (and you probably have more than one), I'm confident this design will lead you to the same right path. My goal, simply, is to help set you free—and to do whatever I can to help you lift off and *fly*.

Through the pages of this book, I hope you give yourself permission to look at the business of life, and the life of business, in a different way. To perhaps rediscover or rethink a few of your perceptions and perspectives. To find comfort in our shared connectedness, and reassurance about its potential for positivity and growth. This isn't a self-help book, and it isn't a business book, and at the same time, it's both. Nor is it a book about music, or philosophy, or leadership, or the meaning of loyalty, or what it means to lose your parents, though we will brush up against all these subjects and more. Maybe this book is best described as a celebration of humanity.

If nothing else, I hope you finish this book realizing that the boundaries that separate who we are at home and who we are at work are as artificial and learned as the constraints some of you may feel are pinning you down. Like anything invented, those divisions and restrictions can be rethought, reimagined, and improved. Simple is often best. And when it's done right, simple can create a huge impact with shocking ease.

Maybe you're at the same point in your life as I was at the start of this story: fighting off a low-level malaise, a disquiet that doesn't have a name; feeling alone, disconnected, out of sorts, not unhappy exactly, but questioning certain assumptions that so many people around you seem to take for granted; sensing that the rules don't seem right, and wondering, who made them anyway? Is it you or is it the world that sometimes doesn't seem altogether real? Are you out of your mind, or is everyone else? Maybe you are even a little bit frightened. You could be any age, in fact, trying to make sense of how your lowercase-*l* life intersects with capital-*L* Life, how your past connects to your present, how your present connects to your future, and why they don't always match up. Guess what, you're *not* alone.

Finally, this is a book about change, and how the most transformative and sustainable change lies within us all. Ironically, we just have to slow down long enough to allow for that change to emerge. Meaning, sometimes staying still is the most important action we can take. As we get older, it's easy to overthink an overcomplicated world, and forget the natural wisdom and values of humanity we understood intuitively as children. Easy to forget, too, that the right thing to do and the right solution to any problem are, most of the time, right in front of us. Simple, right? But remember, simple can be hard.

Despite everything else going on in your life and in the world, I hope this book provides hope. But not just any hope. Hope that is grounded in reality, based on a story that shows what is possible even when it seems like everything is hopeless. It shows that no matter what the world insists on telling us, the pure, commonsense values, the knowing, we felt as children were right all along. We just need a process, a framework, and a bit of knowledge to have the courage to rediscover them, and to trust that warm, good ache deep inside our chest. We just need to find and trust our red helicopter story, and then lift off with the help of a few friends, the old but especially the new.

Act 1

Life

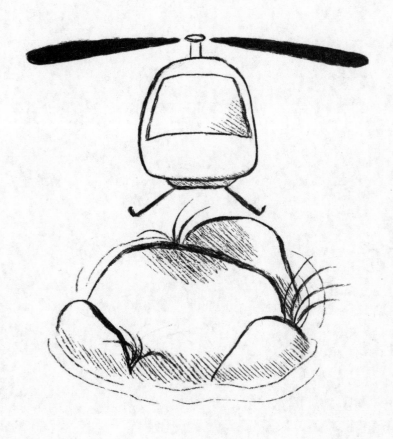

chapter 1

present

A helicopter can land in difficult terrain.

Some people have their revelation in a storybook setting—by an ocean, along a remote mountain pass, under a shady tree. Not me. Mine took place inside a grimy, imposing distribution center with a two-floor office slapped onto it, located in, of all places, Secaucus, New Jersey, fewer than ten miles away from Midtown Manhattan.

The complex was cavernous, and at the same time suffocating. The color palette was mouse gray and mud brown. There were almost no unimpeded sightlines and not much visibility, maybe intentionally. A sea of plastic chairs with faux-leather backrests; dusty file cabinets crammed with two decades of contracts on yellowing paper; cubicle after cubicle separated by imposing partitions. Always a faint stench of industrial soap, failing to cloak the smell of mildew and urine from the bathrooms. There were insects, too—urban-tough water bugs and cockroaches. For around 140 people, this corporate office was where they spent forty hours a week of their lives—all ages, genders, and races, a pretty good sample of the United States of America.

One other thing—there was no Wi-Fi, believe it or not. (It was 2013, by the way.) The only real perk, in fact, was an industrial-size warmer to reheat the employees' packed lunches. This circa-1970s relic sat in a windowless cafeteria, a room that doubled as the site of the rare town hall meeting.

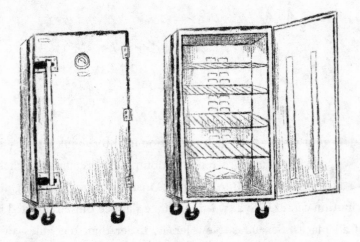

Secaucus is built on a landfill. The name comes from an Algonquian word that means "place of snakes." It's a sprawl of car dealerships, outlet shops, and fast-food and fast-casual restaurants. It's a living, breathing shrine to capitalism, American style. A flash of steel guardrails keeps the traffic moving in and out of the city, which is also populated by low-rise, modular, and uninspiring office buildings. I was to call this place home for the next six months of my life.

I was there on a short-term "salvage" mission, having just agreed to serve as the interim leader of Ashley Stewart, a company on life support. The key word was *interim*. I would be there for only six months, and then I could return to my family and my "high-flying" life and identity outside Boston. For many reasons, I didn't want the company to die. In order to take on this job, I had to resign from my position as non-executive chairman of the board of directors, which is a standard role for a private equity owner to play. It would not be an overstatement to say that my assuming the day-to-day leadership role, no matter how interim, was borderline shocking.

Even beyond this, interim or not, it was a wildly unlikely mismatch between a new leader and a company. Ashley Stewart was a fashion retailer that served plus-size, predominantly middle- and lower-income Black women. Sizes 12 and up. Its stores were in malls, strip malls, and downtown neighborhoods across the United States. With very few exceptions, the workers operating those stores resembled their customers. I was a forty-two-year-old Korean American private equity guy, the son of two immigrants. Though I had leadership experience, I had never been the full-time leader of an operating company. For the previous thirteen years, I had been a senior investment professional in private equity, which means that my firms were paid lots of money by sophisticated investors to own companies on paper and hire executives to run them on a day-to-day basis, with the end goal of selling them for a profit. There was one more small matter. Let's just say that no one has *ever* suggested I have an eye for—or any personal sense of—fashion.

To be fair, my experience was not entirely irrelevant. I had invested in many retail-consumer companies and brands at various inflection points in their life cycles, but it would be a farce to say that I was the right person for the job. Running a board of directors meeting is very different from running the operations of a company.

Owning a car doesn't make you a mechanic, just as buying a new house doesn't mean you know anything about architecture. I'm fairly sure I wore pleated khakis on my first day of work at Ashley Stewart.

Basically, I was one of the least qualified people on earth to assume leadership of a defeated, demoralized company specializing in affordable head-to-toe fashion for a certain segment of plus-size Black women.

I was also dealing with personal stuff. My dad was in and out of a New Jersey hospital forty miles away with a feeding tube lodged in his stomach. My mom was by his side, overseeing his care. My mom had a nursing degree from Seoul National University and had worked for a brief time after immigrating to America. She retired from nursing when I was born, but many years later she got recertified—in English, too, her second language—and went back to work in a Long Island veterans' home, treating ailing soldiers who had fought for her country and saved her life as a little girl during the Korean War.

My dad was in the final two years of what would ultimately be a gruesome and unwinnable fifteen-year struggle with Parkinson's disease. Care was expensive, and my parents relied on the New York State health insurance my mom was vested into through her work at the veterans' home. It was the first time I realized our family had had little to no healthcare insurance when my siblings and I were growing up. Instead, my pediatrician dad had depended on a barter system with other doctors in the area. Needless to say, that barter system wouldn't have been able to handle the expense of treating Parkinson's during a very different era of medicine and society.

My parents were confused by my decision to become the leader of this failed and discredited business catering to plus-size Black women. *What are you doing, James?* What my dad was really asking was, *Why are you ripping up the life Mom and I wanted you to have in this country?* They had lived through the Korean War when they were children, after all. They had given up their lives in Korea and come to the US knowing no one, and barely speaking the language, in search of hope, a new life for themselves, and a future for *their* children.

During the early days at Ashley Stewart, as I sat in what can only be described as a sensory-deprivation zone, I felt so alone on every dimension. Geography. Profession. Gender. Race. I couldn't do anything to fix my dad, either. At least my older brother was a doctor. Me? Well, I knew how to make money investing in private companies. *Great. Way to go, James.* My résumé, one credential after another, a tasting menu of prestigious schools and jobs that concealed the back-breaking work and student debt involved in getting there—it had come at an exhausting cost—meant very little here. Neither did my Rolodex of connections. I wasn't Black. I wasn't plus-size. I wasn't "urban." I wasn't female. I wasn't a retail executive. I wasn't fashionable. In short, on the surface, everything in the world the company and its employees needed for me to be, I wasn't. I'd go so far as to say that I worried my assets would be potential liabilities there. *Two things were dying in New Jersey. And I wasn't qualified to save either.*

Worse, my family wasn't around, as my wife, Meg, and our three young children were at home outside Boston, two hundred miles away. This meant finding nearby lodging. Instead of commuting to Secaucus from a chic Manhattan hotel, I was staying at a local hotel. It felt hypocritical not to. The locks were flimsy; the sheets, threadbare; the bath towels, rags. After work, on the way to the hotel, I would eat dinner, usually at around midnight or 1 a.m., mostly fried and processed foods, almost always accompanied by a large fizzy soda and a side of French fries. That first month, I gained ten pounds. *Why am I doing this*? I thought as I scarfed down all that junk.

My friends were nowhere to be found, either. I had even lost a few. One board member even resigned shortly after my arrival in Secaucus. *What are you doing, James?* was the typical response. (They must have been talking to my parents.) *James, listen: You are a private equity guy. You know how to play the game, and you're good at it. Why are you sidelining yourself? You know, don't you, that this will follow you forever? You will have no goodwill in the deal world. What kind of company is this anyway? Never heard of it. Sounds sketchy.*

In fact, why *was* I there? The surface answer was that I felt accountable to my former firm and its investors. Only three years earlier, Ashley Stewart had filed for bankruptcy after nearly two decades of corporate futility. Failed execution by wave after wave of retail executives, backed by various private equity firms deploying the standard playbook, had resulted in nothing more than a bloated company hemorrhaging cash and contending with lawsuits, unpaid vendors, and antiquated technology. As a private equity investor, I was the person who had backed the then-existing management team to save Ashley Stewart from that bankruptcy and give it one last shot. My firm had installed me as non-executive chairman of the board to oversee the full-time professional operators from behind a desk in Boston, as is customary. But here we were again. By my calculations, the company was potentially only six weeks away from liquidation. What's liquidation? It happens when a company is worth more dead than alive. The body of the company—it's even called a *corpus*—is chopped up and diced into smaller parts. Every organ or limb, no matter how trivial, goes to the highest bidder. Jobs and people are beside the point. In short, it's the business equivalent of death. A dismal death.

As a seasoned deal veteran with a lot of experience investing money in struggling and down-and-out companies, I thought maybe I could buy the company some time by wringing out some loose change, avert liquidation by gently placing it into an orderly Chapter 11 bankruptcy, and entice a larger company to save frontline jobs by buying the neighborhood stores. Doing so, I reasoned, would also likely maximize cash proceeds for existing shareholders, meaning, my former employer and investors. Once that was done, I could go home and resume my life outside Boston. That was my *intent*. The situation required leadership—even if the leadership came from a strange source.

The executive team was in denial and battling one another. It seemed they were more concerned about deflecting blame and protecting their reputations than facing the harsh truth that no money was left. The board of directors just wanted the truth so that we could come up with a plan. So I resigned as chairman, put my life on hold, and signed up for six months to lead Ashley Stewart as a full-time operating executive.

Worse, the company was being besieged by angry clothing vendors who had gotten burned in that first bankruptcy just three years before. The distribution and logistics company, which received and shipped out the merchandise, was now threatening to shut off their services until its overdue invoices got paid. A few months later, I ended up having to hire an armed police officer to patrol the downstairs lobby, with its bulletproof glass, chipped tiling, and sad-sack carpeting. He was the first responder in case a vendor tried to assault an employee in the parking lot, which flooded nearly two feet during heavy rainstorms. This was how tense and fraught the situation was.

The whole thing was like a horror movie. This was capitalism, American style, at its worst—and there was more to come. The restructuring lawyers and advisors, members of the "professional class," hadn't yet appeared to take their pound of flesh. This is the ugly, unhinged side of the capital markets that the public rarely sees. I was a member of that professional class, too. I was well aware that US bankruptcy laws prioritize the interests of financial capital and corporate entities, not uninformed workers, let alone communities that benefit from the social dynamics created by local commerce.

In retrospect, there were other reasons why I was there—reasons that went beyond professional accountability and proximity to my dying dad. Maybe I was looking for something I wasn't getting from my private equity identity and life. I loved what I did, but sometimes I didn't love *how* I did it. Maybe I had an instinct that a jewel was hidden in the rubble. Maybe the obvious mismatch in firepower between the core workforce and customers of Ashley Stewart and the professional world I was part of brought up certain memories from growing up, not least the struggles of my own immigrant parents and the troubles they had experienced fitting in, being seen and acknowledged, and just plain surviving. In the end, it was all those things, and more. I just knew that I didn't want this company to liquidate.

But at the time, I couldn't put my finger on why I felt so strongly about it. All I knew, as I prepared for my town hall speech on the first day of work, was that I remembered the story of the red helicopter. Yup—*that* was my revelation.

I hadn't thought about it for years. It was irrelevant. Too cute— corny even—and even a little embarrassing. Childish, too. Overly idealistic. A branch snag in my otherwise relentless pursuit of success. If you're a man, especially an Asian American man, who attended prestigious schools and works in finance, at some point it's no longer cool, or a badge of honor, to be the red helicopter kid. From experience, I knew that adulthood and towering office buildings meant hard numbers, suits, briefcases, and turf wars. Not little red helicopters.

Why look to the past when your life is supposed to be a straight line, up and to the right? Isn't that what we are taught growth and success look like? The red helicopter was a toy from my childhood, and I had a family of my own now. I was a "big shot." I and everybody else I knew were busy racing around accomplishing "things," making money, competing for titles, trying to get to *that place*. Occasionally I had thought about the red helicopter, only to brush the memory aside.

So imagine my surprise when it showed up in my head. A small plastic helicopter whose rotors I used to flick with my fingers to make it spin and "fly." Mostly I remembered how it made me feel— that warm, good ache deep inside my chest. My friend's dad had rewarded kindness without cheapening it. With an object and a simple, intentional set of actions, he had made kindness tangible. He had recognized and rewarded the little "system," nurtured by

Mrs. Griffith, that encouraged a mutually positive relationship between two little boys in a public school classroom somewhere in eastern Long Island, New York.

Maybe this memory came back into my head because my dad was dying. Or maybe it was because I was about to embark on something so new, bizarre, and uncharted, so I had the space to allow for reflection. All I knew was that the red helicopter felt like a lifeline at a time and in a place that otherwise felt hopeless.

I didn't know that over the next seven years (yes, those six months turned into seven years), I would reimagine and redefine a lot of things I thought I knew but didn't. I would rediscover certain truths I believe are inside us all. I would grow to understand the difference between knowledge and wisdom, and the limitations of the systems in which I belonged, and the unnecessary suffering they inflict on the most vulnerable members of society. I would reevaluate and redefine the meaning of *success*. And even *hope*.

It was a good time to think about how I had gotten there.

At age eighteen, I left the suburbs of Long Island to attend college.
After a five-hour car ride to Cambridge, my mom and dad dropped me off at Harvard Yard. As they drove away, my mom was crying, though trying not to show it. Up until that point, I had been a public school kid whose parents had immigrated to the United States. From that perspective, enrolling in Harvard was a huge deal. It was humbling, too—an introduction to a new arena of social stratification. Big money. Ancient lineages. Invisible networks. Prep school boys with flannel shirts, khaki pants, and braided belts. Prep school girls from Manhattan, who smoked cigarettes and had their first cocktail at age fourteen at one of the bars on First or Second Avenue. According to

the socioeconomic norms of the Ivy League, I was starting out near the bottom.

Over the next four years, I studied American and English history and literature from King James to World War I (1603–1919), with a focus on the late eighteenth and nineteenth centuries. Adam Smith. The American Revolutionary War. The US Constitution. Jane Austen. Charles Darwin. Frederick Douglass. Ralph Waldo Emerson. Herman Melville. Charles Dickens. The US Civil War. The Industrial Revolution. I studied economics and philosophy, too. And for the first time, I formally studied Korean, spending the summer of my freshman year at Yonsei University in Seoul, Korea. I was eager to travel, and see the world, and transcend the specific in favor of something bigger. What I didn't realize at the time was that I was studying how countries, leaders, civilizations, and peoples behaved under the relentless pressure of change over a three-hundred-year time period—a mixture of politics, philosophy, and economics. I learned how leaders and ordinary citizens debated, fought for, and brought to life concepts like capitalism and liberty using a symphony of numbers *and* prose.

It wasn't always easy being a Korean American student in college. I got used to being the only nonwhite person in my social group. After all, that's how I had grown up. As a public school kid, the added twist of having no prior exposure to the invisible systems of socioeconomic hierarchy undergirding campus life was at best tiresome, and at worst exhausting. Nor did I have any idea what I was going to do after I graduated. Luckily, my parents didn't seem all that concerned that their son, who they hoped would have a safer, more predictable life than theirs, was putting his passion for math and science on pause. In retrospect, I am sure they privately fretted about the value of a degree in the humanities.

After I graduated from college, it wasn't a popular decision at home when I took a job teaching high school, at a yearly salary of $12,600, plus room and board. My parents' reaction was puzzled and slightly pained. Many of my classmates were hurtling toward law and medicine, with some of them planning to make lots of money as investment banking and consulting analysts—and I was going to teach high school? My mom and dad had mortgaged their one and only meaningful financial asset, our house, to pay for all four years of college (they didn't own any stocks or bonds for most of their adult lives). And this was the return on their investment?

But I *wanted* to teach high school. After four years at Harvard, I felt I needed some distance between me and the brand, the credential, and all its expectations. When I was growing up, my mom always did our family's laundry, and a week or two into my freshman year, I tried out my first load. The dryer opened to reveal a jumble of pink clothes, lightly dyed by the crimson T-shirt I had been given during orientation. Harvard had stained my identity, too, lightly and indelibly, in the same way it colored my shirts and socks. I needed to rinse off a bit. I liked Harvard, and was proud to have gone there, but I didn't want to *be* Harvard. Upon hearing that name, people had instantaneous associations and judgments. But that was *them*; it wasn't *me*. I needed to test myself. Maybe even teach students who were potentially *not* on their way to college.

So I found what felt like a struggling private high school located in western Massachusetts. It was composed roughly of half day students and half boarders. I would say that a third of the student body was economically disadvantaged, the second third was international, and the last third included a fair share of underachievers. I taught history, culture, and a course in basic financial literacy;

helped run a dorm; and served as an assistant coach for swimming, football, tennis, and baseball.

It wasn't a "name" school. The baseball uniforms hadn't been upgraded in a very long time. This became clear at away games, when the other teams would saunter onto the field dressed in what looked like summer linens. My players would look at me questioningly. "So what?—this school has a lot of money," I said with a shrug. "Let's just go out there and play."

I understood the importance of credentials, especially as someone who had grown up without any, but at the same time I've never been quite able to buy in fully to the cult of names, or brands, or institutions. During my Harvard graduation ceremony, held on a patch of lawn between Widener Library and Memorial Church, I was greeted with the words "Welcome to the fellowship of educated men and women." I always wished they would put it another way—one that emphasized wisdom, not education, a reminder that education without grace and respect for life experience is a short path to arrogance and elitism.

After two years teaching high school, I told myself it was maybe time to do something else. When September came, I enrolled in Harvard Law School. My parents were overjoyed, thinking that I was back on the fast track and would become a corporate attorney. Unbeknownst to them, I was thinking about using what I learned to become a public defender. I didn't know this was the start of a pattern: learn something, a system or school of thinking, as deeply as I could, and then leave before it turned into a prison. Once I figure something out, I connect it to what I've learned before to identify patterns, correlations, possible breakthroughs among seemingly disparate disciplines and ideas. It's the creative and the scientist in me, the little kid who loves coming up with a hypothesis, testing it with information, and then sharing it with others, especially those looking in from the outside. Back then I didn't know the term *systems thinker*. I wish someone had told me.

I never ended up practicing law. The more courses I took, the more I realized there were things I didn't know and *needed* to know about money. *Where do I learn that? Oh wait—you say you don't teach that at the law school? But I can learn it at MIT and Harvard Business School? What do you mean I can't cross-register and take those classes? Well, I'll figure out a way, even if it means pleading my case with the registrar.* Courses in accounting, finance theory, and corporate financial management at the MIT Sloan School of Management and Harvard Business School soon followed. The best part of my time at law school, though, was meeting my future wife. Meg comes from an affluent family in North Carolina and came north to attend Phillips Academy Andover for high school. Different as our backgrounds were, it took me only a couple of weeks to know she was the one. It wasn't just that she was beautiful and brilliant—Meg is the smartest person I know—she was also refreshingly honest and direct. I pursued her hard. One afternoon, we found ourselves on a beach in Maine. *Why not me?* I asked her in a rare moment of vulnerability from those days.

Our different backgrounds, however—Meg is white, by the way—shed light on our differences, too. It was spring break, close to the end of my first year there. I would ultimately be chosen to be an editor of *Harvard Law Review*, but I still couldn't manage to find a paying summer job. Most big law firms wine and dine students during the summer of their second year, but before that, unless you're lucky, or know the right people, it can be hard to catch a break. And I *needed* a job. I was racking up forty thousand dollars a year in debt, and I had two more years to go. My parents were in no position to pay for me to go to law school, and I didn't expect them to. When I went home to Long Island over the March break, I couldn't hide how stressed out I was.

"What's wrong, James?"

"I can't get a job."

"But why?"

In their eyes, I was doing everything right. According to their formula for success, everything was set. I had checked all of the boxes on "how to be a successful boy in America," so why couldn't I get a job? I explained to them how rare it was for a first-year law student to find paid summer employment at a firm, but they kept pushing. "Don't your friends have summer jobs?" Yes, I said, most of them did, adding, "But my friends tend to be pretty connected people." Many, in fact, had landed paid internships. Others, with family money, had parents who were willing to "float" them for a summer and could afford to work without pay.

Meg, for one, had a paying summer job. Her dad, who grew up poor on a farm in Ohio and later became a prominent businessman and philanthropist, introduced her to someone he knew at his former law firm.

"If Meg has a job, then how come you can't get a job, James?"

"Because I don't have the right connections, that's why," I said at last.

My parents became silent. My dad said, "You mean, *we* don't have the right connections." They were sorry they couldn't help me, they said. They were sorry they didn't know those kinds of people in this country. I hated myself for this. I had hurt their feelings without meaning to, so I told a breezy lie, that a lot of recruiting happened after spring break, which it didn't.

The next day I was flying to North Carolina to meet Meg's parents and sisters for the first time. Knowing Meg came from a distinguished family, my dad abruptly announced he was taking me to Macy's.

My dad hated shopping—which meant something else must have been on his mind. In the men's department, he pulled down an inexpensive blue spring jacket. I still remember the way he put it on me, his hands smoothing both sides, making sure the fit was right. It was as though I were still a little kid, and he was gift-wrapping a special present he hoped would be well received.

He didn't say a word, but I could almost read his mind: *I hope they're nice to James down in North Carolina. I've done everything I can to prepare him. But as much as my own life has been hard, maybe my son won't have as easy a path here as I thought.*

I picked up all his pain, his regrets, his worry. I tried to hide mine from him, too. No matter how much you try to prepare them for life, your children will get banged-up, and overlooked, and hurt. They are your children, but sadly, the world seems increasingly to care less. It's our own cognitive dissonance at work. We want our children to be happy—while forgetting we are surrounded by other people's children.

I never became a public defender. In fact, I'm pretty sure if I had become one, I would have spent the rest of my life paying off my student loan debt. Sadly, even back then, based on my research, doing good, taking care of other people, *teaching* other people, just didn't seem to add up from a financial perspective. Responsible for what would ultimately balloon to be more than $125,000 in law school loans, not including the interest accruing at more than 7 percent a year, I began attending meet-and-greets at Harvard Business School in preparation for a classic business career and trajectory. *Who are you?* I was asked. *You taught high school? Why? You went to law school but never practiced law? Why?* I sent off my résumé to a bunch of well-known investment banks and consulting firms. If they showed interest, I insisted on a face-to-face interview.

"I know this sounds kind of weird for a twenty-something-year-old person to say," I said to anyone who would listen, "but I think you're measuring things wrong."

The analogy I gave was of the plus-minus rating used in ice hockey. It's easy to measure how many goals a team scores and gives up when a certain player is on the ice. The plus-minus rating is the difference between those two numbers. Though it has its detractors and limitations, it's a rating that attempts to measure a player's holistic contribution to the system that is the team, rather than more obvious individual stats, like goals scored or goals assisted. "I think I have a high plus-minus rating," I said. "I think I'm someone who makes things better for everybody." Slightly more brazenly, I added, "But maybe you just want to judge me on what's on that 8.5-by-11 piece of paper."

Despite my lack of experience—I could barely use Microsoft Excel—I got a job offer from the consulting firm McKinsey & Company and a second one, which I accepted, from an investment bank that housed one of the top mergers and acquisitions groups on Wall Street. My bold thinking, or perhaps my assertiveness, must have appealed to them. I think I was that group's first-ever direct nontraditional hire out of law school—and Meg went to McKinsey!

After a few years of intense transactions, I left investment banking in New York to move to Boston—Meg was still living there —where I secured a position with what was at the time one of the elite private equity firms in the United States. The firm had a war chest of $3.5 billion that it deployed to invest in growth companies in the consumer products, healthcare services, and retail sectors. There were only six senior deal people, so I had a great opportunity to cut my teeth on some of the firm's most high-profile deals, without too many layers of bureaucracy. Later, one of the senior partners told me he had no idea why they hired me—they just did. It was the same thing I had heard at my previous job, and before that, at the high school where I taught. *We're not sure why we're hiring you.* It wasn't clear to me, either.

The firm had a great run. Then, in my seventh year, some below-ground tensions about power and economics came to a head. A few of the most senior partners were squabbling over silly money. Three of us just sat there, shaking our heads.

My closest friend in the partnership was a self-made guy from a suburb in Pennsylvania, the son of a widow. Though he had a lot more experience than I did, I thought of him like a younger brother. Once a week, he and I went out for beers and burgers and pool, and later, when he got married, I was a member of his wedding party.

One day, another colleague and I were told that my close friend was no longer welcome at the firm. Hoping to stir and stoke the corporate killer in us, I guess, we were offered full partner titles and a guaranteed amount of money that eclipsed what my dad had made over the previous twenty years or so from his practice as a pediatrician.

Hoping to save my friend's job, I basically said, "But he has a high plus-minus rating." It didn't work. Worse, none of the senior partners in the firm had the decency to tell my friend directly. Apparently, that was our job.

That weekend, the three of us met downtown for a beer. When we told my friend he was being let go, his eyes watered, and his voice broke. We told him we were probably going to quit, too. Over the next two weeks, the three of us went back and forth, ruminating. *This is ridiculous*, we agreed. *We're not selling our souls for this stupid firm.* Looking back, I wish I had paused to breathe, and taken a month or two to figure out what I was going to do next. But I didn't. I left the company, joined a doomed-to-begin-with start-up, and was soon unemployed. My friend moved to New York, and the other guy rejoined the firm we had just left.

The next few weeks and months were difficult and dispiriting. Meg was supportive as always. "You were right to do what you did," she said, reminding me that she had married a high school teacher. But we both had practical life concerns, including a jumbo mortgage. We had three children under the age of five. In fact, I had told Meg I was thinking about quitting my cushy job literally only a few weeks before our youngest, Lila, arrived. (Only years later would Meg confess how secretly, quietly stressed-out my quitting had made her, though she did a good job of hiding it.) One day I was sitting on the back lawn, watching Lila's two older siblings playing on our family swing set. Years of snow and humidity had blistered and damaged the wood. *We need a new swing set,* I thought, followed by, *but I don't have a job, so I probably shouldn't be thinking about that.* Then, *You idiot. You know perfectly well you can afford to buy a new swing set. But no matter how much money you have in the bank, what if after buying a new swing set, you never get another job? The real problem, James, is that you don't know what's coming next, and your <u>uncertainty</u> terrifies you. It's the scarcity mindset at work, that there's never going to be <u>enough,</u> that it could all fall apart any minute, when the truth is, you have so much compared with most of the people in the world.*

In hindsight, I didn't acknowledge how much the value system my parents had insisted on could be a burden. I continued to be the only Asian in most of my social and business circles. A former high school teacher doing mergers and acquisitions. Remember, I went to law school thinking there was a strong possibility I would become a public defender. Now, here I was, in hand-to-hand combat in private equity. *Which one of these things is not quite like the other?* I would sing quietly, the lyrics borrowed from the old *Sesame Street* jingle. I was always *that guy.* On some level, of course, I was aware of it. I had never given myself the grace to acknowledge that the life of an outsider isn't going to be as easy or smooth as that of someone born to the inside—no matter how many fancy degrees you have. And that maybe the life my parents wanted for me wasn't the life *I* necessarily wanted. I never wallowed in it, or saw myself as a victim, but mixed in with the good times were harder ones, too. I didn't know that these differences, and so-called liabilities, would someday turn into enormous assets.

But back then, as I stared at the splintering swing set, unbeknownst to everyone, I felt like I was drowning in my own life—and I knew what drowning felt like.

My best friend in elementary school was a skinny, happy, brown-haired kid named Joel. In the same way the close-knit Jewish community in the Bronx had tutored my mom and dad when they first came to the US, the local Jewish families in my childhood hometown helped raise me, too. One of them was Joel's family.

One afternoon, I rode my five-speed bike over to Joel's house so that I could go swimming in his backyard pool. Soon, Joel, who was a much better swimmer than I, was paddling around the deep end, as I inched my way around the perimeter, holding tight to the spongy blue ledge. At some point, my fingers slipped on a wet spot, and I lost my grip and went under.

Even now, it's hard to put into words what drowning feels like. Most people think it happens at the bottom of the water, many feet from the surface, but it doesn't. Only a few inches were between me and the air, but by then I was already taking in water. The Russian word *polynya* basically refers to an area of open water surrounded on all sides by solid ice. If for some reason you're trapped under the ice, a *polynya* is the only way out. The little kid me didn't know that word, of course, but in hindsight, later on, wasn't I looking for a *polynya*? Maybe we all are.

A big irony of drowning is that it happens in an element that sustains life. So, you see, even the most life-sustaining assets can be liabilities, too. It all depends on the context, on the *when* and the *where*.

Joel had never seen anyone drown before, much less one of his friends. *Mom!* he shouted. *Mom!* Luckily, his mom was sitting on the deck overlooking the pool. She jumped in the water, grabbed me by the hair, pulled me out, and started pumping my stomach with two hands. I wasn't breathing. Water began flowing from my mouth, and then I was coughing and choking and crying.

I was understandably wary about getting into the water after that. But my mom and dad enrolled me in a swim club, and for the next few years I ended up swimming competitively. A psychologist would call this "exposure therapy," where you're forced to confront the thing that scares you, over and over again. It's probably why I seem to be up to whatever challenges life throws at me and am at home in so many different and difficult circumstances. It's an intangible asset, born from necessity, whose value I was only just beginning to appreciate in myself and in others.

And now I was heading to Ashley Stewart for my first day of work, not as chairman of the board, private equity owner, or consultant, but as a full-time employee. The situation was so dire that this implausible and somewhat comical solution was the best the board of directors could conjure up. I had achieved a high level of success in a lot of prestigious arenas. I was happily married with three beautiful, young children. My parents were both still alive. My dad's Parkinson's wasn't good, but he hadn't yet fully lost his ability to speak, write, walk, or see. He was still *Dad*.

But underneath it all, in addition to feeling accountable, I was clearly searching for something. Trapped below the water, feeling worn-down and disoriented, at war with my own life and beliefs, looking around me for a *polynya*—that's how I felt. *If you just do* _this_*, or get* _that_*, you'll be happy.* If only I worked harder, got that promotion, earned a bigger bonus. Just one more thing—one more—and it will come together, your life will gel.

In fairness, I also felt, for lack of a better word, *dismayed*. Was there no way to balance the values of a high school teacher or a public defender with those of a financial investor or CEO? Were they meant to be perpetually in conflict? Were the values of my caregiver immigrant parents irreconcilable with achieving the conventional success in the US that they also wanted, if not insisted, for me? It sure felt that way at times. Was the point of private equity to make money for investors no matter the cost to anyone else? From what I saw firsthand, it sure seemed that way. The easiest path was to *stop* caring for people, especially the people who worked at the companies we owned. A spreadsheet makes headcount reductions incredibly easy. Delete row and subtract, calculate the cost savings. Done. Harboring pangs of guilt or regret? Nothing like a trip to a casino or the local bar to numb those feelings. Until the rush of adrenaline from the next deal, that is. Other than Meg's father, no one had shaken my hand and congratulated me for standing on principle and lobbying for my friend at that elite private equity firm. No toy red helicopter showed up in the mail.

There's a famous story about the authors Joseph Heller and Kurt Vonnegut. They were both guests at a party given by a mutual friend, a hedge fund billionaire. Vonnegut teased Heller that their host made more money in one day than Heller had made his entire life from his literary masterpiece *Catch-22*. "Yes," Heller said, "but I've got something he can never have. The knowledge that I've got enough."

Enough. Was it enough for me to have been high school valedictorian and named the best student athlete, and to have played violin in the chamber orchestra and sung in the elite jazz ensemble? Enough to have accumulated two fancy degrees? Enough to have worked in tony firms, and flown around in private jets, and slept in the finest hotels, and socialized with swanky people? Did everyone's life feel as uneasy and dissociated and cinematically unreal as mine did?

I'm not impressed. It was a recurrent refrain in my brain. I had been exposed to "success," and I wasn't impressed. *So many people I know are unhappy,* I thought, *and some are even miserable. And because of that, they seem okay with making other people unhappy and miserable. I respect some of their professional accomplishments, but I don't covet the lives that they are leading. They seem lonely, maybe even a little angry.* The world of private equity seemed to be asking me to not care, to push through the doors every morning while mumbling over and over, "It's just my job."

I couldn't do that. Most people would say that's a weakness, but I didn't see it that way. I was like an actor refusing to go onstage because the tough-guy role I was being asked to play was in contradiction to the person I knew I was, or wanted to be. It didn't just feel hypocritical to me, it felt disingenuous. At the same time, my own cognitive dissonance annoyed me. *Can't you just knock it off and play along like everyone else? What's <u>wrong</u> with you?*

The truth is, the hypocrisy involved in being asked to inhabit a bunch of different identities over the course of our lives is exhausting. It creates a low-level malaise, and disappointment, and alienation from the world. Some people get around it by meditating, but what is meditation for if not to find some sense of unity, or a connection with something larger? Others go in another direction and commit to consuming or acquiring *more*—more houses, more cars, more possessions. They are addicts, just in a different way. Some employers know this and ply their workforce with free yoga classes, massages, billiards, and laundry service. But I recognized drowning when I saw it.

Calm. **Perfectly, weirdly calm. Never had I felt more out of my element**—like a fish rolling around in the sand—or more bizarrely at peace. As I walked into the well-worn lobby of Ashley Stewart, my orange backpack on my shoulder, toward what I knew was complete chaos and blinding uncertainty, I had never felt so calm in my life. I even had a smile on my face. As well as no expectations. I'd just spent a dismal night in my dismal hotel room, but I was overcome by an inexplicable tranquility. I didn't understand any of it.

It might have had something to do with the room and the building itself. Its modesty reminded me of the family room in my house when I was growing up, and the lack of any safety nets. *In this whole country, there is just our family to take care of us. There are only the five of us,* my mom and dad used to say. Over and over again, especially when I fought with my brother or sister. Meaning that if something went wrong, if one of us got sick, or was in trouble, no one else was out there to help. So they thought, at least. Later, I would discover they were wrong. There *were* more than five of us, *always.*

I also recognized the feel of an environment that was a beat or two behind, a half measure off the mainstream. A few months down the road, I would watch my executive assistant, Gina, host a Thanksgiving potluck, and a wildly diverse employee group show up with their favorite homemade dishes from their home countries. I couldn't help but recall the neighborhood potlucks from my childhood. The other moms would bring their store-bought potato salad, cold cuts, hamburgers, and hot dogs, whereas my mom always brought *jap chae*, a Korean dish of stir-fried cellophane noodles, carrots, onions, spinach, beef, and mushrooms. She always put tremendous effort into making her *jap chae*. I used to eyeball the potluck table to see if any of our neighbors was gracious or brave enough to sample such a different-looking dish. And I was disappointed when my mom brought her *jap chae* home and set it on the counter, mostly untouched. Today, Korean cuisine has become popular and hip, but when I was a child, it was a neon-lit emblem of my family's Otherness, not to mention of my mom's insistence on putting effort into making things, not just buying them.

The challenges Ashley Stewart was up against—I felt I intuitively understood them. In part because I was an experienced investor, but more so because of my life outside work. We all have a childhood. We all have a life outside work. And I was about to let life into work, not the other way around.

The first town hall meeting took place in the windowless cafete-ria with the industrial food warmer. When the day came, everyone assembled in uneven rows of metallic folding chairs. Gina, who had served as the executive assistant to three previous CEOs—one of them used to make Gina walk her dog—dug up a microphone that worked and connected an AV screen to my laptop, which sat on another nearby folding chair.

"I'm James," I began. "I've never done something like this before. I'm a man, not a woman. And yeah"—I then pointed to my face, and smiled—"I get it." In other words, let the record show I am Asian. There was knowing laughter.

I was qualified in some ways—but, in most ways, *un*qualified. My only operating experience in retail had been bussing tables at a couple of restaurants as a teenager, and a short stint washing dishes at a local Red Lobster for $3.35 an hour before my mom noticed the burns on my hands and put an end to it. "Do you understand how bad things are here?" I continued. "I wouldn't be here if things weren't really dire. But there must be something here that has kept Ashley Stewart alive for the past twenty-two years."

"When this town hall is over," I continued, "I'll be going through there"—I gestured at the door behind me that connected the cafeteria to the distribution center—"because I have to find stuff—*anything*—to sell so that we can just make payroll." Excess scrap metal, shelving, printers, waste—anything Ashley Stewart had booked as an asset we needed to sell off to raise cash. Otherwise, those non-value-producing "assets" were, in reality, *liabilities*, I explained. The next words that came out of my mouth surprised me. "But I don't want anyone in this room to panic. Because I think if we can center kindness and math in this company, we can get out of this mess together."

Kindness. Where the heck did that word come from? It wasn't a word I used regularly or, let's be honest, ever. Not since Sunday school, when I was preparing for confirmation. I wasn't asking them to be *nice*, or *polite*. I asked them to be *kind*.

In the corporate landscapes I worked in, you never heard that word. I didn't hear that word in college or law school, either. *Kindness* meant *pushover*. *Kindness* meant you were about to get sucker punched or kneecapped. But clearly there is a reason why I said what I said. I'm sure that I had my mom and dad in my mind. The word just emerged and came out of my mouth.

I picked up the low hum of skepticism in the room, especially among certain members of the senior leadership team. Half the room, I suspected, was quietly laughing at me. What did kindness have to do with the workplace? People are supposed to be miserable at work—after all, they have to pay you money just to show up, right? Misery is almost built into the word *work* itself, or so we are conditioned to believe. Kindness happens, if you're lucky, in your personal life, or a place of worship, or in small pockets at work around the water cooler, or through a shared meal with colleagues when the day is done. It doesn't take place at scale. The world won't allow it. You'll get eaten alive. You'll get run over. You'll *lose.* Those are just the rules, right?

Then I threw out a question whose answer I felt I already intuitively knew. "What is this company providing its customers? What is it really selling?"

"Clothes," a few people called out, and "fashion." But during my time on the board of directors, I had studied Ashley Stewart. And my instincts told me that clothes were the least of what the company sold. On the surface, this company sold plus-size clothes in predominantly urban strip mall and downtown locations, often alongside a convenience store or hair or nail salon, and sometimes a liquor store. For the most part, the stores were welcoming and managed by gregarious women who lived in the same communities where their customers did. I think it's fair to say that it can be tough for plus-size Black women to find stylish clothes in a welcoming environment. The world does not exactly give them permission to be seen, much less celebrated—here or in many other facets of their lives. They went to Ashley Stewart stores for something more than a blouse. I couldn't help but think of my own mom.

For my entire life, starting when I was a child, I saw my mom as vulnerable, and isolated, kept back by her poor grasp of English. But there were certain punctuated moments when I felt I had her all wrong. One happened every year, when our family drove to Manhattan to see a Broadway musical, and on the way home we stopped in Queens to shop at a simple Korean grocery.

The moment she entered the grocery, my mom's bearing changed. You could see it in her shoulders and the line of her neck. She was in charge. Gone were the stresses of having to speak and understand English, the anxiety she felt about not fitting in, or not understanding what was going on around her. Once a year, the tilt of her head told the world she was at home.

My instincts told me that Ashley Stewart played the same role in the lives of its customers as that Korean grocery did for my mom. A safe place. A fresh spring that renewed confidence, respect, and self-esteem. How did I know this? Because as chairman of the board, I had visited a handful of stores with my fellow board members. I've always been good at picking up vibes. There's even a Korean word—*nunchi*—referring to the quicksilver ability to understand the subtleties of what is being said versus unsaid. *Nunchi* is a mix of intuition and knowledge, the rational and the irrational, the things that can and cannot be measured, high-speed pattern recognition that even artificial intelligence would find borderline impossible to pick up. My *nunchi* is what enabled me to detect some of the emotions my father found it difficult to express in words.

Basically, it's a kind of X-ray vision about feelings. I've had it my whole life, and it's only grown stronger with time. During those store visits, I *knew*—but I can't tell you why—that the female store managers had something on their minds. They weren't altogether happy. Something was wrong. They wanted to tell me what that thing was, but it wasn't the right place or time. As is sadly common in many corporate cultures, they also seemed a bit scared of the executive team. During an otherwise performative tour of one store for the board of directors, a customer came in and, seeing my blue blazer and khakis, decided to target *me*.

"These clothes are terrible!" she told me. "I want to return these! I want my money back! They're wrinkled and unironed. This is ridiculous!"

With an obvious twinkle in my eyes, I teased, "Are you done? Is there anything else you want to unload on me?" Everyone, including the other board members, was watching me in disbelief.

"Yes, I'm done," the customer said. I told her I was so sorry, and of course she would receive a refund, adding, "Just so you know, I don't work here." Then it was the customer's turn to apologize. She was having a bad day, her son was giving her problems, nothing was working out right.

"It's okay," I said. "We'll fix everything that went wrong." A few minutes later, she and I were walking around the store as if nothing had happened, shopping and yapping and laughing.

On the way back to the airport, a fellow board member finally broke the silence. "What *happened* back there?" I sort of shrugged. *What?* A twinkle and a tease don't show up on a spreadsheet. There is no obvious plus-minus rating for measuring such things. There is no formula for them.

Kindness. I didn't fully understand the meaning or even the reach of that word, just as I didn't altogether understand the reappearance of the red helicopter in my thoughts. But in that town hall meeting, in that moment, they spiraled together and gave me an element of calm, of transcendence above the chaos.

As for the math part of kindness and math, that was easy. There are good reasons why some things are for profit and others aren't. I wasn't saying, *Hey! It's great that you've hemorrhaged money for decades. Who needs Wi-Fi when you have kindness?* I'm good with money. I've made a lot of it, for both my investors and me. Believe me, we discussed the hard measures of true profitability, balance sheet management, and what was about to hit this company, too. (We'll go over some useful frameworks for this in Act II.)

But maybe, using kindness *and* math, we could come up with a plan to save Ashley Stewart from liquidation. It's how I ended our first town hall meeting. The details behind the plan were yet to come, but no one left that cafeteria uncertain about what the two governing principles would be from that point on out.

There was a buzz in the room. I could feel people working hard to reconcile the apparent contradiction. As for me, I was starting to understand why I was there. A connection had been created between the red helicopter, kindness, and whatever it was I was looking for. It had been a long time since I had felt that way. I wasn't overthinking things or putting on some veneer of how I was supposed to act. My colleagues were getting the unvarnished, full me. The answer, I knew, would come from going into my own story and owning it. Before asking my new colleagues to be honest with themselves, I knew that I needed to be honest with *myself*, and that meant uncovering who I was and where I came from. In the end, I had more similarities with the women of Ashley Stewart, and especially with their children, than I thought.

chapter 2

past

The word <u>helicopter</u> comes from the French word <u>helicoptère</u>, which combines the Greek words <u>heliko</u> ("spiral") and <u>pteron</u> ("wing").

Knowing your own past is crucial. History, whether it's personal or collective, really *does* matter. To be fully present, we need to come to grips with our past in an honest way. Easier said than done because facts can be slippery and memories equally unreliable. In addition, our desire to fit into a broader prevailing narrative can cause us to distort or compromise essential elements of our own peculiar past. Sometimes, then, gathering the facts to construct *another's* narrative can force us to see our own story more clearly. Certainly, that was true for me, as you will come to appreciate further in this chapter.

My first few days and months at Ashley Stewart involved digging and excavating, and a lot of learning. The corporate headquarters was like a mausoleum of scattered, disconnected data and storylines. I would find one answer in this department, and a conflicting answer in another. It felt like trying to wrap a gift without tape or twine to bind everything together. There was no central repository of truth—hey, is there ever? But in this case, it seemed to me that there was a collective and concerted effort to cover up the truth. Was that the cause or the effect of the horrific financial results during the previous two decades? As is usually the case, the answer was *both*.

My college studies of history and literature had always come in handy for me as a private equity investor. Before discussing the present or the future with a management team, I always focused on the origin story, theirs and the company's. Why? Because there is always a narrative, a chain of connectedness, and, ultimately, a root cause. Sometimes there's more than one, but it's been my job to distill and make the storyline as simple as possible without gutting the truth.

What *was* Ashley Stewart? Or perhaps most poignantly, *why* was there an Ashley Stewart? How had it even gotten to this point? No one could give me a cohesive, comprehensive narrative. I started gathering information, all kinds—talking to people, exploring all those dusty file cabinets, sifting through contradictory numbers. And this is what I pieced together.

Two decades earlier, observing that a high percentage of Black American women were "plus-size," and seeking tenants for his urban properties, a young real estate developer launched an apparel chain. He called it Ashley Stewart. The "Ashley" came from Laura Ashley and the "Stewart" from Martha Stewart—ironic in retrospect. The first Ashley Stewart opened in Brooklyn, followed by stores in other predominantly Black neighborhoods across the country. There ultimately ended up being more than two hundred

Ashley Stewart stores across the US, with a few off the mainland in the Virgin Islands.

What the founder got right was that the fashion industry, along with so many other industries, is based on a certain standard of what is desirable and aspirational, thus providing the explanation for the name Ashley Stewart. Anything deviating from that standard or *perspective* is seen as Other. In the case of fashion, the prevailing standard is pale, narrow-hipped, and hollow-cheeked. Other body types—and races and cultures—often get edited out, even though most American women across all races and ethnicities wear sizes 14 and higher. For most women, then, shopping for clothes can be challenging, a constant reminder that they don't measure up to an impossible ideal, that they are Other. Such is the power of storytelling, controlling the narrative, and shaping perspective.

At the beginning, Ashley Stewart understood what its customers wanted. Whereas most clothes designed for larger women were intended to camouflage and eclipse the women's bodies, Ashley's clothes were tight, dramatic, and vivid. The fashion pieces were body-hugging and extremely colorful. Sexy, but also appropriate for church services. Ashley Stewart was for a curvy woman who was proud of the way she looked and was not afraid to flaunt it in the many different identities of her life.

For two decades, Ashley Stewart grew and changed. A porous operational foundation undermined the company, and the lack of a galvanizing and consistent origin story did it no favors, either. There was a constant churn in leadership. Each time the business required funding to plug cash flow deficits, some private equity firm would stroke a check and take over. There was even an ill-fated attempt to expand into the Hispanic market. Why not create a separate holding company, Urban Brands, for all Othered women? Uh, that's certainly *one* extremely oversimplified idea. Would it surprise you if I told you that there was evidence of a fair amount of corporate greed, poor oversight, and private equity arrogance—private planes, suspect real estate deals, and questionable executive behavior? I had grown used to seeing that as a private equity professional. But in this case, maybe because the target demographic was so under the radar and without voice, the behavior from on top was rumored to be worse.

When I had first become aware of Ashley Stewart, it was obvious that the frontline workers hadn't been able to catch a break in a long time. How had the company managed to survive as long as it had? Camouflage. Credit the store managers who overcompensated for all the corporate ridiculousness by nurturing and preserving their relationships with customers and their communities in spite of everything.

There was one other truth, though, that needed to see light. It became very clear to me that Ashley Stewart was created for *a certain segment of <u>Black</u> women*. Black women who happened to be curvy. Not the other way around. From the perspective of the prevailing narrative in history books and media outlets, it was a brand for the consummate Other: female, Black, curvy. But because of the lack of trust and directness in the company, people would flinch anytime I said the word *Black*. Especially the human resources people.

If you find yourself in a mess, there is rarely time to be anything other than direct. Directness does require trust, however, which in turn requires mutual confidence in intent, or a shared understanding of the *why*. It's a two-way street. In this case, I felt extremely confident about my intent. I had to do my best to focus on the *how* in order to ensure my straightforwardness was received with relief and not defensiveness.

In the spirit of that same directness, I will say the quiet part out loud: Korean American and Black American communities historically have clashed. There's been a pattern of animosity, resentment, and sometimes violence. The armed standoff between the two groups during the Los Angeles riots of 1992 is well documented and annually memorialized.

But there is more nuance, as we usually find when gathering facts. The renowned movie director Spike Lee tried to convey this in his timeless film *Do the Right Thing*. During the movie's climax, when an entire neighborhood turns against itself in a fit of rage, there's a gripping scene where an elder Black statesman protects a Korean grocer and his wife.

"I Black, you, me, same!" implores the Korean shopkeeper.

"Leave the Korean alone. He's all right." Amidst chaos, one voice, that of the elder Black statesman, saves the store.

My parents' ability to immigrate to the United States owed a great deal to the courage of Martin Luther King Jr. and the change in perspectives ushered in by the Civil Rights Movement. The passage of the Immigration and Nationality Act of 1965 repealed the national-origins quotas that, for nearly a half-century, had severely restricted the number of Asian people allowed to immigrate to the US. Even after the country opened its doors, immigration officials remained selective about admitting people who had no family already living in the country, which meant there were still de facto restrictions on Asian immigration. Doctors, however, were seen as a desirable class. Sitting in that Ashley Stewart warehouse, I realized for the first time that my pediatrician dad left Korea exactly one year after the passage of the 1965 act. That was not exactly in my school curriculum growing up.

Clearly, to accomplish what I set out to do for Ashley Stewart, I needed to do more homework about my own past. It wouldn't be long before I realized how little I really knew about it or had been willing to acknowledge.

My dad had come to the US first, leaving my pregnant mom be-hind. Roughly three months after giving birth to my older brother, John, my mom boarded a Pan American airplane and joined my dad in Pittsburgh. She left John behind in the care of my grandmother. I have a picture of my mom cradling her baby at the airport on the day of her departure. Sadly, this was not atypical for that era, or even today in many immigrant stories. In Korea, grandmothers helped raise children because they lived with their adult children. My im-migrant parents were also light on money and heavy on uncertainty and stress. They must have reasoned that they needed to get estab-lished in their newly adopted country first before sending for John. Five years after my mom arrived, my dad met his firstborn son, and one-year-old me met my older brother, for the first time. Another four years after that, in 1976, my little sister, Jennifer, was born.

For nearly any immigrant, coming to the United States is incom-prehensibly challenging. Is there any form of entrepreneurship that is of a higher order? For a different race, especially one historically excluded on the basis of prejudice, I am sure it is even harder. My parents had to learn a whole new set of rules, a brand-new game that their US-raised children knew how to play better than they did. In Korea, they were graduates of prestigious academic institutions, but here, in practically everything they did, they were often a beat or two behind.

What do I mean exactly? I'll give an example that's both funny and sad. When my dad finished his pediatrics residency in Pittsburgh, he and my mom moved to an apartment in the Bronx, New York. The older local Jewish residents took an interest in my parents and their new infant son (me!).

When the holidays came, many of the storefronts and apartments were decorated with brightly lit menorahs. Thinking this was a good way to assimilate into the neighborhood, my mom and dad went out and bought their own menorah. Why wouldn't they? Menorahs are beautiful.

My mom took me out every day for a walk in my stroller. Apparently, the older grandparents who lived in the neighborhood would always stop to coo at me. A few days after my parents positioned their new menorah in the window, one of the elderly Jewish women said to my mom, "Do you know that menorahs, as well as being beautiful, also have a religious meaning?" No—my mom didn't know that. It wasn't said in an accusing way, or to imply that my mom had made a mistake. It was said with kindness and respect, in the spirit of teaching my mom something new about her adopted country.

But my mom and dad were embarrassed all the same. Growing up, my mom had been raised a Buddhist. But when she and my dad moved to the suburbs of Long Island a few years after I was born, they couldn't help noticing how many Catholics there were. So they decided to enroll us all in Sunday school so that we could convert to Catholicism and get baptized. The new Catholic name my mom chose for herself was Matilda. My dad selected Clement. They took the additional step of selecting new "everyday" American names. My mom's given name was Hwa Ja, but she would introduce herself as Phyllis. My dad's given name was Youchan, but he started to use the name Matthew. When they went to neighborhood potlucks, assuming the other parents wouldn't be able to pronounce Hwa Ja and Youchan, they went around introducing themselves using their new names.

Where and how did they come up with those names? I have no idea. None of the names, except maybe Matthew, was a particularly obvious or conventional choice. Like so many issues and confusions my parents faced, it was bittersweet, both funny and sad.

In part because of these moments of embarrassment and periods of trauma, my mom and dad kept much about their lives here and in Korea private, even from me, John, and Jennifer. Upstairs in my house is a packet of handwritten letters my mom received from her family during her most trying times as an immigrant. They're all written in casually scrawled Korean, which has made it impossible for me to read them. I discovered them after she died—she had kept them hidden. It's so strange to have in my possession evidence of my mom's inner life that I can't understand. Out of respect for her privacy, I've never had them translated, though I know if I do, they'll reopen some old wounds.

As children, we were cut off from our past. My mom and dad expunged big parts of their own history—things that were too painful, or that they thought would interfere with our assimilation, not to mention their own. It's why they never insisted we learn to speak Korean fluently, and why my mom hid any traces of *kimchi* when I had friends over after school and why she apologized to them for any of its lingering smells in the kitchen.

Some things, especially connected to the Korean War, I learned only in bits and shards. The war was always a delicate subject, its meaning conveyed in odd silences and mournful expressions. My parents almost never talked about it out loud. When the war broke out, my mom was nine years old, my dad ten. Later I pieced together fragments of the dark role it played in their lives, especially in my mom's.

When Seoul was invaded by North Korean troops, many adult Korean men of fighting age, including my mom's dad, were evacuated to avoid capture while women and children were left to fend for themselves. My grandfather was a senior officer in the Seoul police force. But as he was being evacuated, he disobeyed orders and leaped off the truck, arriving home in the middle of the night by foot. *How can I leave my family*? he sobbed as he rapped on the door. As Seoul was being overrun, he hid out at a neighbor's house, but not before instructing my grandmother to burn all photos of him for fear of his wife and children being shot by association. No one ever saw him again. The rare times my mom talked about that night, she would stare off and say something like . . . *And yes, he never came back.*

My grandmother was left a widow. Like many Korean women of that era, she was barely literate. She had no occupational training. But somehow, by herself, she raised four children, including my mom, in postwar Korea. All four of those children eventually went to college. I don't know how my grandmother did it. She never lost her spirit, or her energy, or her loud, hoarse cackle. Never once did I hear her complain about her life or flatter herself for what she had done. She was too busy preparing meals, cleaning the house, and hand-washing the laundry in the cleaning basin.

I also knew that my dad, the oldest son in his family, had been a rising medical star in Korea, a highly decorated student at Seoul National University, which he attended for both his undergraduate and medical school education. I knew his mom died when he was in his twenties, and his memories of his father were mostly unpleasant. One was of a dry, subarctic winter's day when my grandfather slapped my dad in the face. "I still feel the sting of that slap," my dad told us a few times, usually after a few drinks. Out of all possible medical specialties, was it my dad's burning passion to be a pediatrician? It didn't matter. *Pediatrician* is what his immigration visa said, and that's what he became. And so my parents left their poverty-stricken country for one that held out the promise of hope, even limitless hope.

Why did my parents keep so much from their children? Because they wanted us to have a different life. A much, much better life. They didn't want us to feel what they had felt most of the time—alone, apart, fearful, hungry. The stories I *do* know are only a tiny percentage of what they probably went through during their lives. Stories about my dad pawning his watch so he could eat during medical school. Or about my mom stepping over dead bodies while escaping from invading Communist forces. Both in Korea and as immigrants, they had experienced *real* suffering, uncertainty, and loss.

I don't want you to get the wrong idea, however. There were plenty of moments of joy in our small family room, too—watching my dad grimace while holding our pet hamsters or listening to my mom sing made-up songs about my little sister ("Jennifer" morphed into "Jennipa-pa") in half-Korean, half-English. But to this day, my most poignant memories are of my outwardly strong parents sharing their worries with each other in hushed Korean when they didn't think their children were watching or capable of understanding.

I was especially attuned to my mom's suffering. She was always my person, and I was always hers.

Why did I feel that way about her more than I did about my dad? I don't know the answer. I know only that from early on, I felt I understood her on a soul level. Her silences, her mood changes, the shifting meanings in her eyes, her mouth, her hands. Mostly I was aware of her sadness. I felt it as if it were my own. Try as she might, she couldn't hide anything from me. And I felt pangs of frustration and guilt not being able to fix it.

Sometimes, but rarely, she would even admit to it. She would speak about her loneliness and the discomfort she felt being singled out as a non-English-speaking Asian immigrant woman. When she disembarked from the Pan American plane and joined my dad in a rented room on the top floor of a suburban home outside Pittsburgh, I'm sure she desperately missed her newborn baby and felt isolated as she waited for my dad to return from his work as a pediatric resident. People would stare at her on the sidewalks, she told us. She said she felt like an exotic animal in a cage.

I can only imagine how hard it was for her navigating the practicalities of a country where everything is new, and everyone knows things you don't. How do you enroll three children in public school? How do you read a street map? What is the English name of this fruit or vegetable or cut of meat, and what do you say to the supermarket butcher when he says *Next*? How do you buy your children the right clothes for school, and what do those clothes even look like? How do you pay utility bills, and understand the fine print on your checkbook and bank statements?

Since there were almost no other Asian families in our Long

Island suburb, and ours was the only Korean family in the neighborhood, my mom had to figure those things out by herself. With my dad at work, and us at school, she was alone every day. In the mornings, she prepared our lunches, and after the bus picked us up, she went home and spent the next several hours running the business of our lives. When school ended, she drove the three of us to lessons, playdates, baseball games, and ballet rehearsals. She was always on time, never late. Her devotion to us was complete and undivided, but it also meant her English, at least as it was spoken in the world outside her family, never got any better.

It could be funny sometimes. In my junior year of high school, for example, I got a job as a busboy at a family-owned seafood restaurant in Port Jefferson, a few towns over from ours. (The restaurant was even shaped like a ship.) I was saving up my tip money to buy a denim jacket, which I couldn't stop talking about. Eventually, I had enough money. When I got home from the mall, and modeled it for my mom, I noticed she had a funny expression on her face. Finally, she confessed that for the previous few months, she had thought I was saying, "I want a damn jacket! I can't wait to get a damn jacket!" My cursing in front of her had disappointed her, she said, though she had kept quiet about it. It was a story we retold, and laughed and laughed about, once a year at least, for the rest of her life.

More often than not, though, the language barrier was frustrating. So much of what I was picking up at school I couldn't communicate at home. Which meant sometimes I couldn't express my whole self. Humor. Irony. Puns. Pop culture references. Anything layered, or with a double meaning. On the other hand, the language barrier between me and my mom probably intensified our connection. Compensating for her English, and my Korean, our eyes, mouths, and hands stepped in. I learned to choose my words carefully. Everything clear and simple. All while watching (and listening with my eyes) to see whether my mom understood what I was telling her. To this day, I find complex rhetoric obnoxious. *Welcome to the fellowship of the educated.* Words like that almost always conceal the truth or attempt to exclude others with a sense of superiority.

Words, eyes, mouths, hands. I might have found a multisensory way to communicate with my mom at home, but I couldn't always help her in the world. The small slights that happened every day. A cashier's cocked head and thin lips. A reply that lightly mimicked her accent. Even some of my "friends" weren't always that nice to her. One day I remember my mom saying, "Do you know that your friend made fun of my accent today when I was waiting to pick you up from school?" I said, "Oh, yeah?" The next day, I took the friend aside and told him never to do that again. In the days before cell phones, when my mom would leave a message on our answering machine, one or two of my Harvard roommates thought it was okay to imitate her heavy Korean accent in front of me.

I must have been twelve or thirteen when my mom picked me up one day from my violin lesson in our family's red Volvo sedan. It was late afternoon, autumn, and the sky was darkening. When I got into the car, my mom didn't turn to greet me, even when I began fiddling with the dials of the car radio, trying to find her favorite Lionel Richie song, "Hello." The high collar of her wool coat hid her face. She pulled away from the curb, but I knew something was wrong.

"Mom, stop the car," I said. Then, "Are you *crying*?"

"*Gwaenchanha.*" It was her usual answer when I asked about her emotional state. *Gwaenchanha.* Meaning, *Whatever, it's fine. It's okay. Just let it go.*

"You *are* crying. What happened?" And then she told me.

All summer long, I'd been complaining about the rust on the basketball hoop in our driveway, especially around the hinges. Wanting to do something about it, my mom went to a local hardware store. She didn't know how to say *rustproof* or *anti-rust.* The clerk got exasperated with her and even raised his voice. "I don't understand what you're saying. Anti-*what*?" He made my mom feel like nothing. She had grown accustomed to absorbing slights, but this one was too much.

"Mom," I said, "we're going to the hardware store *now.*"

I was a teenage kid, who felt pretty tough as a member of the wrestling team. When we got to the hardware store, I got out of the car, went inside, and found the clerk. He was a grown adult man, and twice my size, but I faced him down.

"Why did you do that? Why did you make my mom feel so bad? You know you made her cry, don't you? Seriously, what's your freaking problem?"

He was infuriated. He swore at me, and I swore back. We only barely avoided getting into an actual fistfight. When the store owner overheard us, and asked what was going on, I told him, adding, "You should be ashamed of yourself." Defending my mom, advocating on her behalf, sometimes even volunteering to be her bodyguard—that was my role growing up.

Ironically, the hardware store was owned and staffed by immigrants from somewhere in Eastern Europe. I don't know how, but the store owner tracked down our phone number and that night called to apologize to my mom. He also said he fired the store clerk.

He was embarrassed. I'm sure he was someone who saw common-
ality, not difference, with his own life experience. What happened
didn't reflect the values of his small business.

Despite my dad's stature as a widely respected physician, and his
strong English speaking skills, he was not immune to incidents like
this, either.

A few years before, our family had gone out fishing in a small
boat. A lot of our neighbors spent their weekends fishing on Long
Island Sound. This must have seemed to my dad like a good way to
assimilate. On a sunny weekend, the five of us piled into the boat for
a long, relaxing day of fishing. But my dad was a novice at the helm,
and, panicking as he exited the harbor, he lightly bumped into another boat by mistake. "You idiot!" the two guys on the boat yelled.
"Go back to your own country! We don't want people like you here!
You don't even know how to steer!"

The trip was ruined. For the rest of the day, in the open waters
of the sound, as we kids ate the *kimbap*—seaweed-wrapped rice
rolls—that my mom had prepared and dropped little umbrella
hooks into the water to attract bluefish, my dad sat quietly by himself. His sadness felt private and beyond words. Nor did his mood
get any better when the same two guys who had yelled at him pulled
up alongside our boat and apologized. They felt especially bad, they
said, saying what they had in front of my dad's family. My dad accepted their apology graciously, but his face remained fixed in sadness. How alone and defenseless he must have felt. Years later, he
told us that when he saw the boat approaching, he assumed the two
guys wanted to hurt us, out there in the middle of the water, with no
one around to help.

For my dad, taking care of people wasn't just what he did as a pediatrician. It was part of everything he did as the founder of his own small business, meaning his medical practice. But it even extended beyond this. When I was a kid, a national pizza chain became famous for its delivery guarantee. If you ordered a pizza for delivery and it didn't show up in thirty minutes or less, your pizza was free. Lots of speeding tickets and car crashes later, the pizza chain abolished this policy. But when I was young, I found the free pizza guarantee incredibly exciting, like living inside a real-life video game. My brother and I would hover on the doorstep checking our watches, barely able to contain our delirium, hoping the driver would get lost, or overwhelmed, or stuck in traffic. If the driver was one minute late, we would do a dance and insist on the freebie.

When my dad saw us doing this, he called us into the family room. "Don't ever do that again," he said in a stern voice. "In a few years, that delivery person could be you. He is someone's son. Put yourself in the shoes of his parents. I don't want people to treat you like that one day." And then he would give the driver a huge tip.

Like so many men, my dad did not like to show his vulnerability. But the memory of that day on the boat, or even the pizza delivery lesson, painted a clear portrait of his existential worries and fears—a father of three, whose wife was equally vulnerable, if not more so with her poor command of the English language. When my dad came down with a severe flu one winter, he and my mom fretted openly about the future. Was any contingency plan in place if he died? What would his family do for money? But five years after the birth of my sister, it was my mom who got sick.

Her thyroid. The diagnosis was so bad that my dad's colleagues at the Port Jefferson hospital thought she might die. I could almost hear my dad thinking: *If she dies, what am I going to do? In this whole country, there is just our family to take care of us. There are only the five of us.*

When things are at their worst, though, it's often the case that seemingly ordinary people show how exceptional they really are. During my mom's hospitalization and recovery at home, a young Italian American nurse, who worked in my dad's office, and her boy-friend, took care of us. They loved my dad. They volunteered to come to our house to babysit and treated us to a lot of steak sand-wiches at Burger King. This young couple (her boyfriend was a burly guy who quarterbacked his flag football team) would always help my parents navigate the ins and outs of America. They especially helped my dad with American idioms. "Carol, you're pulling my legs," my dad would say, and instead of rolling her eyes, or correct-ing him, Carol would say, "Dr. Rhee—if I pulled both your legs, you would fall! That's why we say, 'pulling your *leg*.'" Hearing this, my dad would fall down, laughing. Like the elderly grandparents in the Bronx, Carol was always so gracious and generous.

My mom made a full recovery, but her hospitalization under-scored the fact that my siblings and I lived with a different type of existential vulnerability. It wasn't a war, but there was trauma. Be-fore moving to my childhood home one year before my sister was born, we lived in an apartment fifteen minutes away from my dad's single-shingle pediatric office. My brother and I scooted around on our Big Wheels, aware of the tension and uncertainty in the air—arguments about money, and whether my parents would have to move back to Korea. In those early years, one Christmas I received a single present: a store-bought plastic net stocking filled with can-dies. At the time, my parents still didn't know much about Santa

Claus, or the commercial aspects of Christmas. They were also at the time extremely worried about money.

In retrospect, we lived in a household with a cloud of scarcity permanently hovering over it. If my dad's medical practice was going through a slow period, it was DEFCON 1. But paranoia also was grounded in reality. One of my dad's patients claimed that the antibacterial soap my dad had prescribed for her had damaged her baby's brain. She sued the manufacturer and added my dad to the lawsuit for good measure. This puzzled him. *Dr. Rhee is the best, most caring pediatrician I know*, he recollected her saying. Then why was she suing him? Quite simply, my dad was collateral damage. More surprising to him was learning how happy one of the local doctors seemed when he heard about the lawsuit. If my dad lost in court, he could lose his malpractice insurance, which meant he could not practice medicine anymore. He would be forced to go back to Korea, and the other doctors could gather up the spoils, his patients. To a doctor who always went the extra mile and gave his fellow physicians as much coverage as they needed, this seemed monstrous.

"That's not fair," I remember my dad saying at the time. When he was dying of Parkinson's disease, he said it again. He had worked hard his whole life. His plan was to retire at age sixty-five so that he and my mom could do things together. Ultimately, there wasn't a single day during his retirement when the disease wasn't attacking the neurons in his brain and tormenting his body. I can still hear him saying, "This isn't fair."

The lawsuit, and the uncertainty it brought, hung over his head for almost fifteen years, as he was dragged feet-first through the US legal system. "I'm sorry, Dr. Rhee," my dad's attorney told him, "but this is just how the system works in this country." I heard him tell my mom a few times, "Maybe we can't make it here." The suit was dismissed just in time for my dad to be diagnosed with Parkinson's.

The experience was damaging. And panic-inducing. It gave rise to a low-level terror, the fear that everything might be pulled out from under the five of us at any time, even after decades of building a successful life in the US. It was one reason why he always wanted me to lead a safer, more predictable life than his, since success and money can be safeguards, *to a certain extent*, against the guaranteed volatility that life hands all of us—as he found out firsthand with the malpractice lawsuit. I'm sure that played a part in his worries when I couldn't find a job after my first year of Harvard Law School.

During that time, my mom withdrew even more. She would sometimes wrap herself in a private cocoon. When I picture her with her non-Korean friends, she is standing among them. The others are talking and laughing and gesturing. My mom's smile is, as always, incandescent, but her eyes are inward-looking and cast to one side. I knew those eyes from school. They were the eyes of kids who hoped the teacher wouldn't call on them. The eyes of kids who didn't want to be put on the spot and laughed at. *I'm not here*, those eyes said. Of all things, that look of hers pained me the most, even more than when my "friends" thought it was funny to make fun of her accent.

As I hurtled through life, gathering prestige and status, my resentment of anyone who treated my parents badly now and again became something else: embarrassment. It horrifies me now to admit that. But that embarrassment swirled around, like an inlet joining bigger waterways of anger, and protectiveness, and outrage at the way the world treated them, and in the end, it was hard to tell the feelings apart.

In retrospect, part of what silently moved me to enroll in a Korean language class in college and spend the summer after freshman year at Yonsei University in Seoul was to uncover the past that my parents kept from us. I even stayed at my aunt's house, rather than the party dorm for expats.

Every country, every culture, has an essence that can't be easily explained in another country's words. You need to immerse. There are words and feelings that have no equivalent in other languages.

Korea is no exception. Korean culture is the embodiment of resilience and survival. It's been invaded something like nine hundred times over its two-thousand-year history, suffering through dehumanizing periods of colonization and torture. After the Korean War, the country was divided into two by an armistice—note that Korean leadership was not even invited to the final negotiations. Perhaps for this reason, Korean culture can be raw and sharp, like *kimchi*. Words can be very direct and biting. There's a survivor's mentality. But at the same time, because of this, neighbors and virtual strangers will feed you their last grain of rice if you need it more than they do.

When I was in Korea, I finally understood a part of me that I had not understood before. And I finally had the vocabulary, the framework, to explain and express it. First to myself, and then to others. I think the dynamic balance created by the uniquely Korean concepts of *han* and *jeong* best captures all this.

Han can be defined as an unrelenting, bottomless anger, sorrow, frustration, and grief born of too much suffering. *Han* is both personal and collective. Many Korean families are aware of some degree of *han* in their own history. *Han* can last after a person dies and endure in their children and grandchildren. It's a form of generational trauma. *Han* is the pain of a past that won't let go. Is there a relationship between *han* and the fact that Korea has among the highest rates of alcoholism and suicide in the world? Probably.

Thanks to immigration, I guess it's fair to say that *han* can cross oceans and transmute. I'm referring to the indignities my parents, and other immigrants, had to put up with every day. The incidents at the hardware store and on the boat both added to the proverbial *han* balance sheet of my parents and their children. Do you think perhaps I recognized *han* in the souls of my colleagues at Ashley Stewart?

As nature knows, all things are balanced by an opposite force, and *han* is no exception. The other side of *han* is *jeong*. *Jeong* refers to a connectedness infused with love, empathy, warmth, compassion, and friendship. But it's more than that. *Jeong* is a statement of interdependence, of mutual coexistence, of cooperative living (though it can go too far; there *is* such a thing as bad *jeong*). There is no English equivalent, but I think the closest English word is *goodwill*, whose meaning we will circle back to later in this book.

Jeong. It was created when my mom overstuffed the Halloween goodie bags with the larger-size candy bars for the neighborhood kids who flocked to our doorstep. Why? Because she hadn't had any as a refugee escaping invading armies during the Korean War. When one of our neighbors left to enlist in the navy, my mom had him over to our house and fed him *kalbi*, beef-on-a-bone that's associated with Korean barbecue. She grilled it in front of him, on a small makeshift indoor grill, the *kalbi* wrapped tightly in aluminum foil to enclose the drips. We rarely ate *kalbi*, because it was too expensive.

Jeong was in the lunches she packed for us every day, and in the warmth of her gifts. A wool scarf, a cozy sweater, V-necked and crew-necked undershirts to keep us from shivering in the snow, winter coats, mittens, and hats. (I still have the gray, elephantine Eddie Bauer down jacket she gave me during law school, as she apparently was worried I would freeze to death in the winter.) My mom's *jeong* extended to anyone who came to our house. If plumbers or electricians showed up to do some work, she would serve them a tall glass of cold water or an icy Sprite, presented on a tray. They were always so surprised and grateful.

Jeong was created when she picked me up from nursery school and the two of us went to McDonald's. Our order was always the same. For me, a hamburger, a small fries, and a Coke. (The Happy Meal hadn't been invented yet.) For her, a Filet-O-Fish sandwich and a small coffee. *Who would ever choose the Filet-O-Fish?* I always wondered.

In Korean culture, words can be sharp, even abrupt. It's in the action, the doing, where the underlying generosity manifests. The depth of *jeong* is matched, and made possible, only by the depths of *han*. The *what* may have sharp sides, but the *how* is gracious. In Korean restaurants (the real ones at least), the servers can be quite impatient with customers. *What do you want?* But when the food comes to the table, it's served with such respect, attention, and care. It's all about the *how*.

When I was growing up, *how* my siblings and I did something was just as important as what we did. If I told my mom that a friend's mother had treated me to an ice cream cone, she wouldn't just ask whether I had thanked her. "Did you thank her *graciously*?" If I was studying for a test, she would gaze at me from the doorway. "Are you preparing *correctly*?"

The Korean language is complex, nuanced, with different pronouns and verb endings depending on whom you're talking to—peers, younger people, elders. You have to use the right word, conjugation, and emphasis. Verbal communication is often paired with a series of highly scrutinized and choreographed physical gestures. Two hands are used while pouring a drink for an older person, for instance.

My mom's *jeong* always felt super personal—but that is a beautiful characteristic of *jeong*: the way it makes another person feel seen. My mom's *jeong* was in the pink-and-white-striped, cotton ball–stuffed cushion she sewed me when the commercial neck support I used when playing the violin didn't work. Even her hands conveyed *jeong*, whether they were rubbing an upset stomach as she sang a soft, traditional Korean song—*My hand is medicine, my hand is medicine, there, there, there*—or stroking my cheek if I was upset about something.

Years later, concerned about my financial well-being during my entrepreneurial days, she always slipped a twenty-dollar or one-hundred-dollar bill into my jacket pocket. *Yongdon*, or pocket money, is a Korean custom where older people pass along money to younger people. Not a lot—just enough to ease a younger person's worry or suffering. How the recipient receives and spends *yongdon* matters as much as the gesture itself. Through *jeong*, *yongdon* transforms money, a transactional thing, into social currency, a gift that imparts warmth, which is one reason why my mom insisted on using crisp white envelopes whenever she paid for any services or lessons.

As for my dad, he never turned away a patient who couldn't pay for care—that was how he created *jeong*. Rereading the letters his patients sent him after he retired, I could clearly see they experienced that *jeong*. In his interactions with his patients, and especially with my little sister, I saw his quiet generosity and kindness. But with his sons, I think it's fair to say that he had more difficulty expressing this *jeong*. Or maybe we, his sons, weren't good in recognizing or receiving the form it took. Among the three of us, we never fully developed a shared language or a framework for emotions.

What could be more natural than my dad wanting me to live a safer life than his? *You took so much risk to allow me to take risk*, I used to tell him. I knew he thought I overdid the risk part. I knew my life made him anxious. He wanted better things for me, but I always thought that my academic pedigree should give me the courage to live more freely. *It should be freeing, not burdensome*, I thought. My degree from Harvard College—that was on *them*, with immense gratitude. But what I decided to do with it was on *me*. My mom and dad used to have fights about me, in fact. She would tell him, *Yeobo, gwaenchanha. Sweetheart, it's okay, just let him be.*

Other than my mother, the person in my life who most taught me the beauty of *jeong* was my older brother, John. As children, he and I were extremely close, partners in crime. He provided me with the emotional, and sometimes physical, security that all kids need. He made me feel safe in a way my immigrant parents could not.

John is a little less than four years older than me, but remember, he didn't really meet our parents until he was almost five.

One Christmas morning, he got very upset. My sister, Jennifer, was still essentially a toddler. John and I woke up early and made the usual barreling rush for the tree in the corner of that same family room where my parents had questioned me about the red helicopter a few years earlier. I remember the disappointment on his face when there was only one present under the tree for him—a board game called Carrier Strike, which no one then or since has ever heard of. I had a pile of presents. My parents had wrongly discerned that John didn't need many presents because he no longer believed in Santa Claus. But that's not how it felt to him.

All Christmas morning, he cried. He was inconsolable. He cried so hard his nose started bleeding. And it wouldn't stop. It was bad enough that my mom, who was a nurse, had no idea what to do. She had to call my dad at his office, where he was tending to sick Christmas Day patients.

I watched intently. It's hard to see your older brother, your hero, in that condition. Because he knew I still believed in Santa Claus, he couldn't tell me why he was sad. During the next year, I saved up my coins in a plastic tin to buy my brother something good for Christmas. Twelve months went by, and a few weeks before Christmas, my mom agreed to take me to the local record store. I bought *Zeppelin IV*, the iconic Led Zeppelin album with "Stairway to Heaven" on it. On Christmas Eve, I clumsily wrapped the album and tucked it under the tree in our family room.

Early the next morning, the two of us, now joined by my little sister, raced for the tree, tearing through our presents, barely pausing to enjoy one before reaching for the next.

"We're done," my brother said finally. He was the boss.

I shook my head. "No. There's another gift, I think—"

"No, we're done. There's no more."

He hadn't seen my present because records are flat, and the tree branches were also in the way.

"Oh, hold on," he said, "I think there *is* one more." Slowly, he tore off the paper. "Is this from you?"

"Uh, yeah," I said.

I will never forget that Christmas. It was the first year any of us kids had given a sibling a present. Up until that point, Christmas belonged completely to Santa Claus, not to parents or brothers and sisters. My brother extended his hand for a handshake, trying to act like a big brother, but I could tell he was emotional.

To this day, I tear up when I picture the two brothers sitting next to the tree in the tiny family room, the older one hugging *Zeppelin IV* against his pajama top. It's still the best present I've ever given anyone. (I'm pretty sure the red helicopter is the best present I've ever received.)

So you see, *jeong* is powerful. It's dynamic. It lives and breathes. But its life force comes from suffering, from *han*. My brother and I aren't those two little boys against the world like we once were, but every time I hear a Zeppelin song, I am transported back through space and time, and I am grateful for how much he loved his kid brother.

Piecing together the Ashley Stewart corporate narrative forced me to come to terms with my own history. In that gloomy converted distribution center, I experienced more clarity than I had in years. Inside that room, there was still chaos, but I was also finding peace.

A stillness within the frenzy. Underlying the calmness was the permission I gave myself to allow opposites to coexist. And, dare I say, thrive. I opened up space for the symbiotic connection between *han* and *jeong*, high school teacher and financier, Korean and American, and ultimately, past and present. It was A *and* B, which created an organic C.

From that vantage point, I saw the differences *and* similarities between the lives of my parents and those of the women working for or served by Ashley Stewart. Especially my grandmother and my mom. Also, were my dad's existential fears all that different from those of the white widowed father who came into my kindergarten class to give his son's friend a toy red helicopter?

I was hundreds of miles away from my own family. My social life and identity were fewer than ten miles away in the restaurants, clubs, and office buildings of Manhattan, but Manhattan felt as far away as the moon. I was literally apart from my life, in what was most certainly an unwinnable situation. But surprisingly, as I said, I felt at peace. I felt aware. I felt alive. I felt present.

In the end, by mortgaging the stuffing out of their one long-term financial asset of substance, our childhood home, my mom and dad sent all three of us to college. We graduated debt free. They received no financial aid, when in reality I wonder if they might have qualified had they been equipped to read and comprehend the small print. Yes, they struggled, but their life was authentic. They created and earned every ounce of joy that assuaged their pain. For every slight handed them, they forged friendships with people like Joel's family, Carol, and their other friends from Seoul National University who came to America when they did. They had real friends. My parents had tried to protect us from their childhood and adult suffering. But perhaps that is where they erred. Maybe by sharing more of their past and embracing the ugly with the good, their three children could have made more sense of their complicated reality and found real joy in forging a path through their own suffering. I know that for me, for the first time in a long time, sometime during that first month alone at Ashley Stewart, I gave myself permission to breathe and to give myself grace. I was born only six years after the passage of the Immigration and Nationality Act of 1965. How many lives, historically speaking, were like my own? How many role models did I have? There was no playbook. (Granted, there's no real precedent or playbook for *any* of our lives.)

A month after arriving at Ashley Stewart, I knew in my gut what I had to do. My intuition told me that I had to strip off my armor. Until that point, I hadn't truly realized how heavy and burdensome it had become. I needed to venture out even further from my comfort zone, out of the warehouse and corporate headquarters, where what fragments of truth there were existed only in stale and misleading financial reports. I needed to head out into the stores and spend time, a lot of time, with the women who I instinctively knew were going to be so much like my grandmother and mom. The exchange I had with the dissatisfied customer during the performative board visit replayed in my head. I knew I needed to show up not as a former board member or private equity guy, or even as their new boss. But instead, as James, all of him. With my armor off, I could only hope they would see and accept me for being me.

chapter 3

future

A helicopter can fly in six different directions (up, down, left, right, forward, and backward).

By now I knew that reconciling my past was key to understanding my future. And that my future, in turn, would be influenced by my own history. But I was also determined not to be shackled by the past. After the first town hall, the present took center stage. There was only the *now*. I had to *do*. I didn't have the luxury of overthinking things. But, as is often the case, the most important things were what I chose *not* to do, the *words* I did *not* say. During uncertain times, sometimes the best thing to do is to receive, not take. To choose to float instead of thrash. With time in scarce quantity, I focused my intention on *creating space* to allow for time to unfold in a different direction.

Most of us are conditioned to think of space as physical. At work, *space* is defined by an office, a desk, a room. Having told everyone I wasn't altogether qualified to be their leader, I wasn't about to add, *So would you mind showing me to my corner office, please?* I not only didn't stake out the nearest or best office, but I didn't lay claim to *any* office.

We did not have the budget to break down the physical walls and buy furniture that could allow us to see one another. So I did the best I could. I found a small cubby in the middle of the second floor, overlooking the bulletproof glass–protected entrance, and asked for the lowest set of dividers in the building. People coming to work in the morning and leaving at night couldn't miss me. Nor I them. Next to the cubby, I positioned a small oval table with a cheap laminate overlay to create a tiny, makeshift conference "space." And voilà, we had designed a regal executive suite.

The conversations reminded me of the ones I had had with my mom over the years. I did a whole lot of listening with my ears *and* my eyes—not just with the people who oversaw key functions, but with everyone. One by one, my new colleagues took a seat at the oval table. Some were curious or had ideas they had swallowed for fear of being dismissed or ridiculed. I didn't turn anyone away. Meetings happened organically. I noted who had the courage to grab a seat, and I gave them that space. Generally speaking, it was the people who had something on their minds. Something that was bothering them. Something they wanted, *needed*, to get off their chests. People who cared.

What's your name? What do you do? Why do you think I'm here? Why are you here? Why are you <u>still</u> here? What kind of music do you listen to? What do you do for fun? While listening to the answers, I gained insights into a few other implicit questions. I felt like my dad with his Socratic methodology. *What are you good at? Do you truly care about the outcome? How willing are you to learn new things? And <u>unlearn</u> others? Do you have a history of overcoming obstacles? Are you willing to suspend disbelief and keep an open* *mind? Maybe embrace contradictions?* And, fundamentally, *Are you willing to take this leap with me?*

That said, I made my share of declarative statements, in a voice whose timbre and pitch were distinctive from my everyday one. Against the backdrop of a disarmingly casual environment more typical of a kitchen than a boardroom, the statements had an unmistakable gravity and clarity. *This is a new system,* I said. *A clean slate. With a different intent. Your reaction is your choice, not mine. Unhappy people usually end up firing themselves,* I added. I would give those people the time and space to do just that.

I used a decrepit whiteboard, rolling it into the cafeteria on its squeaky wheels, to show everyone how the company invested what little money it had. This much for rent, this much for payroll, this much for merchandise, and so on. Someone in the information technology group shared his eureka moment with the whole room, explaining, his voice loud with excitement and bewilderment, that the company, as structured, had been losing millions of dollars a year. I smiled serenely. It was important that this conclusion came from someone who *wasn't* me, *wasn't* someone in finance. Collective ownership of the numbers had begun. My intuition was right. Rather than panic, people expressed relief. Rather than shrinking, they rose to the occasion. The cat was now out of the bag. Secretive meetings and hushed voices had created more harm than good. They were now in the past.

Sensing the positive electricity in the air, I seized the opportunity to say something that might have been received poorly but for the buzz created by this new level of transparency about the financial situation. Meaning, I was very aware and intentional about how my various statements and their respective tone formed an overall composition.

"If you lie, cheat, or steal from this company," I said quietly and matter-of-factly, "you will be prosecuted to the fullest extent of the law."

I let my eyes carry the message. If this sounds harsh, or unkind, remember that I was very much aware of the company's rocky twenty-two-year history. In addition, no one who sabotaged their colleagues' right to start over was permitted to stay. It's one thing to be miserable, but intentionally undermining someone else's right to make an informed choice wouldn't be tolerated. It would help no one to hide my intention and reasoning. I was completely transparent. Saying what I did, in the context of sharing the company's financials, helped people better understand the relationship between kindness and math. No one in the cafeteria that day left with any doubt of the importance of behavior vis-à-vis financial results.

A month went by. The culture started showing gradual, unmistakable signs of change. The makeshift conference space became the new hub of decision-making, pushing the windowless boardroom into irrelevance. More often than not, the best ideas came from those colleagues who had previously been conditioned to remain silent. I saw a few new leaders emerge. They had passion and hope, practical skills and concrete ideas, as well as life experience in how to maximize results with the scarcest of resources, which was rare among or forgotten by many of my private equity peers. Most were first- or second-generation Americans, all genders, races, countries of origin, and ethnicities. They knew what *entrepreneur* meant, not from business school but from experience, from their own lives. Like my parents.

One was a young, whip-smart assistant fashion buyer named Tamara, who commuted north of two hours daily from Brooklyn. As she sat at the oval table describing what she did, mentioning almost as an aside that her background, and her *passion*, was in marketing, *in getting the word out*, it was obvious she was in the wrong job. "You should also be spending time in marketing," I said.

"Right," Tamara said, laughing, "and I don't want to be just an assistant buyer!"

We decided we could integrate her fashion savvy into our nascent marketing efforts. Tamara beamed. And, as time went on, we started filming Tamara in our home office, wearing our clothes. "Hey, ladies," she would say, "it's Tamara. And I'm wearing *this* today," and she would twirl around with a knowing look in her eye. It was the show *within* the show that was our corporate ordeal. These clips would then be posted to our newly activated social media channels, which were run by a young white woman who had grown up in rural America. The executive team's fear of the unknown, namely digital marketing, had led to her being sidelined, where she was drowning helplessly under the ink of print advertisements and circulars. Way down the road, after we upgraded the music playing in the stores, she helped Tamara broadcast her melodious speaking voice over the store speakers. Basically, for some, Tamara became the face *and* the voice of Ashley Stewart.

I was glad to find talented people in-house—since we had neither the time nor the money to bring in anyone new. During my private equity career, I also generally discovered that sustainable solutions are typically found from within. More often than not, substance beats credentials. That said, in this case, I did make two external hires.

The first was Randy. Half-Irish, half-Dominican, Randy grew up poor in Brooklyn, was raised by a single mom, and ultimately worked his way to an Ivy League degree and a series of top finance jobs. He had been part of my team in Boston. "I'm coming to help you," Randy announced my second or third week at Ashley Stewart.

From then on, he and I ate every breakfast, lunch, and dinner together, calorie for calorie.

Donna was next. The daughter of Chinese American immigrants, she had been bored at her job at a Manhattan investment bank and was in a period of transition. Donna and I had met during the failed capital-raising process for Ashley Stewart that had necessitated my unlikely appearance in Secaucus as interim leader. Somehow, she caught wind of the goings-on and reached out to me. "Come say hi and check out what Randy and I are doing," I told her, a little ambiguously. One day, Donna, intrigued, appeared in our office. "What are you guys doing?" Then, "Are you kidding me?"

In fact, we had already prepared a laptop for her. Donna took a seat in a cubby on the other side of the oval table and never left. Just like that, with the addition of Randy and Donna, I had successfully turbocharged the world of Ashley Stewart with the language of Wall Street. Internally, several bright individuals had subject matter expertise in accounting, finance, and computer systems, but they lacked the experience and exposure to the lingo and analytical conventions of Wall Street. Randy and Donna would serve as trusted translators and pass along the hands-on training they had received on Wall Street, only ten miles and a moon across the Hudson River.

Being the new person is never easy. Remember the first day of school? Summer camp? College? Remember my mom? The same goes for CEOs. They need allies, advocates, and translators, too. It can be isolating. But even one person can make all the difference. Stepping in to play all those roles for me was Gina.

Gina is a bilingual Dominican American woman. She is a single mother whose son proudly served in the military. Born with a knack and talent for calling out nonsense when she hears it, Gina also served as the unofficial office manager and a roving therapist on twenty-four-hour call. Immediately upon my arrival, Gina was able to intuit that her new role was to verbalize those things I didn't say out loud but instead communicated intentionally with my eyes, face, and hands. (Evidently, Gina, my mom, and I had taken the same multisensory language class in advanced, executive-level *nunchi*.) Gina also took it upon herself to vouch for me. "He's real," I heard her say a few times in English and in Spanish. "He cares. And you better be ready. Don't let the calmness fool you. He's relentless."

With Gina's encouragement, the town hall meetings turned into a regular series. They were unscripted, and always light in tone. During one, I explained the lesson of the three-legged stool.

The three-legged stool is a metaphor—obviously—and a big one, too, with applications for your life, as well as the life of a company. The first leg of the stool is your work life. The second leg is your family life. The third leg is what you do in your free time, when you can just "be," from your social life to your hobbies. These three legs are never perfectly level, or even. One leg is always wobbly, and un-aligned, and threatening to give, but if the other two legs are kept reasonably steady, the stool can remain standing. How? Through *action*, because balance actually requires perpetual motion. It is never static. And as we will see throughout this book, it is an incredible relief when that action comes in the form of friendship or a helping hand from someone else.

"I'll give everyone here a head start," I told my new colleagues. "I'll do everything I can to help keep your work leg stable. I can't promise financial results. That's our collective responsibility. So how will I help? I will do my best to make sure this culture rewards those who care enough to be curious, honest, generous, and willing to keep learning." In my head, I was thinking about the plus-minus ratings in ice hockey, and the part they might play here. I was looking for people who made other people *better*, just as I had told the investment bankers years earlier when they gazed quizzically at my résumé.

What I *didn't* say, not wanting to trigger anyone's sordid memories from high school geometry class, is that there's a good reason why two points make a line but three points create a plane. Lines are rigid and straightforward and tend to be binary, but planes have dimensionality. *Three's a crowd*, people say. Yes, but isn't the third child, the third friend, the third at the dinner table usually the one who shakes things up, oftentimes by defining the nature of the balance between the two other people? Two is a partnership. Three is a system.

With a small nucleus of new leaders in place, and a loosely framed narrative already forming in my mind, I now had the confidence and wherewithal to go where I needed to go: to the stores, and the women in those stores, in those Black neighborhoods across the country. I needed to follow and trust my intuition. The one intersecting with my past, and my mom and grandmother. But there was another thing, too. And it frankly puzzled me.

Financially, something wasn't adding up. According to the

company's balance sheet, we had a surplus of inventory. (More about this in chapters 4 and 5.) Tons of "assets." But our initial sales momentum had stalled and was now declining. *The store managers aren't selling hard enough*, the executive management team told me. *It's on them, not us.*

Even people who hate or fear math can't help but spend their days surrounded by numbers, documents, and data tables. Bank statements. Restaurant and gas station receipts. Top ten lists. By definition, those numbers, like accounting, reflect only the *past*—the twenty dollars you just withdrew from the ATM, the gas tank you topped off. More important than the crumpled white slips in your pocket, however, are the decisions, or actions, that led to them in the first place. Casting your mind back to *those* makes it easier for you to change the future.

For the previous couple of weeks, dressed in my fashion denim (I had upgraded from the pleated khakis after some light teasing from a few of the younger fashionistas), I'd been staring at numbers that made no sense. If we had so much inventory, so many "assets" on the financial books, why had sales suddenly stalled? The executive team couldn't, or wouldn't, help me understand the *how* of those numbers, or their root causes. In fact, the executive team, paralyzed by the negative sales numbers and unwilling to hear bad news, had canceled the weekly feedback calls from the store managers. In doing so, they both knowingly and unknowingly cut themselves off from the truth.

I got behind the wheel of my company car, a gray and aging Nissan sedan that had seen better days. Time to go searching for root causes. *We have so much inventory—so what am I not seeing?* Sometimes you find the answer to the most mystifying riddles in the strangest places, and when you least expect it, too.

• • •

I had "met" the store managers before. Shortly after that first corporate town hall, I set up a second, similar meeting via conference call. Remember, we had no Wi-Fi. No Zoom or Microsoft Teams. The best that the in-house technology group could muster was a Starfish phone with an old-fashioned, multidigit, dial-in number. After a few minutes of static and multiple beeps, the store managers assembled on the call. "I trust you," I said as the conversation ended, "and I look forward to meeting you. You know these stores a lot better than I ever will."

Meaningful silence. But good silence. The store managers were scattered around the country. We weren't speaking face-to-face. But they understood. It was a big leap of faith on everyone's part, my own included. Without my coming out and saying it, I had just told them everything they needed to know. Left unsaid, but heavily implied, was that without their having shielded the truth of the debacle that was the corporate entity from customers, Ashley Stewart would have gone out of business a decade before.

The Nissan sedan and I logged a lot of miles together. I visited as many stores in and around New York, New Jersey, and Philadelphia as I possibly could before racing back to Secaucus in the early evening to review materials at headquarters. As Thanksgiving grew nearer, I flew to farther-flung stores around the country—Dallas, Atlanta, Detroit. Every store was different. So were my interactions with the predominantly Black female store managers. They were happy to see me, but also surprised. A chasm had always existed between the company's corporate side and its customer-facing colleagues—*Us* versus *Them*. Not anymore. We were in this together. And, in my mind, a pattern began to emerge. My first visit to one store in particular captured its essence.

Brick Church is a neighborhood in East Orange, New Jersey, not that far from Secaucus. Ninety percent or so of its residents identify as Black or African American, and Brick Church also has one of the highest percentages of Caribbean Americans in the United States.

The Brick Church store was narrow, with a slightly worn appearance. Tan wallpaper, yellowed lighting, wall-to-wall animal print carpeting. A lot of clutter. In some areas, strips of masking tape pinned down untidy spots where the carpet had torn away. The cash registers were a decade old. But like a popular, well-loved family room, the store gave off a feeling of hominess and cheer and welcome, thanks to the store manager, Chary, and her assistant manager, Shelley.

With no videoconferencing, no one could possibly know upon seeing me that I was the new leader. During our phone call, it wasn't as though I said, *Hi—I'm James. Here's how to recognize me. Ready? I'm Korean American, dimpled, around five-foot-ten, and 175 (and counting) pounds.* At one point, Shelley playfully asked to see my phone in order to confirm my credentials as a company employee. She began fiddling with it, as the three of us continued chatting and joking around. Finally, I said, "You know that I'm *that* James, right?"

Chary and Shelley couldn't have been more different, but they had one thing in common: they loved people. And they cared for each other deeply. Chary had been with the company for fifteen years. Nothing made her happier, she said, than making another woman feel good about herself. "A woman might come inside the store not feeling so great—but when she leaves, she feels good," she told me. "There aren't enough people in this world who say, 'You can do this, you got this, you are amazing.' That goes a long way."

Shelley was a self-described "ball of fire." Born in Barbados, she was twelve years old when she came to the US. Her dad died unexpectedly when she was eighteen. "I lost a piece of my soul that day," Shelley told me. Like my mom, hers was a nurse. Like Chary, Shelley had worked in retail her whole life. She had three children she doted on, and followed the New England Patriots. She loved that I lived outside Boston and was profoundly disappointed that I didn't hang out with Tom Brady.

I can't explain why, but two seconds after meeting Chary and Shelley, I knew the three of us would be friends forever. More obvious was the affection, respect, and love between them. Just being around them made me feel good.

For the next few hours, I immersed myself in their world. Anyone who came through the door—Chary and Shelley knew that person's name. And with the few they didn't know, in no time at all the customer was calling them "baby" and telling them what she had planned for Friday night. Sons, daughters, boyfriends, girlfriends, husbands, mothers, fathers, grandparents, grandchildren—Chary and Shelley seemed to know everything about everyone. The customer who was raising two boys by herself, another whose marriage was rocky, a third whose daughter just had a baby. I overheard pockets of conversation. *I'm worried about my son. I got a hot date tomorrow night. My job interview is next week. My dad is doing much better, thank you for remembering.* After listening in, I wasn't surprised to learn that Chary visited customers in the hospital if they had no local family.

Before I left, Chary and Shelley gave me a tour of the back room. Like your closet, or attic, the back room of a store is usually home to the truth. It was there that I observed a few seemingly irrelevant things that crystallized everything I couldn't quite put my finger on while studying spreadsheets from my makeshift office in Secaucus.

One of the culprits was the operations manual, a thick, disheveled paper pile held loosely in place by a broken binder. Biweekly updates spilled out of it. Apparently, all new hires, including part-time sales associates trying to earn extra money during school vacations, were supposed to sit down and study this thing. Seriously? I scanned random pages. Do this. Do that. If this, then that. It must be done *this way*, too. Or else. Then, after you do it, prove it. Confirm it. Mail the evidence back to us. Or else! This prescriptive, heavy-handed attempt to control everyone's behavior in the store extended to how managers were supposed to treat their customers. Needless to say, the operating manual said nothing about visiting customers in the hospital or asking about their jobs and children.

Again, seriously? How can any person feel a sense of ownership and agency at work if someone is jamming a rulebook down their throat? It was beyond ridiculous and incredibly condescending. "Does anyone actually *do* this?" I asked Shelley. "Do you or your customers really think this operations manual is worth anything?" She gave me a *you've gotta be kidding me* look. "Hey—check this out, Shelley," I said, and tore up some of the more painfully inane directives and store signs. We laughed, Shelley the loudest. But inside, I was seething.

On the lighter side, have you ever watched as a grown man only a few weeks weaned from wearing pleated khakis receives a crash course in women's fashion? I'm proud to say I left the Brick Church store newly aware of the differences between a *Marilyn* (a dress that Marilyn Monroe made famous), a *shark-bite* (a dress that looks like a prehistoric predator took a huge munch out of one side), a *peplum* (a blouse that is generous in the back and provides ample "coverage"), and a *keyhole* (another style of blouse with a hole in the center to minimize a different sort of "coverage"). Learning all of this brought the numbers to life. The financials were literally dancing in my brain. So was the red helicopter. It was *at home* in that store.

The other culprit was more troubling. Back inside the company car, heading back to Secaucus, I now understood why Ashley Stewart was so inventory-rich but sales-poor. Stashed in the back room were piles and piles of black and white camisoles. For the uninitiated (that was me that day), a camisole, or cami, is a basic undergarment worn as a layering piece underneath a blouse or a sweater. You buy a cami so that you can make another piece of clothing stand out—on its own, a cami isn't the type of purchase that brings you joy or makes you feel beautiful or celebrated. By my calculations, Brick

Church had around a year's worth of these plain camis stashed in the back room. This was suicidal math on the part of the management team. They assumed that buying in bulk meant they would get a better deal, on a cost-per-cami basis. They were right that the cost-per-cami was lower, but they couldn't have been more wrong in not appreciating how calamitous it was that they had tied up cash in "assets" that were just sitting in the back room, collecting dust.

A fundamental rule of finance and economics, and all of life, too, is a concept known as *opportunity cost*. The opportunity cost of something of value refers to what you must give up to have it; every choice we make means we give up one or more options in favor of the one we choose. Example: You get the opportunity to go out partying with friends the night before your final exam. You beg off and study instead. You ace your final, but it comes at the opportunity cost of a night spent dancing and socializing. Or you love your daily takeout salad, but the costs add up. What else could you have done with the money? Was the opportunity cost worth it? Did you choose wisely, and did you maximize value? The concept also applies to matters of the heart. I moved to Boston from New York because my future with Meg was more valuable to me than my career on Wall Street.

In the case of the camis, management had tied up cash in stuff that was collecting dust off the sales floor for months. *Instead*, they should have used a portion of that cash to buy fewer camis at a slightly higher cost-per-cami that could sell faster, and invested the rest of it in marketing or the type of merchandise that would drive incremental traffic. Worse, our store managers were being blamed for not achieving sales goals, which affected their compensation when they couldn't sell the oversupplied merchandise. Even though the accounting team dutifully booked the camis as an "asset," they were in reality just the opposite. They were toxic liabilities. Further, the store managers had not made the initial decision to purchase those camis. *They* were being held accountable for poor decisions made by the corporate leadership. The balance sheet (inventory) was at fault, not the income statement (sales).

I could only shake my head. I'd seen this absurdity so many times in my private equity career. I also knew that most business schools and mass media focus on the *income statement*, otherwise known as the profit and loss statement, which tracks the revenue, expenses, gains, and losses of a business over a finite period. This is where the lower cost per cami would have looked great in reports. But this is different from the *balance sheet*, which reflects a company's assets, liabilities, and overall equity at a particular time. From this perspective, the management team had turned cash into what were for all intents and purposes *dead assets*. But hey, I get it—revenues are a lot sexier to talk about and easier to measure than balance sheet productivity. At Ashley Stewart, however, the mindset was about to change. A *lot*.

In the course of my travels, the same interactions and observations I'd had at Brick Church generally repeated themselves. Fear and camis concealed in the back room quickly gave way to relief, action, decisiveness, and recommendations. Other findings, too, gave me confidence that I was right to believe fashion was the least important thing happening inside our thirty-five-hundred-square-foot stores. The interactions I saw revolved not around clothes and shopping, but around key moments in the lives of generations of women—moms, daughters, sisters, cousins, aunties, grandmothers. On Sundays, families stopped by a neighborhood store after church, with mom or dad paying down an outstanding balance with a check. Many customers dropped by the stores two or three times a week, and left feeling better with or without a shopping bag, assured that whatever their perceived flaws might be, or however their lives might be going, someone had their back and was cheering them on.

Abundance was the word that kept coming to mind. Along with *warmth*, *graciousness*, *generosity*, and yes, *kindness*. Other words that kept coming up were *character*, *accountability*, *leadership*, and *entrepreneurship*. Chary, Shelley, and many of the other frontline women I met were more like small business owners and innkeepers than store managers. They were their customers' best friends, close confidantes, relationship counselors, life coaches, keepers of secrets, and trackers of family histories. Strangers who'd been given their number would call them after hours, or over the weekend. *I'm going out with my husband. Do you have this dress in stock? What about that blouse?* Even if she was in her car, or hanging out with her family, Chary would volunteer to call the store. *We have it*, she would report back. *But you have to bring me a Pepsi in return. You better have my Pepsi, or you're not getting your dress.*

In some stores, customers addressed managers simply as "Miss Ashley." It was patently obvious that Chary and Shelley acted no differently in stores than they did in their family rooms. They gave permission to their customers, not to mention me, to do the same. And by doing so, they tapped into a reservoir of authentic power that warmly invited in a common humanity that softened the angles of that place we call work. If Chary hadn't seen a regular customer in a while, she would call or text to make sure that person was all right. As for the stores themselves, they were safe havens. Oases. Community centers. Neighborhood check-in stations.

At some point during those first few months, I don't remember exactly when, I started calling the company *Ashley* and *she*. *She* was real. *She* was human. *She* had feelings. It was hard to look at the cavalier attitude of past ownership and leadership toward this company, toward *her*, and not take it personally.

Mind you, I saw bad leadership and purely transactional interactions in the stores as well. Not every store had the magic I saw in Brick Church. But I saw enough of the examples of the good things. There was *potential*. When customers came into one of our stores, a change came over some of them. A new ease. A confidence. The feeling they were among people who saw them and valued what they saw. I saw the relaxation in shoulders, the loosening of tension around necklines. Confident voices, firm steps, deep and hearty laughs. Community. Belonging. Safety. When I shut my eyes, I saw and heard my mom in the Korean grocery, or imagined my grandmother needing a break from her trials and tribulations in postwar Korea and sharing a moment with her neighbors while squatting low to the ground in a classic resting position.

Against this backdrop, and in those moments, the meaning of the red helicopter also came to life. I knew—I *knew*—what *I* was experiencing. I had *felt* this feeling before. Inside my chest. There were so many reasons for these women to have rejected me. But they did the exact opposite. They gave me permission not only to see but to participate in their safe place. They gave me an incredible gift. Faced with this generosity, the weight and defense of my own armor fell away. How could it not? Cast to one side was the onus of having to be someone I wasn't. I was *myself.* The women in the stores liked me. I liked them. Ours was a human connection—not one based on a job title, a fancy address, an academic pedigree, or a work credential. My abilities and experience were important, and helpful, make no mistake. But they were not defining.

With friendship and trust also comes directness. The women and I talked about family a lot. I told them about my mom and what was going on with my dad. I even met a few customers' children inside the stores. I thought of my dad taking me to Macy's to prepare me for my first trip to North Carolina.

At that time, I had no close Black friends. Acquaintances, sure. It wasn't a conscious choice. It had everything to do with geography and proximity, or so I told myself. I hadn't worked with many women, either. In private equity, female colleagues are hard to come by. The elite Boston firm where I had worked once came close to hiring its first and only female investment professional, but in the end, she reneged on her acceptance to stay in New York with her new fiancé. The general attitude in the conference room implied a sentiment something along the lines of, *See, this is why firms like ours shouldn't hire women investors. They aren't serious about their careers.* Another way to look at it is she weighed her opportunity costs and decided that our firm wasn't as valuable an option for her after all. She ultimately landed a job at a great private equity platform headquartered in New York.

Yes—Ashley Stewart was a safe place that was worth saving. But the actual business *funding* that safe place was dead on arrival. I used to joke that the company was an awesome nonprofit. Nor was it lost on me that raising financial capital from the worlds of finance and big law would be an enormous challenge. Precious few investors and players in those systems either looked like my customer base or would have the courage to let themselves admit to, much less embrace, similarities of their own life experiences.

Fall hardened into winter. By then I had settled into the routine of my weekly travel schedule. At 4:00 a.m. every Monday, I woke up in Boston in time to board the 6:00 a.m. JetBlue flight to Newark. Barring delays, we touched down at 7:20. A taxi dropped me off at the Secaucus office at 8:15. I worked there all day Monday, flew out to visit another batch of stores on Tuesday and Wednesday, returned to the office on Wednesday night to prepare for Thursday, and then flew back home to Boston to be with Meg and our children late Thursday evening. I never missed a flight, though I was always the last person to board, shoes in one hand, belt dangling from the other because I hadn't had time to put them back on after clearing security. In Secaucus, every morning, Randy and I had the same breakfast of a coffee and a chocolate frosted doughnut from the Dunkin' drive-through, or a bacon, egg, and cheese bagel from the rolling coffee-and-bagel cart stationed outside the warehouse—the only early morning sign of life anywhere near our headquarters.

Randy and I were always the first ones in and the last out. Now and again, we would hear one of our colleagues complaining about their commute. No other response but to smile. Some nights, though, it would all catch up with me, and I would quietly lose it— *What the heck are you doing, James*? and *Why did you agree to do this? You're so stupid!*—especially when a storm grounded my flight back home and had me trudging through the snow in dress shoes, looking for someplace open for dinner in Secaucus. More often than not, though, I surrendered to the absurdity of the situation. Randy and I would have a beer and spend the next hour laughing and smacking our foreheads.

By early November, we had scored a few victories. First among them were the bonds between the members of the unlikely leadership team that had been given space to emerge at headquarters. There were moments of inexperience and errors in judgment, but I was always grateful for the earnest effort and unimpeachable intention of these people to save the company. I loved my team. They cared. I called them Misfit Toys because, seriously, what else were they? What else was I? And together, we were *relentless* Misfit Toys. With no money to hire outside experts, we had managed to rewire a big chunk of our technology, and in only a matter of months we mapped out the plumbing for what would be an entirely new digital commerce strategy down the road. And yes, the headquarters now had Wi-Fi!

Next up: marketing. Content wasn't the problem. We had plenty of that from interactions among customers and store managers. We approached marketing like an unscripted show chronicling the humor that coexisted with our struggle to survive. Meaning, we blurred the artificial lines and identities drawn by commerce. We treated our customers as *teammates*. People, not consumers. Literally weeks before Thanksgiving, we somehow completed the implementation of a new, state-of-the-art e-commerce platform. We paid for it with the cash that was freed up by selling tens of thousands of camis through clever (and necessarily steep) promotions. We had successfully swapped "dead" assets for a *true* long-term asset. In the run-up to Thanksgiving and Black Friday—always a huge volume day for retailers—I drove to an Ashley store outside Boston.

"What do you want me to do?" I asked.

"What *can* you do?" teased the store manager. I shrugged and looked down. She and her assistant decided that the best use of my time was to begin unpacking jewelry from boxes and hanging pieces on the display case. Seeing the haphazard results, they couldn't stop laughing. Warmly. Endearingly. And wouldn't you know it, but that year the company ended up having a record Thanksgiving weekend.

• • •

But all wasn't wonderful. On so many other things, we fell short.
Reality slapped us in the face every day. Not surprisingly, the
company was in worse shape than I had thought. And I had been
expecting the worst. Achieving what we did to create a record
Thanksgiving galvanized everyone, but it couldn't offset two decades of shortcuts and futility. The foundation of the company—the
bones, pipes, furnace, cracked cement, and unkempt wires—was
just too ramshackle and broken.

For the previous few months, I had been selling any and all
assets, including warehouse scrap metal and racks, to "jobbers"—
liquidators who dispose of unwanted materials—just to make
payroll and fund projects like the e-commerce platform. Everything
that could be sold had been taken away. Even our record Thanksgiving was bittersweet. We actually sold too much of our inventory,
leaving us with not enough to sell for the remaining weeks of the
vital holiday season. We had a little more cash because of the sales,
but we couldn't buy enough additional inventory or get it made fast
enough to generate future profit. The feedback loop was broken.
The vendors had been burned too often to agree to sell us anything
on credit. They smelled blood. Around this time, I made the painful
but necessary decision to hire an armed police officer to patrol the
downstairs lobby and preempt any potential aggression from agi-
tated vendors sick and tired of not getting paid.

Most of our vendors were small business owners. If Ashley
Stewart didn't enjoy the best reputation, theirs was, in some cases,
also less than sterling. But I was honest with them. In time, many
of those owners became my friends. We chose not to forget things

like integrity, truth, and the importance of long-term relationships even though our predicament begged us to take expedient short-cuts. Stated another way, despite our tenuous situation, we were careful not to let our handling of short-term liabilities imperil critical long-term assets like trust.

I sat down with our vendors. "Given the company's past behavior, we don't deserve your trust," I admitted. "From this point on, though, this company will honor its commitments. But we expect the same from you." Years later, we would end up getting some of the best payment terms—which determine how much time a company has to pay a vendor for delivered services or goods—in the industry. But at that moment, we had to pay cash up front. And I didn't blame them for insisting on it.

Having lost our faith in the inputs and outputs of the existing financial reporting systems, we had built an entirely new set of equations and series of reports from scratch. The most important schedule was the first one: a simple model that tracked the inflows and outflows of cash from our checking account—the same kind of basic math each and every one of us is familiar with in our personal lives. Complex financial accounting can lie, but cash never does. You either have it or you don't. You either spend it or you don't. And if you spend it, you generally want it to come back, with a profit, as soon as possible. We kept these new, simplified numbers far apart from the main systems and made them transparent to our team. We wanted everyone to see plainly the connection between a decision and its impact on cash levels. I asked everyone why they should have any confidence in a Byzantine financial system that contributed to a pattern of behavior that drove two decades of corporate futility and disrepute. Good question, they answered. To influence the future, it's important to remember that a change in behavior often requires a change in reports. It's that simple.

Around this time, we also parted ways with a few of the most senior executives. Other than one person, there had been no terminations or layoffs up until that point. Trust me, I wanted these senior executives to be successful. How else was I going to be able to leave at the end of my six-month contract? But much to my chagrin, I couldn't let them stay. Their negativity drained the energy from the camaraderie and momentum created by the Misfit Toys. From my perspective, they were unwilling to hold themselves accountable for poor business decisions, and they refused to acknowledge the ugly truth plainly painted in the cash model. It was almost as if they had an image of how a professional executive should walk and talk, insisting on sticking to a stilted script even when the situation called for the type of improvisation and agility born of realness. The contrast with Chary's and Shelley's effortless authenticity couldn't have been starker. For this reason, it shouldn't surprise you that my initial instincts had been right: the women in the stores were indeed intimidated by, if not downright scared of, these executives.

I faced each of them directly, and relayed some additional observations and lessons from all the time I had invested in relationships across the country. Ashley served a particular subset of *Black women*—women who weren't always given the respect and visibility they deserved. Similar to how I had advocated for my mom against the slights and insults served up by the world, Chary and the other managers protected and championed women who didn't have enough advocates. And no, despite what the executive team believed, Ashley Stewart's customers didn't *just* need wardrobe basics like low-priced camis. More important to them were clothes that were fashionable and formfitting. They wanted pizazz, and they were willing to pay for it if they found it. *Hey, what are you looking at?—And wow, look at me!*

In sum, I explained to those senior executives, they had failed to identify the single most important asset of the company—the *why*, the *root cause* of this company's uncanny ability to persevere through corporate incompetence and borderline negligence.

I told them: *The most important product our predominantly Black female customer is looking for is companionship, safety, a dose of confidence. A judgment-free zone where she can breathe, take off her armor, and be seen, finally, for who she is. But how can she feel this way if our own store managers aren't being treated in this way? Why are they scared of you? Why did you cut off the store feedback loop? The essence of Ashley is in those relationships, not the clothes. The relationships are the capital-P Product, while the clothes are merely the product. I see it everywhere I look. Can't you see it? Can't you feel it?*

I looked closely at each of them. There were a few expressions of belated recognition. But not enough. They had allowed the sensory deprivation tank of an office to fool them, along with the taped-down rugs. They hadn't seen, or visited, the places or moments where magic happened (whether they *couldn't* or *wouldn't* didn't matter at this point). Not all the time. But enough of the time.

So we parted ways. And the way in which the Misfit Toys rose to the occasion made me proud, even as I mourned the reality of how lonely the spotlight of leadership now felt.

The beginning of December made things official: we had no money. No surprises there. I had spoken repeatedly about the three-legged stool, for the company and everyone else. But other than Randy, no one knew how wobbly and imbalanced my own life was.

I missed my family. I felt like a bad husband and a bad dad. Every night when I was growing up, my mom and dad made sure we ate dinner together. My dad worked late, treating sick kids, but he always made it a point to come home and sit down for dinner at the kitchen table. In this, I fell short. No one told me that the glamour of private equity meant spending more nights than I wanted to away from home, in sterile, random hotels, socializing with owners and management teams. In the present, thanks to Meg, we were okay. Six months was doable, we agreed. So it wasn't my marriage or my kids I was really worried about. It was my dad.

He was fading. There was one close call after another. My phone would ring, I would rush out of the office, and speed to the hospital or my parents' small condo an hour away. My mom was doing everything for him. Bathing him, helping him to the bathroom, cooking and shredding his food for the feeding tube, giving him his medication. Hoping to give her a reprieve, my sister and I had hired a few home health aides. None lasted long. My mom didn't like having people around. It made her uncomfortable. The situation was too intimate. Besides, she was a trained nurse, she would say. *I know how to take care of my husband.*

The first symptoms of my dad's Parkinson's disease had shown up on my wedding day, around a year after I had moved up to Boston from New York City. Our family had gathered in North Carolina, where Meg's parents were hosting a beautiful wedding. My new father-in-law had arranged for a morning round of golf. My dad was a good golfer, but he had trouble hitting the ball that morning. "Are you nervous," I asked? "No, it's okay," he said. I thought he felt intimidated by the social environment. He had introduced himself as Matthew. My dad told me he was fine, not to worry. Only later did he admit he had trouble moving his muscles. He was sixty-one years old. It was now a dozen years later.

Like many men, I had a complicated relationship with my dad. My brother, John, followed his path and became a doctor, so they had that connection, and John could offer sound medical advice, which he did faithfully for both our parents as they aged. My sister and my dad were close in a different way. Jennifer gave my dad permission to show the same heart and compassion that also fueled the adoration he received from three generations of patients. I loved seeing the two of them together.

I wasn't a doctor, and I wasn't my sister. I had a thoroughly impractical profession that rendered my day-to-day life hazy to my parents. *Investor*. What could *I* do to give relief to a dying man? To my parents, *Harvard grad* was synonymous with *success. Investor*, with the money, status, and success it presumed, was additional icing on the cake. But when your dad is locked inside his body, what good is *success*? The world that prized that definition of *success* was the same one that was about to crush Ashley, the same one that made teenage kids risk their lives crash-delivering pizzas, and the same one that had nearly stripped my dad of his livelihood as collateral damage in a malpractice claim that was finally, after years and years of worry, dismissed.

During those visits, I marked time in the hospital room or the condo hoping I could find some opportunity to help. I should have been there more, regardless of how absurd and overwhelming the demands were in Secaucus. The language barrier between my parents and me was making matters worse. In a life and death situation, meaning gains even more importance, and meaning kept getting lost. *Dabdabhae* means *frustrating* or *stifling* in Korean. Not what you experience in traffic or when taking a final exam. *Dabdabhae* is more visceral, and suffocating. A pain in your chest. A feeling like drowning. A sharp ache quite distinct from the warm, good ache I associated with the red helicopter. I felt *dabdabhae* as I watched my mom tirelessly do her best to alleviate my dad's incurable suffering.

Helping to assuage the pain of my dad's dying, and the faltering Ashley Stewart, were the bonds I'd created with my new colleagues, and especially with the women in the stores. In my mind, the past was playing out in the present, just in a different context and with different faces. With women like Chary and Shelley, it was a gift to relive some of my childhood moments and to have textured conversations in fluent English that I never could have with my own mom. We spoke about feelings and emotions, using a vocabulary to which I never had access in conversations with my mom and especially my dad. I did it better this time around. I had the compassion and empathy of a grown man, a dad with three young children of my own. Chary and Shelley had accepted me, stripped of all credentials. If I'm honest, there were times when I wasn't sure my dad accepted me even *with* those credentials. Maybe that's another reason I didn't feel like I had much to offer him during those late stages of Parkinson's. I felt useless.

For all those reasons, I was finally unambiguously clear about why I had felt compelled to sign up for this six-month "salvage" mission. The sky inside my head was unclouded.

December was colder than usual. Wreaths and colored lights began appearing across Secaucus. My hotel put up a listless tree and a plastic menorah on the lobby counter. Both felt slightly mocking. I thought of my dad and his father slapping his face. Life felt cruel to me.

We had failed. Rather, *I* had failed. We had done momentous things in the previous four months. But it was too little too late.

The truth is we were broke, frightened, and exhausted. The restructuring advisors were lurking in the wings. Only Randy and Donna were familiar with the full-frontal assault about to be unleashed on this hobbled prey of a company, but they were still junior, and relatively young. I felt especially bad for Chary, Shelley, and my other frontline colleagues. Their hard work and commitment had created a lot of goodwill in the communities we served. But after two decades of corporate ineptness and poor behavior, Ashley had no goodwill in the *financial world* to draw upon. Wall Street wasn't exactly about to bend over backward to fund a company like this, the Misfit Toys, or women like Chary and Shelley, who lacked any of the "right" connections.

Gina organized one last holiday party. *Failure or not*, I thought, *Ashley will exit the world gracefully, gratefully, and in style.*

The holiday party was held at the Brooklyn YWCA, which has provided a safe haven for survivors of gender-based violence, teens, and immigrant women for more than a century. Tamara's sister was a senior executive there. It was a cold, rainy night. I showed up wearing a suit, which I never wore anymore. (I had begun the process of begging for money from Wall Street contacts.) The gathering was hardly extravagant—a few cartons of doughnuts, some light refreshments. A boom box played dance music and hip-hop. It was a family affair, honoring the residents of the YWCA.

We donated about two dozen boxes of merchandise samples,

clothes that manufacturers send a company for approval before putting them into production. Other than that, we had nothing left to
give. Instead, we chose to give back to the community what was intangible, and collective. Our time. Our hearts. Earlier in the holiday
season, I had created a sales competition whereby the top forty
stores earned the right to donate $250 to a local charity of their
choice. These two things, the party and the sales competition, were
my way of thanking the local neighborhoods and communities that
had supported this star-crossed company for twenty-two years.
Gina also learned about two local girls whose apartment building
had recently burned down. We bought them bikes for Christmas so
that they could ride to school come springtime.

It was an emotional night. I was quiet, reserved. After some
coaxing, I danced the Wobble and the Electric Slide with a handful
of colleagues and YWCA residents who showed up to celebrate. It
was an outpouring of generosity, of music and movement and joy
and sadness.

Then Tamara shoved a microphone into my hand. Everyone was
probably expecting the usual jokey, plastic CEO shtick. That's not
what they got. For the first time in public, I told everyone exactly
how I felt. I thanked everyone. "You were incredibly generous to
me," I said. "You didn't judge me. You welcomed me. You saw me in
the same way I saw you. I did the best I could. *We* did the best we
could." After a mumbled apology, I shuffled off the makeshift stage
with my head down. Sensing an end to things, a lot of people wept.
Tamara, suspecting I wasn't coming back, was especially upset.

I'd given everything I could to Ashley, but I'd gotten much more
in return. I was looking for something real. And I had found it.
Those women gave me back *myself.*

I liked the person I was when I was with them.

It was still raining as the cab took Randy and me to LaGuardia Airport for the flight home to Boston. I felt despondent. We had made incredible strides in four months, but I hated myself for building up false hopes. *For sure*, I had thought, *some of my money connections will step in to help*. But no one had come. Just Randy and Donna.

"What's wrong?" Meg asked when I stumbled through the door that night, and I spent the next hour or two explaining.

Only two months were left on my six-month contract. Was there any point in returning to Secaucus? My only option was preparing Ashley Stewart for a crisp bankruptcy-turned-liquidation filing. The lender was agitating in the wings, knowing this was the best way to ensure its loan was repaid, and I could oversee the liquidation from Boston with a few phone calls. From experience, I knew the carnage that would ensue. Distance—being in Boston, not Secaucus—would make it less real. I could put my armor back on, explain away the previous four months, and wrap myself up in the security that not caring might afford me. I could retake a seat behind a desk and let Chary, Shelley, and Gina go back to being faceless numbers on a spreadsheet. Besides, the investment bankers were calling me already about some new potential deals in the market. As the economists would say, those four months had been a *sunk cost*—meaning, an investment that can't be recovered. Maybe it was time to fold the hand and walk away.

It wasn't a very joyful Christmas vacation. I spent most of it lost in thought. By that time, there was no question in my mind that kindness was the ultimate form of strength, and kindness had a much deeper role to play in business. We had only scraped the surface of being able to execute my system, one that integrated kindness and math through a new and different set of behavioral nudges and measurements more consistent with life outside the contrived formalities and legalese of work. I saw patterns amid the convergence of so many seemingly different lives and stories, gaining clarity from and finding beauty in the natural harmonies and melodies of the chaos that is the present, past, and future of life. I also knew that the red helicopter was far from merely being a silly memory from my childhood. And yet, I was tempted to look the other way. To rejoin the easier path. This slump in my own courage—I hated it. Meg, I remember, said something like, *This doesn't sound like you. The James I know sees things through.*

Shortly after the new year, Randy and I flew to Secaucus and then drove the beleaguered Nissan sedan right back up to Boston for a meeting with a team from the lender. They agreed to give us a little more money if we agreed to prepare bankruptcy papers and hire a restructuring advisor. They proposed a particular advisor. Just so you know, advisors are hired by the company but spend weekends playing golf with the lender. Get it?

It was the beginning of the end, but we had no choice. I believed in kindness, but I couldn't hide from math. Bankruptcy was certain. Liquidation was likely inevitable. But at least this arrangement would buy me two months to try to figure out a way to salvage as many jobs as I could. In finance, we would call this an *option*. And options have value.

I knew exactly what we were up against. I also knew how unlikely it was that anyone would believe us or, frankly, care. I knew what the systems of the world did to little red helicopters. After all, I was a card-carrying member of that system.

Act II
Money

chapter 4

agency

A helicopter is harder to fly than an airplane.

Not long after he helped save me from drowning, my friend Joel introduced me to a series of books called Choose Your Own Adventure. Inside each book, you could make different choices that would lead to different sets of pages, with different outcomes. In one book, the choices I made led me deep underwater, where a monstrous octopus annihilated my submarine. More happily, I also could have discovered Atlantis. Oh well. Because the books had only a finite number of pages, they got stale after a while. The outcomes became predictable. But, like the copy of *Aesop's Fables* my dad gave me, the books did a good job teaching kids like me about the importance of choice, of agency, and its relationship to consequences and chance within the constraints of a specific system.

Today, interactive video games expose children to a more realistic simulation of agency. Each player is subject to the never-ending choices and behaviors of *other* players, which in turn create a seemingly infinite number of potential outcomes. What *others* do is just as important as what *you* do or don't do. As a group, the players effectively co-create new scenarios. Their own actions and reactions shape the very system in which they are asked, repeatedly, to make choices. Players' ability to figure out *others'* intent, and make clear *their* intent, is a critical determinant of the outcome. Nonetheless, as players, we still feel in control. Because in video games, the feedback loop between action and consequence is concise, and the results are clear.

Unfortunately, life lacks this same concision and clarity. The impact of our decisions can take longer to play out, and the results are often more ambiguous. Our estrangement from direct causality can sometimes lead to despair or a feeling of hopelessness. In our attempts to impose order, we sometimes forget that agency is about making informed choices toward a desired, worthwhile outcome. Agency is *not* about controlling and guaranteeing outcomes for either yourself or others. In fact, real agency often begins with the understanding that we *lack* control over many, if not most, things. We like to think this isn't true, especially as it relates to work life. But it is, no matter what the squawking pundits say on television. And as for home life? Well, anyone who's coached a soccer team of kindergarteners doing cartwheels on the field during a "crucial" game knows this to be true.

Yes, as humans, we tend to forget we are tiny specks at the mercy of much larger natural systems that collectively have very little regard for human-made controls, or rules. (As a species and as individuals, we like to put ourselves at the center of the narrative. But sometimes, as we shall see, playing small and positioning ourselves slightly *off*-center, and to one side of our own narrative, can generate surprisingly "big" results.) This humbling perspective can actually give us the courage to take on even the most imposing human-made systems. By naming them, we remind ourselves that they are merely conventions. Unlike, say, the ocean tides, gravity, or the phases of the moon, they are not immutable. They are elastic. They can be bent. They can be changed. Why? Because we are the ones who invented them.

Understanding what agency *is* and what agency *isn't* is a good defense against anyone trying to sell us the elixir of certainty, omnipotence, or permanence. Life is unpredictable, random, and chaotic. Which means that exercising *true agency* over our lives also requires letting go. True agency ultimately entails a certain degree of surrender.

This is likely why the time my family spends every summer on a barrier island off the North Carolina coast has played such an important role in my own understanding of agency. The island is as beautiful as it is raw. Its shape is always changing. A few decades from now, it may not even exist. There are no lifeguards, and my children learned to swim and surf in and around hidden riptides and sudden afternoon storms. Being there provides the humbling perspective I just described above. It's a good reminder that I am at the mercy of things unfathomably greater than my own image in the mirror.

This could also be why the barrier island is the site of so many lasting memories—moments of hyperclarity and, yes, agency. I got down on one knee and proposed to Meg there, for instance. And one summer, in almost the same spot, in the same house, I saw my oldest child's face crumple when he came face-to-face with the dissonance created when made-up rules conflict with and override the better inclinations of humanity.

Jared and a few of his older cousins were playing the classic game of Monopoly around a glass table. Though he was only seven or eight years old, Jared could already fend for himself, calculating rents, paying the luxury tax, and buying properties. He understood what the little property cards meant in terms of the cost of building houses and hotels, and the implications of collecting elevated rents as a return on his investment. Though he knew the rules of the game, I kept a casual eye on his play because his cousins were older.

In the early rounds, Jared had the only monopoly. As his little pile of money grew, I noticed he was giving his cousins money on the side. Whenever they came close to insolvency, Jared would hand them a few bills or issue a verbal IOU. That way, they could keep playing and going around and around the board. Jared was having fun. Everyone was having fun. There was a social compact, an implicit agreement of reciprocity around the goal of everyone "surviving," so to speak. Without the specter of "elimination," everyone was thriving.

Then I became aware of a small commotion. Whispers and giggling. Before long, Jared's cousins, led by the eldest, had exchanged properties among themselves and created their own portfolios of monopolies. The momentum turned. Before long, Jared's pile of cash had shrunk into a scattered assortment of scraggly one-dollar and five-dollar bills. I watched as he rolled the dice, landing on his oldest cousin's monopoly. Jared gazed hopefully across the table. *I helped you. Won't you help me?* But no. He had to hand over his cards to fulfill his debts. A few rolls later, Jared was out of the game, his little token hitting the bottom of the empty cardboard game box with a muted thud.

Have you ever seen a child's face crumple? Jared's cheeks wobbled. His eyes watered. Then a sound came from his mouth. It wasn't the cry of a kid angry at himself, or the wail of a poor loser. It was more anguished than that. "Daddy," Jared choked out, "I just really wanted to keep playing."

There was more to it than that, however. In his child's logic, and given his past actions, Jared had made the wrong assumptions. First, he learned the hard way that some invisible possibilities (like collusion) aren't in Monopoly's instruction booklet and can be understood only in real time. But I think what upset and surprised him most was the collective behavior of his older cousins. Usually they doted on him—but the unspoken rules of *that* game, in *that* space and time, nudged or permitted different behavior. His cousins were fully within their rights to make the decisions they did. Because of the difference in their age and life experience, Jared and they simply had different perspectives on what *winning* meant. The fictional world created by Monopoly dramatically drove this distinction home.

After Randy and I returned from the emergency lender meeting in Boston at the start of the new year, I needed to educate the Misfit Toys about the real-life Monopoly game we were playing. They were ecstatic that the bank meeting went "well," that the company's lender had given us a little more money and breathing room, but my sober face quickly dispelled any notion that the bank meeting was anything other than a formal death sentence. I then saw the same crumpled faces that I had seen that day on the barrier island.

The now-somber Misfit Toys were about to get up close and personal with the truth of American-style capitalism. To minimize fear of the unknown, I gave them a crash course in distressed investing and bankruptcy law. I knew from our detailed cash model that by early March, Ashley Stewart would realistically be unable to fund payroll, which meant we needed to spend the next two months preparing for a bankruptcy filing. Given the company's history and reputation, that bankruptcy filing would probably result in a quick decision by the court to follow the recommendation of the restructuring advisor, with pressure from the lender, to convert the bankruptcy into a full-out corpus-dissecting liquidation. The lender didn't care about us. It just wanted the loan repaid. These were the rules of this particular Monopoly game.

One of the Misfits had two follow-up questions: *I still don't understand. Then why in the world did the company's lender give us a few extra dollars and two additional months? And, by the way, what does it mean for a lender to be "asset-based"?* It wasn't an act of generosity, I explained. The lender was, justifiably, looking out for its own best interests. Asset-based lenders are the equivalent of hard money lenders—that is, lenders whose loan is secured by specific identifiable assets. Think of a car loan, or a house loan, more commonly known as a mortgage. If you don't honor the terms of the loan, at some point the lenders can seize the car, or the house, hire intermediaries to conduct an auction, and turn the asset into cash. Quite literally, liquidation means turning an asset into water, or cash, which is the most "liquid" asset. By fronting us a few extra dollars, the company's asset-based lender was getting us to March, at which point the going-out-of-business sales would attract more shoppers emerging from their winter hibernation. In other words, thanks to the heightened demand from spring shoppers, the value of our inventory would be higher in March. My voice trailed off as I mumbled, "This so-called asset has become our greatest liability."

Seeing they didn't quite appreciate the irony, I explained in further detail. To protect themselves, asset-based lenders have rigid appraisal formulas (this is literally called lending "inside the box"). Built on huge amounts of appraisal data from countless prior transactions spanning decades of going-out-of-business sales, these formulas can accurately predict the cash value of specific assets in liquidation proceedings. The independent purchasing decisions of tens of millions of individuals from the past can be reduced to a single number, or percentage. Amazing, right? This means that at some point, if you don't honor the terms of your car loan, or your mortgage, the asset-based lender is mathematically confident that it can fully recoup its loan by just seizing and selling your car or house—or in our case, the camis, peplum blouses, shark-bites, and the rest of the inventory. A lender just wants to get its money back. Which means that an asset-based lender is in effect lending to the *asset*, not the actual person or business in custody of the asset. This *also* means that, in the event of a crisis, if the assets have too much value and the lender can turn them into cash and pay off its loan, the lender has every incentive to liquidate the business rather than keeping it afloat and taking on incremental risk. For the borrower, then, these so-called assets can become, oddly enough, liabilities. Or death warrants, to put it more directly.

This was hard for the Misfit Toys to swallow. *Do you mean that all of our hard work overhauling operations and streamlining decision-making these past four months did nothing to undo twenty-plus years of damage?* "No, not quite," I said, explaining that our decisions and actions prevented what was almost certain liquidation during the previous fall and had earned us two additional months of *option value*, namely, an incremental sixty days of *time*. There was more grimacing. Faces crumpled further. Then I took the opportunity to name and demystify what was to come.

A week from now, I went on, a team of young people, mostly men in suits, will be roaming the halls of this office. These are restructuring advisors and lawyers. They will try really hard to blend in (in fact, I called them before their first day and asked them to wear fashion denim, not suits, hoping it would minimize my colleagues' anxiety levels). Their mandate is to execute on the reliable (and somewhat tried-and-true) process of preparing Ashley Stewart for bankruptcy, and to try to find bidders for the assets, whether in pieces or as a whole.

January and February were understandably tough months. While running a business on fumes, the team also had to prepare for a process they had never experienced and didn't want to have happen. Worse, they knew the overwhelming odds were that they would end up unemployed and without healthcare coverage. In our favor, transparent and calm explanations went a long way. Self-deprecating humor went even further. Amid the general tension, there were absurd moments of levity. Always. During one of our many late nights, we discovered that the size 16 faux-leather green vest hanging near my "executive suite" fit me perfectly. There was also the time I coaxed a few of the male Misfit Toys to change outfits after they came into the office wearing super-starched, oddly patterned business shirts and ties, because that's how they thought bankers dressed. I thought of my mom buying me clothes for school when I was in junior high, well, before I took over that responsibility my-self. We all doubled over in laughter.

But mostly, there was heartbreak. Later in this process, I had to gather everyone in that same cafeteria with the industrial-size lunch warmer to read them the Worker Adjustment and Retraining Notification Act, known as the WARN Act. I was legally required to do so because a hundred people were at risk of being laid off. The lawyers wanted me to start the sixty-day-notice clock ticking. Usually, the WARN Act notification is just sent through the mail. We sent that mail, but I also made the choice to read it directly to everyone while looking them in the eye.

As you can imagine, my colleagues were scared and upset. Still, I wanted them to feel they had some modicum of agency with regard to the situation. The WARN Act letter was legalese. I wanted to make it real to them. That was the least they deserved. Unlike Jared's cognitive dissonance caused by Monopoly, this was not a game. True, everyone in the room bore some culpability for what had happened to the company. This was on *everybody*, including me when I served as the chairman of the board. Our failures, our actions—and inactions—had contributed to what would be Ashley Stewart's second, and most likely fatal, bankruptcy in three years, but that didn't mean this had to be a *punitive* process.

I was surprised and gratified by the number of proactive, constructive questions I received—a far cry from the first town hall, when nearly everyone, conditioned by the prior written and unwritten rules supporting a hierarchical management structure lifted from some business school textbook, had stayed silent. This time, people rose to the challenge of the situation.

What does all this mean? How does the system of bankruptcy work? So I told them, just as I have now taught a generation of students both in the classroom and on Wall Street.

Like all human-made systems, the US bankruptcy system is de-signed around an original intent that is set down in rules that have evolved over time, in ways both written and unwritten. No different from video games, it is *people* who actually bring the system to life. Let's start by looking at the intent.

Who doesn't like the idea of a second chance, or a do-over? Whether you're a person or a business, bankruptcy laws allow borrowers to structure a new agreement with creditors and lenders so that the future isn't drowned out or permanently held hostage by the past. Everyone makes mistakes. It certainly beats an old-fashioned debtor's prison. And let's be real: Wouldn't entrepreneurs maybe think twice if they thought their new start-up could land them in jail if it faltered and they couldn't pay back their debt? And, from lenders' perspectives, sometimes the rational thing to do, after they have analyzed their opportunity costs and sunk costs, is to *forgive* a portion of the debt in the hopes of getting back what they can. At its best, then, the bankruptcy system allows for a pause, and for cooler heads to prevail.

On the other hand, the bankruptcy system has an *extremely* clear pecking order, both in law and even more so in practice. Secured lenders (the least risky loan, thanks to their legal claim on specified assets) take the first bite of the apple, followed by all the *un*secured creditors, who generally include riskier debt holders without a claim to a specified asset and vendors who provide anything from telephone services to real estate leases to . . . camis.

Anything left over after that goes to the equity owners, which makes sense since they own the company and had all the ownership and thus upside in the first place.

The cafeteria was silent. *What about us? What about all the people who work here, who do the actual work?* Well, I explained, you are an *unsecured* creditor, no different in the pecking order than the cami vendor. Under the rules, and even though it's doubtful anyone thinks this way, employees are assumed to have theoretically *loaned* their labor to the company. (I know—it sounds nuts.)

"That's why I had to send you the WARN Act," I went on. "That's why you have no right to make a claim against the company for severance or continued healthcare coverage. In our specific case, the lawyers and restructuring advisors have determined that there are likely no proceeds—no money left over—for any biters of the apple other than the secured lender.

"Does that make sense?" I asked. "Do you now see why the clothing vendors insisted on cash up front, and why some of those who didn't were angry and anxious enough that I felt compelled to hire a police officer to sit downstairs in the lobby?"

More silence. *That doesn't seem fair*, said the body language of the room. Well, unfortunately, that's just how the system works. *Who can we talk to about this?*

I sighed, thinking about my dad's travails defending himself against the medical malpractice suit. *Congress*, said my inner voice.

In a smaller group, one of the Misfit Toys later asked me about the astronomical fees charged by the perfectly pleasant young men in fashion denim who had now commandeered a corner office. I explained that there was a group, given the name *estate administration*, that was even higher in the pecking order than the most secured senior lender. And that upon a bankruptcy filing, a company—like magic, just like that—changes form. It undergoes a bizarre metamorphosis. It is now known as the estate. The estate administration has to get paid or there won't be anyone to run the bankruptcy process, maximize proceeds, and prevent total chaos.

The Misfit Toys glanced over at the well-dressed contingent. If this corpus got divided up, the estate people would be the first ones to bite into the apple, followed by the lender. As a group, the Misfit Toys finally realized that despite all their blood, sweat, and tears, they were lowly unsecured creditors, standing in line with the cami vendors, hoping for a few apple scraps to fall to the ground.

In that moment, I could have pointed out that as unfair as the corporate bankruptcy system might seem, it was more lenient to a company than its parallel system was to individuals filing for bankruptcy. (In fact, I would say that much of my law school education underscored how advantageous it was to be a corporation rather than a person.) I could have added that at least, in this case, Ashley Stewart was so insolvent, so down-and-out, that the estate professionals would have little financial incentive to drag things out and run an extended process. Meaning, because there were so few assets and such little cash, death would be mercifully swift. I also could have noted that the way bankruptcy works in practice is less by law and more by backroom dealings and negotiating among repeat players (meaning, the lenders, the lawyers, and the restructuring advisors, who all play golf together and who work in a mutually beneficial manner, sometimes at the expense of the unsecured creditors, including employees).

But I kept quiet about those points. I sensed what the Misfit Toys really needed were the same words of comfort I had given Jared after he absorbed the real rules of Monopoly. The young men in fashion denim were just following the rules of the system governing this space and time, in the same way Jared's older cousins had done around that glass table on the barrier island. Being angry at them wasn't a productive use of energy. We needed to focus on what we could control.

In that moment, I was tempted to tell the Misfit Toys about how strangely applicable the story of Jared and the Monopoly game truly was. You see, the game that inspired Monopoly, the Landlord's Game, was invented in the early twentieth century by a woman named Elizabeth Magie. Her original intention was for participants to play two versions of the game. The first rewarded all the players if they effectively maximized collective wealth, while the second version rewarded only the player who wiped out everyone else. Magie wanted people to play both versions and then compare and contrast the two, with the hope that doing so would inspire their more collective, cooperative instincts to address her generation's growing wealth disparities.

But as fate would have it, decades later a man "adapted" her intellectual property unbeknownst to her and sold it to Parker Brothers, which had great and lasting success marketing Monopoly—the game that today symbolizes a distinctly American version of cutthroat capitalism. The original idea was Magie's, but that man, Charles Darrow, is still widely credited as Monopoly's sole inventor. Would business, and our lives, be different today if the Landlord's Game had hit the shelves and we had all grown up learning about money and life in a different context with a more balanced perspective on winning?

But I chose not to bring that up. As I did with Jared, I stayed quiet. I let my grimace do the talking. Some things are better learned through firsthand experience, and I knew the team would quickly put two and two together as they began preparing the presentations for potential bidders.

When a company raises financial capital, in bankruptcy or not, it is a lot like when a person writes a résumé and submits it to one of those nebulous databases for prospective employers. An even better analogy, I think, is when a person creates a profile for an internet dating platform. I've been married way too long to have used one of those apps, but bear with me.

First, you find a site, or broker. In the case of a company, that means contacting an investment bank or restructuring firm. It provides guidance so you can best tell your story. More important, it brings together a pool of potential suitors who make up a marketplace. Next, the broker posts a short teaser profile, a two-dimensional narrative that shows off your best assets, the ones it thinks the suitors will find attractive. (Not catfishing, exactly, but it's important that you look *good*.) Last, the broker tallies the bites; arranges for dates; creates a longer presentation known as a *deck* (an in-depth and detailed description of a company's present, past, and future); chaperones you to make sure you don't mess things up; and then, after a few more meetings, and if all goes well, marries you off.

Also like a dating site, brokers measure their success by whether a marriage takes place, *not* by whether the union ends in divorce. Not surprisingly, their financial incentive is based solely on consummating as many unions as possible. A pejorative term used to describe indiscriminate brokers is *chop shop*. They have absolutely zero incentive (or time) to take on a "special case," for the simple reason that "special cases" do not ordinarily attract a lot of suitors or get married off easily and efficiently.

Adding another layer of complication was that Ashley Stewart's broker was not accustomed to having someone of my professional background actually running the company. I have been behind the curtain on many bankruptcies during my investing career—I know the written and unwritten rules of the game. On the other hand, the typical operating executive is unfamiliar with the many ways in which deal professionals can maximize profit and minimize work by going through the motions and leveraging preexisting forms, formats, and presentations. Basically, I knew too much, and I butted heads with the broker's professionals as they pulled out that standard playbook.

Now, look, in fairness, summarizing *any* company in ten pages or so is incredibly difficult. Even more so for Ashley Stewart, given its history. Plus, how do you explain the connections among Chary, Shelley, and their customers in words, let alone in *numbers*? From my deal experience, I knew we *were* a special case, and that we needed to run a customized process. The hardest part would be getting a meeting—a first date.

I got into some pitched battles with the lead restructuring advisor and the lead lawyer for the estate. In my opinion, the first version of Ashley's dating profile and the longer deck were lifeless. The story being told was run-of-the-mill, no different from the thousands of standard materials I'd seen during my private equity career. Run-of-the-mill doesn't work when the status quo has failed you for the better part of two decades. Would I want to meet that person for a first date? Nope. They hadn't *found* Ashley—they hadn't even *looked* for her.

Like the four corners of the paper holding it, Ashley was metaphorically presented as a box. A coffin, almost. Secaucus. Plus size. Clothes. Twenty-plus years of existence. Real estate leases. A newly implemented e-commerce platform showing some signs of life. Along with failing to capture the soul, vitality, and humanity of Ashley, this *box* would have left any investor who might consider a company like ours without any appreciation for its true assets, our burgeoning soul, and the seeds of change we'd planted since the previous fall. The numbers just weren't there yet in an obvious way. If we made it all about the numbers, we'd be dead on arrival. We needed to lead with the *story*, and hope for people to pause, pay attention, and invest the time to immerse themselves in it. We needed to persuade potential investors that the future might very well be receptive to Ashley, if she were given the space to fly.

For the most part, in nature, there are no squares or rectangles. A square is a human-made shape—tidy, organized, and scalable. Good for some things that require precision. The barrier island in North Carolina is anything but tidy and organized. Neither are small children. Would it surprise you to learn that private equity investment funds, on the other hand, are generally organized in nice, neat compartments? Distressed, growth, or venture. Distressed private equity firms, which aren't known for their creativity and vision, rely more heavily on cost cutting and financial engineering to maximize cash flow. They tend to lurk around bankruptcy proceedings. Growth and venture firms back big ideas and visions for the future with less of an emphasis on cash flow. They shy away from distressed situations, choosing to build from scratch rather than getting their hands dirty looking for hidden value in messy situations.

After resigning from that elite private equity firm and floundering at the failed start-up (and, yes, I *did* end up replacing my family's old swing set), I had started my own investment platform. I christened it FirePine Group. I wanted the latitude (think lateral, not vertical) to invest in transformative situations with the best potential risk-return profile, whether it was a start-up, a mature company, or a turnaround. In my mind, backing big vision should not be the exclusive domain of venture capitalists. Introducing a venture mindset to preexisting companies sorely lacking direction, courage, and vision can generate huge financial returns without the operational risks associated with starting from nothing. What is a company, anyway? It's a fictional space made up of people who come together to exchange goods and services. This means that, like people, there is *always* something of value, even when things look bleakest. Appropriately, the name of my group, which Meg came up with, is inspired by something found in nature.

Some pine cones seed new trees only after the destruction wrought by a forest fire. Their seeds survive the fire thanks to a heavy resin that encases and protects them from the heat. When the heat of a forest fire melts the resin, the seeds are released. Ironically, that same gluey resin prevents these pine cones from seeding trees during normal times because their seeds are trapped and have no way out. So, you see, in the same way we've discovered that assets are sometimes liabilities, it works the other way around, too. Sometimes your greatest liability becomes an asset when you have the courage to view it from a different perspective, usually at an inflection point in your life. A change in perspective costs zero dollars. Remember how people drown in water, an element critical for sustaining life? Well, a near drowning experience can also create the opportunity to breathe again.

This nuance, which applies to all of our lives, was not, however, convenient to the restructuring firm's desire to run a quick, streamlined, in-the-box sale process. In fairness to that firm, the conventional perspective on Wall Street did not equate being a plus-size Black woman with the word *asset*. But in the absence of any financial track record to speak of, we needed an attention-getting vision.

"This won't work," I told the restructuring firm. "It *doesn't* work. Why are you making me beg for money using this box? I have another perspective, a *different* one."

James, just stay in your lane, was what I could tell they wanted to say, but didn't. Tensions ran so high that the seniormost restructuring advisor went around interviewing some of the Misfit Toys, asking whether I was altogether necessary in this equation. They stared back at him blankly, as did the young men wearing fashion denim, who had quietly grown quite fond of the work environment we had created. In fact, it's worth noting that, as time passed, these young men did everything in their power to bend the process and buy us time to stave off liquidation proceedings.

The restructuring firm went ahead and sent out a fairly standard teaser, devoid of big vision, to hundreds of prospective suitors. We ended up with only a handful of prospects interested in exploratory, in-person meetings. Among them was the original founder of Ashley Stewart, who showed up to roam our halls one afternoon and take a walk down memory lane. The only suitor who came to our Secaucus office more than once was a pleasant young man without a team. He had taken the time to understand our story, especially the big vision for the future, but he had no money, no committed pool of financial capital. My new head of merchandising bit her lip while watching him take third and fourth helpings of the food Gina had brought in. Money was *that* tight.

There were many reasons why the process failed. As beloved as the brand was by its customers, the business reputation of the company on Wall Street was indeed awful. Our recent positive performance was too little too late. And remember, this was the second bankruptcy in three years. Layer onto this the fact that retail is a fickle, low-margin business. Fashion is even more volatile and competitive, subject to ever-changing whims in taste and perspective. Right around the time I was modeling the green faux-leather vest, the leaders of Amazon, Walmart, Costco, and Target were feasting on an entire generation of department stores and specialty retailers that had grown lazy relying on the sales growth fueled by countless lookalike malls. These malls were beginning to close left and right.

But—and this is said without a hint of drama—I think that in the cold light of day there were other reasons the process failed, too. We needed venture-type investors open to a restructuring situation, but we were summarily dismissed by the very few big-thinking, imaginative investors who showed up. They saw a clothing retailer with tired stores in stumbling urban malls just beginning to grow online; they were quite simply unable to spy the potential for innovation in a demographic unfamiliar to them. As a result, they summarily snubbed this opportunity, especially the stores, choosing instead to fund laughably unprofitable e-commerce start-ups run by recent business school graduates shilling novelty and "technology-led disruption."

As humans, we are so accustomed to boxes, processes, and straight lines that we forget sometimes to breathe, pause, and look for things we might not be seeing. We forget that astro- and quantum physicists have shown us that most of what occurs or exists is beyond our ability to see or comprehend in the ordinary course. Or, worse, sometimes in our haste, exhaustion, and obsession for order, we just don't want to embrace the unknown, forgetting that movement and change are core to life.

Against this backdrop, then, I think I was a big part of the problem. If you had been a potential bidder, how would you have responded if I'd shown up in your office?

Hi. My name is James. You know me from my private equity life. We were in the same golf foursome a few years back. I've been making some strides here as a full-time, first-time CEO. I'm willing to stay here for as long as you need until you find a permanent solution. I know, I'm a Korean American man with questionable fashion sense. Now, let me talk to you about

Ashley Stewart. It serves and employs primarily Black, plus-size, moderate-income women.

Let's keep going.

You and I both know the history. The headquarters are in a grim warehouse in Secaucus. Pay no attention to the historical numbers. Past results are <u>not</u> indicative of future performance! We've written a new operating model with different algorithms, measuring different outcomes. We have a venture-type operating plan, all written without consultants, whereby Team Misfit Toys (pay no attention to their slightly unconventional behavior in the meetings) will move offices, virtualize more than a hundred physical servers, streamline the store base with a focus on non-mall real estate, and rewire the technology to create a soulful e-commerce experience. And, if you really study my investment track record, I've doubled as an operating executive at times, in one instance helping set up a company from scratch that ultimately fetched close to a billion dollar valuation.

Bewilderment. A smirk or two. But it gets better.

We can do all of this because we've built a new organizational structure that more closely mimics the chaos found in nature. Controlled chaos, if you will. The real product here is not fashion. It's <u>connectedness</u>. It's humanity. The best part of America. A feeling that will be in increasingly short supply over the coming years based on my recognition of patterns

learned as a student of history and literature. Would you
please take me up on my offer to spend time in the stores?

The above is written in a slightly hyperbolic tone, but in sub-stance that's pretty much what I said after the first volley of teasers yielded us virtually nothing and I embarked on a last-ditch and hu-miliating begging tour. I knew a reinvented Ashley Stewart was ready to emerge if her encased seeds were set free, but everyone could only see the fire. If she, Ashley, were given the permission to be herself—not just in the stores, but as a corporate entity—she would thrive. And trust me, I knew better than to even *consider* bringing up kindness, and my belief in its underappreciated rela-tionship to the laws of nature and math.

Are you surprised to learn the entire world said no, *again*? That the dating system failed? That our profile garnered only a few ad-ditional hits, and those initial, fumbling coffee meetups resulted in no second dates, other than with the guy without any money who ate all our food?

In fact, the verdict from the world's financial systems was unan-imous and definitive. *Ashley Stewart is worth more dead than alive.*

With my investor hat on, I understood the rejections. I'd sat in the seats of those prospective investors. It's difficult for imagina-tion to flourish when money is stored and doled out in boxes. But another aspect of some of the rejections was hard for me to bottle up and ignore. It triggered memories from my childhood. *Jap chae.* The menorah. Clement and Matilda. The medical malpractice suit where my dad was collateral damage.

Some firms said they *weren't familiar* with Ashley Stewart's de-mographic. Ashley Stewart wasn't a *lived experience* for them. Fair enough. But beyond the argument that all humans share a lived experience—don't we all live through junior high school, say, or have a friend who could use a confidence boost?—what happens if there are very few investors from this particular demographic (female, Black, or both)? *It's always just about the numbers, James. Money has no emotions.* Uh, I can tell you directly that this is false. Do you know how often financial projections are fudged to miraculously justify vanity investments in fashion brands, modeling agencies, and media companies? When you own those companies, let's just say that your social life and dating prospects markedly improve. Think about it. Suffice it to say, even for the most hard-nosed investors, it is rarely *just* about the numbers.

What bothered me most was that *not one* suitor, even the few who made it to headquarters for an in-person presentation, took me up on my offer to visit Chary and Shelley just a few miles away at Brick Church. Accounting is just like history. *Past.* Our suitors turned down the chance to see the only thing that had value, in my mind, for the *future*—our relationships, our *social* capital. Things that by definition do not show up on the financial statements. Even with some of my closer friends and acquaintances, it was less what they said than what they didn't say or what they communicated with their faces or intonations when I chose to extend those invitations. And remember, I read that unspoken language pretty much fluently, thanks to my mom. These are people I *know*. And they all said no.

On the weekends during those two cold months, I had a lot of time to reflect on the root cause of the mounting rejections. Our family skied in scenic New Hampshire, a far cry from the metal of

Secaucus, every weekend that winter with one of my college roommates and his family. Raising three young kids, not to mention my
heavy travel schedule over the years, had stripped me of one of the
easiest legs of the three-legged stool for any of us to lose. *Fun-James,
James with hobbies.* In retrospect, I'm not surprised that some of my
clearest thinking happened as I was relearning how to ski moguls
while listening to "Born to Run" on my headphones. (I may be a
Long Island guy, and Bruce Springsteen is from New Jersey, but the
desire to be sprung from cages—*boxes*—is a desire close to my
heart.) Also? There's nothing like an ice patch in a field of moguls to
keep you *present.*

The entire world had just slammed the door in Ashley Stewart's
face. And in mine. I'm not sure the world was ready to see me as
anything but a "private equity guy." They certainly didn't see me as a
backable leader of a business serving Black women. Only the Misfit
Toys and the women in the stores understood how I fit in. They had
given me permission to disentangle myself from my résumé, credentials, and appearance. And I was so grateful for that.

I let my mind wander. Is it fair to say that we don't teach basic
rules and norms about employment law and money to students before we cast them into adulthood? Is it fair to say that many of the
overlapping human-made systems making up the social fabric of
American life were not designed with women in mind? Much less
plus-size Black women? Much less my mom?

Was it a coincidence that a vast majority of the prospective investors had never even *heard* of Ashley Stewart? And speaking of
which, why did the high demand for fashionable plus-size clothing
in these urban areas even exist in the first place? The answer, as I

formulated it, lay at the intersection of multiple systems, anchored in the brain. Let me explain.

The stores were mostly located in low- to middle-income neighborhoods. These areas tend to be noisy, crowded, and underfunded, and they don't have many green spaces. Some of them, based on my study of history, were zoned with that intent in mind. With few grocery stores, healthy or nutritious food is hard to come by and pricey when it can be found. Policymakers refer to these areas, where many of the stores were located, as *food deserts*. I can also tell you firsthand as CEO how much more often basic services like utilities went down in the stores compared with my old offices in Boston. Getting them repaired also always took much longer.

Let's keep going. Living in food deserts can be stressful. Human bodies need glucose, or sugar, to help prepare them for heightened activity caused by stress. Fast food restaurants and convenience stores are more than happy to satisfy this need with affordable, biochemically engineered, highly processed foods rich in calories, sugar, salt, and trans fats. Residents, not surprisingly, put on weight. Many become plus-size. They are now at higher risk of developing diabetes, high blood pressure, and heart trouble, and have a lower life expectancy. The cost of healthcare and health insurance increases. And . . . they need clothes that fit.

For the most part, I'm fairly certain that the people I called colleagues for those six months weren't fully aware of how all of those systems converged to influence a set of behaviors and economic results. To undermine agency. Were *you* aware of this? In truth, how many of us have ever been properly taught about the interconnectedness of systems like wellness, cognitive science, finance, economics, and corporate law? Much less how they work together in silence to influence our daily lives. I don't know about you, but my home economics class in public school probably devoted a bit too much time to how to make a casserole. Plenty of information is out there about happiness and the human brain, but much of it is theoretical and not grounded in the actual language and rules of money and work. It's hard for any of us to have a healthy relationship with money when our first exposure to it is as adults, from a position of unknowing and, oftentimes, fear.

Over time, I did my best to share this knowledge with Chary, Shelley, Gina, and as many of my other colleagues as I could. Like my mom, most had no idea about, or even the words for, what they were up against. Also like my mom, they tended to blame themselves for feeling exhausted and "less than." I admired their character all the more for it, and I saw their self-confidence increase as their growing knowledge gave them the tools to name those systems and exercise genuine *agency* in their lives.

There is a lot of time to think on ski lifts because . . . there isn't all that much else to do. It was there I also managed to put my finger on the reason for some of the low-grade malaise I had been feeling before showing up in Secaucus the summer before.

For much of my adult life, I had been unconsciously operating with two sets of rules, norms, behavioral expectations, and value systems: Work-James and Home-James, each prodding me to behave in very different ways. In essence, Work-James is an avatar, a doppelganger who is protected by all of the corporate laws I learned about in law school. At work, *all* of us are basically avatars, directed to act on behalf of oftentimes faceless shareholders who own equity in a legal construct called a corporation or organization. If not avatars, we're certainly not the same people we are when we're at home.

Most of the time, we aren't even aware of our split selves. But, with technology and 24/7 work culture, perhaps it's our growing inability to sustain this artificially compartmentalized distinction between life and work that creates the discomfort and unease so many of us feel. Maybe the fact that your work laptop tracks your every move while you sit there in your sweatpants in your family room with your children, reading them an illustrated story about caring and character—well, maybe this scene hits a discordant note somewhere inside you. It could be your own innate, intuitive definition of fair play that makes you cringe when you see companies plying college students with credit card applications and casino ads on campuses. There's a part of us, small or large, that I imagine looks askance when we observe the ballooning disparity between CEO compensation and average worker take-home pay.

But, we shrug and accept it. We give up agency without always knowing that's what we're doing. We just trudge forward, and quietly think, *Am I the only one who feels this way? Am I out of my mind?* I'm here to tell you that you're not. *What else are we supposed to do?* you reply. *The world has rules it expects us to play by. It's always been this way.* And I'm here to tell you that's not true, and you should trust your instincts. Fairy tales we're fed about our history conceal the truths hidden in the past, waiting for us to find them like the seeds of a fire pine cone. We've grown numb about accepting inaccurate stories and following human-made rules as if they were as immutable as the ocean tides, versus what they really are—mere conventions that favor an increasingly smaller group of individuals who benefit from them. We have somehow all come to accept that the game of

Monopoly was created solely by Charles Darrow (remember, it was *Elizabeth Magie's* idea and invention, but Darrow is still credited, thanks to a false, widely accepted narrative). In our minds, we let isolated anecdotes about unicorns, rags-to-riches stories, and lottery winners somehow make us numb to record levels of CEO compensation and disparities in stock ownership and financial wealth. In an era of gated communities and deteriorating participation in local civic organizations, when public school teachers increasingly can't afford to live in the towns in which they teach, the bonds that hold us together are fraying. Few of us question the convention of shareholder supremacy, which says that the board of directors (and by implication, the CEO) for the most part has a fiduciary duty only to shareholders, not to employees or the common good. Instead, we robotically parrot the prevailing "truth" that capitalism has always been based on shareholder supremacy—until we find out that this doctrine only first appeared in 1973, two years after the US government unilaterally changed the global monetary system by abandoning the gold standard. Meaning, in 1971, the same year in which I was born, the US dollar became a social construct solely dependent on trust, not on its mathematical relationship to gold.

So, rather than limiting us, or inspiring fear, it turns out that understanding the past can be incredibly *liberating*.

So there I was—back in Secaucus, off the ski slopes of New Hampshire, my earbuds tucked away in my orange backpack. It was late February. Ashley Stewart was fewer than three weeks from filing for bankruptcy. I will repeat: we canvassed the entire world and there were ZERO willing bidders. We had been hoping to find what is called a going-concern stalking horse bidder. This refers to a buyer who commits to purchasing the assets of a company with the intention of keeping it as a running business, rather than winding it down and selling it for parts. Think of it as the low-end bar, the minimum bid. A stalking horse bid helps a company continue to buy and sell inventory in the ordinary course, retain employees, and otherwise keep its lights on during bankruptcy. If we could announce to the world that at least *one* party believed that Ashley Stewart was worth more alive than dead, we might attract other lemmings (I mean, bidders!) and raise more money. But no one showed up.

Randy and I went to a bar after it was all over. He bought me a birthday beer. Maybe even a second. I must have been staring off vacantly. Randy is a burly guy, and I felt his big hand on my shoulder. "Sorry, boss," he said. Randy knew what this meant. Given the company's history, heading into bankruptcy without a stalking horse was a death sentence. Things would quickly spiral out of control. It meant liquidation.

I was exhausted, depressed, and angry—all at once. Six months wasted. The entire world had rejected our plan, scoffed at our math, smirked at our predictions for the future, and placed zero monetary value on the connections among my home office colleagues, store managers, and customers. Not to mention *me*.

"What are we going to do, boss?"

In fact, I had a plan. I knew—*knew*—how to unlock the seed within Ashley Stewart. Of course, there was a high degree of execution risk—but Randy and I both knew what we had experienced in the previous six months. We felt confident in the vision, in the business plan, and in the team. Today, when I tell the story, I point to my heart and then my head, and say, "I knew I was right *here*, and then, after six months, I knew I was right *here*." The trouble was that as

CEO, I was legally conflicted. My sole legal, fiduciary, and professional responsibility was to maximize value for the estate. Not for Chary and Shelley, and not for the women living in the local communities of which Ashley was part. My investment platform, Fire-Pine Group, could not be the lead bidder because of this conflict of interest. Nor did I really want it to be, in truth. I wanted to be done and to go home. I had signed up for six months with a promise to do my best to maximize proceeds and find Ashley her new home. Anything beyond that was not part of the compact I had made with the board, my new colleagues, and especially my family. The problem was that there was no new home for Ashley.

The next day, I called a friend of mine, Steve, who was a partner at a then-boutique private equity firm. *I want to do a deal with you*, Steve had told me over the years. *Find something.* But I hadn't found the right opportunity, and I kept turning down the ideas he brought me. I remembered my father-in-law's sage advice that the best investments are usually the ones you choose *not* to make. Meaning, be extremely intentional about what assets you place on your balance sheet. The point is, Steve and I trusted each other. He knew I had no interest in making a quick buck at the expense of sacrificing principles or our friendship, which was the long-term asset we both valued the most.

I had pushed the restructuring advisors to include Steve in the bidding process as the rejections started to pile up. As a result, he had done a nominal amount of due diligence in case something like this ended up happening. "There's something here," I told him. Silence on the other end of the line. "Is this the one?" Steve said at last. Before we hung up, we agreed Steve would continue with his due diligence. A week or so after the bankruptcy filing in early March, after confirming that no one else was going to show up, Steve's firm signed up to be the stalking horse bidder. The fundamental investment thesis from their point of view? They trusted *me*. They backed *me*.

Deep down, there was a part of me that wanted another bidder to show up and top Steve's bid, which would mean I could go home with a clean conscience and resume my former private equity identity and all the security it afforded me. The world where Work-James and Home-James were *distinct*. I also could have *not* called Steve and just let the liquidation play out. But the investor in me truly believed in the vision of the future we were pitching. And, most important, the human in me knew that I had given my word to the Misfit Toys and especially the women in the stores. *Ride or die?* they asked me during those months of store visits in the fall. I would always nod my head. *Yes. Ride or die.*

In late April, at the final bankruptcy auction, I winced when only the liquidation firms showed up. Steve's firm won the auction by default. Because Steve's firm was an arms-length, third-party bidder, FirePine Group, which included some of the world's most sophisticated investors, was now permitted to make a significant investment as well.

Was I excited, amped up, racing around and pumping my fist, high-fiving the world, singing "Born to Run"? No—just the opposite. I was glum, and Randy and Donna knew why on a level that the others did not. They had met me in the context of Wall Street and high-flying private equity. They knew I was letting go of my private equity identity and all of the signifiers pertaining to educational background and social status accompanying it. Gone were the prospects of wood-paneled boardrooms, catered lunches, and Pebble

Beach golf trips hosted by law firms and investment banks. It turns out that exercising agency is sometimes incredibly painful.

No more "it's just for six months." Now I couldn't pretend this was just a temporary detour from my actual life. This was no longer about *option value*. Suddenly it was all *real*. It was put-up-or-shut-up time. I would be away from Meg and my three kids for too much of the time. Real money was at stake now, and real reputations. My friends had bet big on me, and my Ashley Stewart colleagues were relying on me. The safety net was gone.

Don't get me wrong. I derived some amount of solace from knowing that even if we ultimately failed, at least the company would be alive and more than a thousand jobs would have been preserved for a bit longer, including those of the Misfit Toys and Chary, Shelley, and Gina. But the long-term plan was far from foolproof. Remember, exercising agency doesn't mean that the outcome you desire is mathematically guaranteed. That said, my investors did not back my vision for me to fail them financially. And, what about the "me" part? Yes, FirePine Group owned a significant minority stake in the company. But from the perspective of the world, I was now the chairman, CEO, CFO, and largest individual owner of a twice-bankrupt company that sold clothes to plus-size Black women in urban neighborhoods, only six months removed from not having Wi-Fi. That's what my business card said. All of my eggs were in this one tattered basket. *Exhale, James.*

In retrospect, there were several different occasions since I had first landed in Secaucus when I had tried to avoid agency by hiding behind the security of precedent and convention. But over the course of those six months, my conviction and my courage grew. It was up to me to decide whether Work-James or Home-James played the leading role in my own life story. Appreciating how liberating it felt to accept uncertainty was just the icing on the cake. So the whole world had passed on Ashley Stewart—so what?

When I had come to Secaucus, I didn't entirely know what I was after. Reality, maybe. Authenticity. A better version of humanity. A better *me*. I was sick and tired of dealing with the cognitive dissonance, and of sacrificing real connection for its financial and technological equivalents. I didn't want to be an avatar anymore. In retrospect, I'm sure that my dad's deteriorating health contributed to this. In a life or death situation, there's no time for games, or gamesmanship, or one gamified system after the next that alienates you from your own humanity. Instead of running away from what was real, I wanted to run toward it. And yes, what is "real" is always painful. Joy and suffering are never far apart, just like *jeong* and *han*. I was also pretty sure that caring, or feeling, didn't make me any less capable or smart. In fact, as we shall see, it made me more capable and, I know deep down, smarter. I felt the same boldness I once had trusted so innately as a kid.

Then and now, I believe that any system with rules and norms that pushes us away from our own natures, away from the commonsense laws of nature and humanity, is doomed to fail and doomed to fail us in the long term. I was going to do things a different way. And that way, I knew, would call on a creative and musical side that had been locked away behind more spreadsheets and formulas than I could remember.

Ride or die. I chose the former.

chapter 5
balance

*A helicopter can hover.
In windless conditions, the sum
of the weight and drag forces
equals the sum of the thrust
and lift forces.*

A few days after the deal closed, I gathered everyone in that same dreary cafeteria with the cluster of gray folding chairs and the industrial-size lunch warmer. That same setting had played host to my first town hall meeting and the heart-wrenching WARN Act recital. But this time was different, and the space felt somehow transformed. Even the lunch warmer seemed oddly endearing.

Grabbing my laptop, I placed it on one of the chairs and played my favorite Beatles song, "Here Comes the Sun." I didn't say anything. Everyone just listened. I wanted us all to gather and savor this beautiful moment we had composed together against odds that once seemed insurmountable. With childlike sweetness and optimism, the song speaks of rebirth, clarity, and hope after a long and lonely winter. A new beginning, free of anger, or resentment. *Jeong*, born from *han*.

In the pit of my stomach, of course, I had doubts. Fear, even. But it was the good type of fear, the version that inspires courage. In the past, I might have second-guessed myself, or sat around wringing my hands. Not this time. Why? Because I knew that what I had experienced those previous seven months was *real*. No spreadsheet could possibly capture the *realness* or the connectedness among the Misfit Toys, Gina, Chary, Shelley, and me. No investment banking deck could even come close to explaining how relevant my past and the lives of my Korean parents were to my appreciating the potential of this business. Any honest money manager will tell you it's nearly impossible to outsmart the markets. But here's the catch. That's true *when the markets are efficient*. An important caveat. In this case, there were numerous data points that conventional market measurements and processes couldn't or wouldn't capture. Fundamentally, the markets were unable to recognize the value of this unexpected convergence of people and their respective pasts combining to form a new future. They lacked the historical data to predict the strength of a coalition that had no precedent. And, unlike them, I was fully present. I was *here*, not there. I wasn't sitting behind a desk. And because of this, I saw a future, whereas they saw only a past.

As "Here Comes the Sun" wound down, I knew that agency and kindness were intimately related—but I still didn't have the language to communicate that knowledge properly. Maybe that's why I instinctively chose to let the song speak for me. Our own winter may have been long, but it had become increasingly less lonely. We had all independently chosen to opt in, knowing at the same time that each of us needed the others for this to work. None of us had relinquished agency. For that reason, we had the type of agility that only true collective trust, as opposed to "group think," can inspire. Only later, in a week full of personal tragedy, would I fully understand and appreciate how important these fundamental human qualities were to our business and to my own life.

To succeed, I had to continue to lead in a way that inspired a worn-out, underresourced team to believe in and nurture the reality we were co-creating and actually living. Many of the human-made systems and constructs had done this company, its customers, and its workforce no favors. All we could do was prioritize and stay true to the core values we saw happen quietly in the stores and around my makeshift executive suite. We—the whole company—literally had to stop drowning in other people's perceptions, opinions, and valuations, and instead sing our own uniquely beautiful song. If we could somehow manage to do this, I was confident we would stay true to the Ashley Stewart mission *and* achieve Wall Street's measures of success.

We had no ambitions of changing the world. But as it so happens, by the time it was over, the world would gaze at us, slack-mouthed and shocked. We would smile back amiably, shrugging, our hands in our pockets, and invite everyone, including the doubters, to join us in celebration. But of course, I couldn't see that in that moment. I believed in us, whether the stated odds were in our favor or not. I also knew there was a whole lot to do.

The situation at Ashley called for a radically simple and honest solution—a business that operated more consistently with the "natural laws" of humanity, with the common sense and *knowing* we all remember as kids that the world tries to corrupt, and distort, and tells us we're nuts for remembering and holding up as real. *Those* were the values and principles we prioritized. Only *then* would we apply our knowledge of business accounting, marketing, technology, and organizational theory to amplify, not warp, those values and principles.

Put another way, we were intent on bending human-made systems rather than letting them bend us. We cared deeply about the people inside our ecosystem, and we weren't at all embarrassed to admit it. We encouraged home values to permeate our office and, in so doing, avoided some of the root causes and costs of workplace misery. We challenged ourselves to learn how to play and find a dynamic balance between both versions of the Landlord's Game, rather than solely playing the modern-day game of Monopoly. We shouldered the need to generate immediate positive cash flow because of the very limited runway that was afforded us while also clinging tightly to the bigger vision of replicating at scale the safe place that was the store in Brick Church. We acknowledged our mistakes and imperfections while insisting on excellence. Throughout, we did our best to maintain balance.

Where to start? Well, we needed to go back to the beginning. Literally. Neuroscientists will tell you that children are born learners, wildly imaginative creatives, and natural systems thinkers, at least until they grow up, at which point adulthood places them gently but firmly in those boxes we've discussed. But everyone in that cafeteria, including me, had been a child once. If we could start over, and learn (and *unlearn*) certain things, Ashley stood a good chance of succeeding.

So, how could I persuade everybody to embrace agency? To think with the radical common sense and curiosity of a kid? To unlearn? To drive profitability after two decades of this company hemorrhaging cash? Well, don't laugh, but I taught everyone how to do all this by using the combination of a lemonade stand and a T-account, the central framework used in business accounting. We then sprinkled in a few key tenets of finance and behavioral science. And here's the good news. People already knew most of this stuff intuitively. Albert Einstein wrote that the intuitive mind is a sacred gift, whereas the rational mind is more like a dutiful servant. Good point, from a man who was pretty good at using science and math to discover and communicate truth, no?

Consider what follows in this chapter as a dynamic framework for starting up or pivoting a business—or a life. I promise I'll make it fun and super-intuitive. When we're done, you'll realize that adapting only a few core principles can change the trajectory of a business— and, more importantly, maybe even the business that is *you*. It means exercising agency and then intentionally and accurately naming assets and liabilities, especially the ones that are difficult to track because of the rules of business accounting. As we have seen, sometimes assets turn into liabilities, and vice versa. Accepting this fluidity requires true agility. In fact, in a speeded-up, fast-changing world, agility might very well be the most important asset on your balance sheet.

So, how do we get started? First, let's do a quick refresher course.

The lemonade stand. It's a small business, set in a real community with distinct stakeholders. Real people part with real money. In return, they are given a small cup containing a mixture of sugar, lemons, pulp, and water, and maybe a slippery, dissolving ice cube if they're lucky. The math and operations are firmly grounded in capitalism, but viscerally, everyone knows there are certain differences relative to what we see in the adult world. Profit and return on investment are important in a lemonade stand, but other considerations and constraints often matter just as much, if not more. For instance, even though most lemonade stands sell a slightly "inferior" product (we don't buy the lemonade because it tastes great, do we?), even the crustiest neighbor does not come storming back to demand a refund. Remember the two versions of Monopoly's precursor? A lemonade stand operates in a hybrid space where *work* behaviors and *life* behaviors are allowed to coexist more seamlessly. In other words, Work-You versus Home-You. Of the two Yous, which one forks over the dollar bill to the kid selling the watery mixture in the soggy cup? Both, I think.

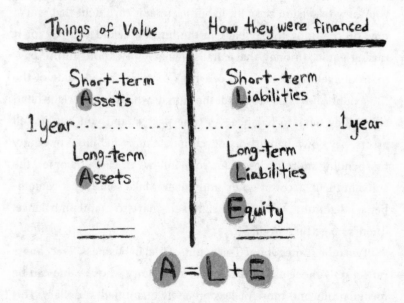

Second, *the T-account.* The T-account is a fundamental framework for organizing and visually presenting a balance sheet. It even looks like a capital letter *T.* The purpose of a balance sheet is to summarize a company's assets (A), liabilities (L), and shareholders' equity (E) at a specific point in time, which facilitates quarterly and annual comparisons. Accounting teaches us that *assets* are those things that create future value for the owner of the balance sheet. The assets go on the left-hand side. Assets whose expected life is longer than one year are grouped together separately and designated as *long-term* assets.

The right-hand side of the T-account tracks how you *paid* for all those assets. There are two ways. You can pay for them with funds that you one day must repay (*liability*), or you can pay for them with funds that give you outright ownership (*equity*). Did you finance your new television set with liabilities (credit card debt that you're now on the hook to pay back in the future), or did you pay for it raising equity (money that entails ownership without future payment obligations)? The sum of what's on the left-hand side of the T-account *always* has to equal the sum of what's on the right-hand side—they have to balance. As time passes, and you buy or sell assets, pay down liabilities, or accumulate more liabilities or equity by spending more or less than your inflows of cash (income), the sums in the T-account go up and down. Make sense? Just remember, by definition, the left and right sides have to maintain balance. There's no getting around it.

Two other notes about T-accounts. First, in business, T-accounts reflect only those assets, liabilities, and equity whose value can be formulaically and more or less precisely quantified in dollars. This means that more human, intangible assets (things like loyalty, wellness, or connectedness versus, say, business assets like trademarks or copyrights) are generally missing from most corporate balance sheets. Second, T-accounts are organized solely from the perspective of the equity—the ownership group, or shareholders. A typical balance sheet reflects the gains and losses realized by equity *share*holders, not the *stake*holders (workers, vendors, society at large) who are part of the same ecosystem. For example, the well-being of workers is absent from the balance sheet, unless it can be precisely measured in dollars. And even then, it would show up from the perspective of the shareholders; meaning, what is the impact of workers' well-being on the value of shareholder equity? So, if a future quantifiable obligation, like a defined pension, creates a positive impact for a company's employees, it would be classified as a liability because the T-account is organized from the sole perspective of the shareholders, or equity owners.

Why am I belaboring this? Because if you're using *business* accounting rules as the *sole* framework for measuring your *life*, it can be easy to lose track of assets and liabilities that simply cannot be measured in dollars but nonetheless play a big part in your overall balance as a *person*. According to the rules of business accounting, these difficult-to-quantify assets and liabilities would not appear on the T-account that is your life. This is an important point to understand, especially if the vocabulary of work is annexing more and more of your life, as it seems to be doing for many of us.

Let's just say that at Ashley Stewart, we worked hard to reconcile the rules of the lemonade stand with those of business accounting and corporate behavior. We did so by establishing a culture and a set of operational standards that challenged us to take into account the human assets and liabilities left untracked by official business accounting rules. In other words, though we reported our financial numbers *externally* to the letter of the law, we adapted a set of *internal* behavioral standards and measurements that were more consistent with those of a ten-year-old's lemonade stand. And in doing so, we exercised agency by holding ourselves accountable to *how* we hoped to achieve our desired outcomes.

Setting Up the Lemonade Stand

Step One: What's the Product?

Setting up a lemonade stand in theory is easy, but actually *doing* it can be scary. Just think back to when you were a kid. It's tough to put yourself out there and be vulnerable. What happens if no one shows up to support you? What if other kids make fun of you? The bigger point is that we all know that the actual lemonade is merely the p-product, whereas the real P-Product is *you*.

Remember how I asked everyone to listen to "Here Comes the Sun"? To put it in lemonade stand terms, what I effectively did was unfurl a new hand-lettered sign reading "Ashley's Lemonade." Everyone in the room knew the meaning behind those words. To underscore this, when the song ended, I repeated the questions I had asked during the very first town hall meeting, including, "What are we serving?"

In response, I heard words like *safety* and *self-confidence* and *friendship*. (*So far so good*, I thought.) "Who's responsible for this company's results?" was my second question.

"We all are," was the answer.

"And how are we going to do this?" I asked.

"Kindness and math!" they replied.

"Cool, we're making progress!" I said.

I pretended like this was no small feat, but in truth, the change in everybody's perspective was the result of nearly seven months of day-in and day-out intentionality. A shift in mindset is a process, not a eureka moment. This shift was real. I had given everyone space to observe, facts to reflect on, and time to form conclusions. The right conditions were now in place for them to exercise agency, or not. The responses I heard weren't canned, or memorized. People said what they did because they had lived it.

From that new vantage point, other changes flowed. No one flinched when I told them that this ecosystem centered Ashley, a Black, plus-size woman, who reminded me an awful lot of my Korean mom. At our lemonade stand, this woman was no longer

Other. Remember, statistics confirm that the majority of American women are plus-size. Along these lines, in this context, I was James, a former high school teacher with private equity skills. As for the Misfits? Well, it was obvious to everyone that they fit in just fine.

At the center of this world were the stores and the relationships among the Charys, Shelleys, and their customers. The stores were the real-life lemonade stands. The corporate office served *them*, not the other way around. This truth also underscored how fundamentally misguided it had been for previous executive teams to foist overly prescriptive rules upon the women on the frontlines, instead of learning from them. By undoing the dam, we freed those waters to flow more naturally, in the opposite but ultimately "right" direction.

If, by now, after everything we'd been through, anyone in the company was unwilling to unlearn the old, and adopt and embody this new perspective while surrendering to its underlying rhythm, they were not welcome to stay. It quickly became obvious who those individuals were. They were too constrained by the past. They couldn't keep up. Rather than floating, they wasted energy and thrashed around. Remember, I know what drowning looks like. In the end, we extended invitations to stay to approximately 60 percent of the individuals who had attended the initial town hall meeting held when I first arrived in Secaucus.

Step Two: Space

What's the next step in setting up a lemonade stand? You pick a spot on the curb and set up your table. But as we've learned, space often has an impact that goes beyond the mere physical. Do you remember how the fresh dynamics around the makeshift executive suite had a hand in slowly toppling a conventional (and made up) hierarchy? Or, for that matter, how creating distance from my life and identity in Boston provided just enough headspace for me to reconnect with my past in a new way? In both cases, a change in space catalyzed a shift in perspective and ideas.

So, one of the first things I did through the bankruptcy process was to inform the estate we wanted nothing more to do with our old headquarters. *Burn everything*, I told my colleagues, emphasizing, *bring only your brains, an open mind, your new perspective . . . and your laptop. This company is now in form and substance a <u>start-up</u>.* Gina gave everyone a little box for personal effects. We had already begun transferring our data to the cloud, which further liberated us from the physical definition of space. Left behind were the dusty filing cabinets, the cubbies, and all other physical reminders of failure and neglect. We also said goodbye to that industrial-size lunch warmer, which I still think about (and laugh about, and sometimes miss) today.

We set up our new corporate lemonade stand on the top floor of a nearby low-rise office building in Secaucus. It was gray, four stories tall, and uninspiring. But on a relative basis, from our perspective, it felt like a mountain resort, despite being a lot smaller and looking a lot like a well-worn Wall Street trading floor. It also came furnished. The spoils included a round (not rectangular) board table that seemed to foretell good fortune. One long-term executive, whose fear for his physical safety ultimately had driven my decision to hire the armed security guard, gazed at the unobstructed sight of a sunset outside his office window and started crying.

"I can't believe this," he said. "After everything we've been through. It's a miracle."

I let him savor the moment, but my inside voice told me no

miracles were involved here. Our path thus far had involved a series of very deliberate decisions about which assets had value and which ones didn't. Agency, imagination, safety, ingenuity, and confidence— those aren't assets that explicitly show up on any corporate balance sheet. By embracing them, we could detach ourselves from the mindset that the most valuable assets are physical in nature. From a financial perspective, we saved millions of dollars in annual costs by shrinking our physical footprint, which was made possible only by mentally recategorizing unproductive physical assets as liabilities, and then taking the necessary steps to detach ourselves and our operations from them.

In our new digs, I found a desk that looked an awful lot like my old desk and positioned it so that it looked over the trading floor. The only difference from my old "executive suite" was that Gina set up photos of the store managers, including Chary, on the faux wall right behind my desk. Most of these women were hundreds if not thousands of miles away from Secaucus. It didn't matter. They were figuratively there with me. I *wanted* them looking over my shoulder as I made decisions on behalf of Ashley. Gina and I also hung a picture from that bittersweet Brooklyn YWCA holiday party. It was a good reminder that there was no freaking way that would happen again, at least not under my watch.

And voilà—we had set up a new "table" in a new "space" that was geared up to support the actual lemonade stands across the country. We couldn't keep them all—we ended up shuttering most of our mall stores, even the modestly profitable ones. Malls can be contrived and impersonal. They feel more transactional and less rooted in their location. Ultimately, we hand-selected 90 stores from a remaining pool of around 115 (50 or so stores were liquidated during the bankruptcy process), focusing on the ones that were most woven into the fabric of their neighborhoods and communities. We did the best we could to retain deserving colleagues affected by the store closures by offering them transfers to one of the remaining 90 stores.

Overall, this decluttering process nudged me to streamline and clarify my *own* T-account. For the longest time, I realized I had mistaken my armor (things like credentials, degrees, my tough-guy image) for an asset. I had confused it for security. And it wasn't. It was *insecurity*. By placing this false sense of security where it belonged, on the liability side of my T-account, I could now take the steps to get rid of it and free up time to invest my energy creating and fostering *true* assets. By forcing myself to reevaluate all my assets and liabilities, I reminded myself who the owner of my life was. Me. Just as the owner of your life is *you*.

Step Three: Assembling the Leadership Team

Like any business, a lemonade stand works better with experienced hands and voices working in unison as a team. Aside from you, who else provides leadership for the stand?

When we're children, the logical first step might be to call your immediate friends, or at least loyal acquaintances. But, as we all know, it's important that our network expands to include those people for whom a friend or loyal acquaintance has vouched. Ultimately, these core team members prove their mettle not with their words but through their actions. They stick with us even when it starts pouring rain. They're there because they want to be there, and not purely for transactional, dollars-and-cents reasons.

Let's just say . . . there are four members of this core leadership team. Running a lemonade stand is a close-knit endeavor. You don't want to work alongside another kid who harasses or bullies you, or who is negative, unpleasant, self-serving, or a know-it-all. You want partners who will work the stand as hard and enthusiastically as you will—even if this means embracing a new kid who looks nothing like you but who acts every bit the part of a co-owner. Would it be fair to say that you don't want to work with anyone whom you don't implicitly trust to oversee the plastic container where the loose dollar bills and change are stored? No manual is required to spell out baseline rules of engagement such as these.

Notably, I'm not saying that adult work environments should be social clubs. Far from it. What I *am* saying is that there should be a basic unwritten social compact that transcends the corporate legalese I learned in law school and private equity, and whose roots are more in the humanities I learned in college. One enforced by your colleagues, not by the company itself. Not some purpose statement designed for a self-promoting press release or media spot. I believe it is fair to say that basic humanity, and the right to be treated humanely, should be equally distributed. And, yes, even in that world we call the workplace. This may sound overly philosophical, but just ask your inner ten-year-old and see what they say. *Fair is fair*, would be the answer. Rather than being exempt, those in a position of authority should be held more accountable in this regard. Leadership is not a prize. Leadership is an obligation, which means that, yes, it *should* feel like a burden.

At Ashley Stewart, we took all this to heart when we chose our team. It was a remarkably easy exercise. Everyone had been given seven months to show their cards and decide whether they wanted to play within the new system. We didn't hesitate to cut ties with highly skilled individuals, or walk away from money-making stores managed by teams who showed little interest in co-imagining a new future. We viewed negativity, an inability or unwillingness to even consider reimagining the future, as a genuine liability on our balance sheet, never mind what the accounting rules had to say. The energy costs of flying with such surplus weight were just too high. After shedding this liability, I knew we had created real equity value.

The original Misfit Toys naturally became the first iteration of the new leadership team. However, we never stopped evolving as a team after we moved offices. A few leaders, who had worked backbreakingly long hours during those first grueling eight months, wouldn't stop complaining about little things, like office size or snack offerings. "Let me understand," I said finally, "you're complaining about things like your office, and most of us here don't even *have* an office. I'm really disappointed. And after everything we've been through, too." But for some reason some people wouldn't let up, and it began to affect their and other people's work performance.

After a while, I'd had enough. "I'll tell you what," I said. "I found a great office for you. It's outside, in the parking lot. Let me know on Monday which of the two offices you want." On occasion, we would decide the parking lot office was the best option, and an individual and the company would part ways.

I gave the store managers the same speech I gave my home office leaders. The same standards would apply. For the most part, they were relieved. Even thrilled. My words, they said, were consistent with that very first conference call on the old Starfish phone. *I trust you. You know these stores better than I ever will. This is _your_ lemonade stand. Use your best judgment. We will do everything to support you on our end. Now go ahead and build your team.* Lemonade stands are fun. Fun is not contradictory with accountability. No one has fun when they are fearful. Many fancy organizational studies show that camaraderie and humor are essential to "productivity." It is a well-documented scientific fact that fear triggers our fight-or-flight impulses, effectively squashing creativity, generosity, and rational thinking. Didn't we all intuitively know this when we ran our first lemonade stand?

Step Four: Trust, Slack, and Redundancy

How are responsibilities divided up for an average lemonade stand? When I pose this question to executives in the various classes I teach, at first they try to assign roles in a logical way. One kid is in charge of pouring the lemonade. Another kid is responsible for combing the neighborhood for potential customers. When I ask which one of the four kids oversees the money and has visibility into the dollars and cents in the plastic container, most of the executives hesitate. *All of us*, they say. When I follow up by asking who among them is the CEO, or boss, inevitably someone tells me with some incredulity that there *is* no boss of a lemonade stand.

It's true, isn't it? Rarely among ten-year-olds do you hear the words *CEO* or *boss*. I then remind the executives that this feeling of being one among equals must reside somewhere deep inside us, and it never goes away altogether. Let's be honest—who *really* wants to work for a boss? For that reason, there is a critical difference between *leadership taken* and *leadership given*. Though it would never appear on a formal balance sheet, *leadership given* is a company asset that is created through the response of everyone who's *not* the actual leader. By exercising agency, the group concludes that the collective functions better with a certain person as CEO. But that doesn't mean they relinquish their agency. As a collective, they still own it. In my mind, then, far from being an asset, *leadership taken* is a company liability, using the same line of reasoning.

In hindsight, one of the most important decisions I made was to tell everyone at Ashley Stewart that my past performance and credentials did not make me qualified to lead the company. My colleagues could decide for themselves whether my leadership deserved to be followed and was worth sticking around for. I did not use my title, education, or professional credentials to foist my leadership onto anyone. Remember, I even told people how woefully unqualified for the job I was. Some misconstrued those words as evidence of weakness, or poor self-esteem. To me, it was the exact opposite. I knew I didn't need some ribbon or badge to validate my authority.

Instead, I distributed that authority. Everyone was encouraged to gain a general understanding of how the business worked. I made it clear from day one that my tenure was finite, and my goal was to make myself redundant. "It's Ashley's book," I would say. "We are just one chapter of a book that will hopefully have a wonderful ending." To reach a certain level of seniority, colleagues were required to prove they understood how the entire lemonade stand functioned on an integrated basis. Everyone can agree that mixing and selling lemonade requires less specialization than, say, building semiconductors or running a quantum physics lab. That said, no matter the industry, wouldn't you want your colleagues to have the broadest possible understanding of how the business works overall? Shouldn't people work in an environment that inspires and rewards curiosity about how their jobs enhance the company's overall levels of innovation and profitability? Shouldn't you want to hire people who think like that, or *want* to, at every level, if possible?

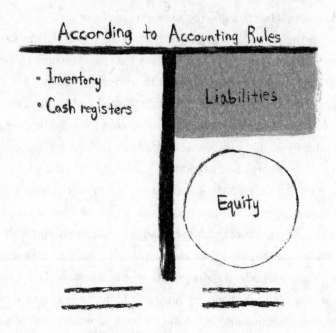

We certainly did, which is why I had posed those open-ended questions in my makeshift executive suite during those first few weeks in the old headquarters. In doing so, we created other hard-to-value assets like *slack* (ease, extra time, extra space, grace) and *redundancy* (back-up, insurance). Cross-functional training, which creates slack and redundancy, allowed people to have peace of mind when they went on vacation or on days when a child was sick. Blurring the lines that defined departments and functions reduced boredom and encouraged collaboration. It also meant that no single person, including me, could ever hold the company hostage, which in turn meant that compensation, not just decision-making, was more evenly and flatly distributed. Hoarding information is

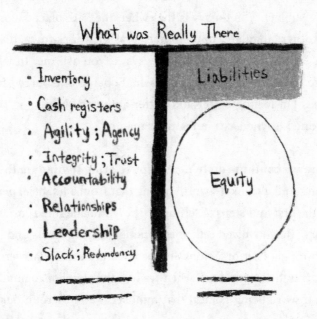

symptomatic of a culture of fear and scarcity. That wasn't us. We encouraged and rewarded sharers.

I want to be clear that I'm not saying that workplaces should eliminate specialization. But it also stands to reason that people should have a well-rounded understanding of how their business—and their own life—works. Being good at only one thing without understanding how it connects to bigger, broader systems at play is a high-risk, high-reward strategy that puts you at the whim of an ever-changing, unpredictable job market. It's something present-day college admissions officers should bear in mind, especially with the acceleration of artificial intelligence. Only a few decades ago, schools sought out "well-rounded students." Today, many schools seek and admit applicants who are wildly specialized in a single subject. The theory is that when they are placed alongside their other "angular" contemporaries, as they are known, they create a well-rounded *class*. Not always, if you ask me. In a world where linear functions are increasingly being outsourced to machines, I'm feeling better and better about the lessons in critical thinking I learned as a humanities major.

Before we continue on to next steps relating to funding the lemonade stand, I think it's worth noting that from a financial perspective, the first four steps of setting up the lemonade stand cost us *zero* dollars. They involved redefining and identifying assets and liabilities through a set of actions and behavioral norms that were once more intuitive to us, back when we had the abundance mindset of kids. If we're being honest, that mindset is still there in our adult selves. We just sort of . . . *bury* it, as I had done with the red helicopter. In the case of Ashley Stewart, the world had used the literal rules of accounting to draw its T-account. That T-account overlooked and (significantly) undervalued countless assets that were in plain view if you chose to look closely enough.

Funding the Lemonade Stand

Step One: Raising Money and Ownership

The lemonade stand needs money so that it can go out and buy the necessary supplies to fund operations. For illustration purposes, let's just assume twenty dollars is more than enough to fund one day's worth of selling cups of lemonade. Where does that money come from?

When I ask adult executives this question, they usually come back with one of two solutions: either all four kids agree to break open their respective piggy banks, with each investing five dollars, or else they each ask their parents to give them five dollars.

In other words, each team decides to raise money (financial capital) by investing a collective twenty dollars of equity—not debt—in the lemonade stand. That means the stand has zero financial leverage, which is a fancy term for *debt*, out of the gates. There are no loans, no liabilities, to pay back. Why? Because if your parents gave you the five dollars, it's highly unlikely they would demand the return of their "seed" capital. I like to remind my students that the five dollars they got from their mom or dad is the cheapest, easiest "friends and family" capital they will probably ever see. Call me if you ever find equity investors who demand zero ownership!

Generally speaking, each team member assumes that the others should contribute their fair share to the overall pie. That's five dollars per kid. It's only fair. This helps ensure buy-in from all the participants, otherwise known as skin in the game—which we tried to offer at Ashley on a direct and indirect basis. Let me explain.

I gave the Misfit Toys the opportunity to invest the equivalent of their own piggy bank money alongside Steve's firm and FirePine Group. They had earned that right. They were also familiar enough with the overall business to assume that risk fairly and knowledgably. In other words, they had the information and understanding to exercise true agency around that decision. With the approval of the board, I also granted a slightly larger group of individuals equity ownership through the issuance of stock options, which awards ownership over time without requiring anyone to break open their piggy bank up front. To this day, it's one of my bigger regrets that given our challenging path, we did not have the wherewithal to properly evaluate and implement an employee stock ownership plan (an ESOP).

That said, we did our best to take a more expansive view of the word *equity*. Ownership in stock isn't the only form of ownership that matters, though financially it is obviously very important. Too often, people who don't own stock *feel* they have no agency. That their contributions or actions don't matter or count. The fundamental tenet of agency is ownership of your actions, which we took great pains to identify and reward. For instance, at a companywide level, we went out of our way to teach everyone that the cost of healthcare and other forms of insurance was the result of the aggregation of each person's individual choices and actions on a daily basis. Year after year, we consciously drove this point home by showing the connection between our collective behavior and renewal rates. At the store level, we recalibrated the cash compensation system to modify what were purely sales-based bonuses to include nonsales goals and requirements more appropriate for lemonade stand *owners*. For instance, the measurements we used to determine these supplemental bonus awards were based on how well a store leader managed her balance sheet, including tangible assets like inventory (remember the camis?) and intangible assets like employee retention, community relationships, and character. This bonus system came to be known as the CEO Citizenship Award, whose winners embodied the principles *Act like an Owner, Be a Good Friend, Be a*

Good Mentor. The cash payouts were intended to track the appreciation in value of the "stock price" of a particular store. We will revisit this in chapter 6.

Step Two: Using the Money to Invest in the Business

After the kids raise twenty dollars in seed capital, what do they do with it? A logical response would be they invest that money in supplies (cups, lemons, sugar, and so forth). I'll use very easy numbers here. If one saleable cup of lemonade costs fifty cents to make (including the cost of the cup itself), the team can produce forty cups (twenty dollars divided by fifty cents). If the kids charge one dollar per cup to customers, and sell everything they produce, they can generate sales of forty dollars (forty cups times one dollar). Basically, they've doubled their money (twenty dollars has become forty dollars). And since the cost of the saleable cups was twenty dollars, the team's gross profit—the profit from the actual p-product, that is to say, the lemonade—comes out to a tidy twenty dollars.

This also means that every dollar that does not *directly* contribute to producing a saleable cup of lemonade results in lower gross profits. Meaning, if you are going to spend money on things like tables and chairs (long-term assets), you'd better think long and hard about how valuable they are to selling cups of lemonade in the long term. And, because there are no labor costs (the four kids are owners without salaries), no marketing expenses (the kids already have felt-tip markers and construction paper, and foot traffic is a wonderful thing), and no rent (curbs are free), the overall *net profit* is equal to the *gross profit*. What I'm trying to say is that every dollar spent on marketing or anything other than a saleable cup of lemonade would reduce gross profit and net profit.

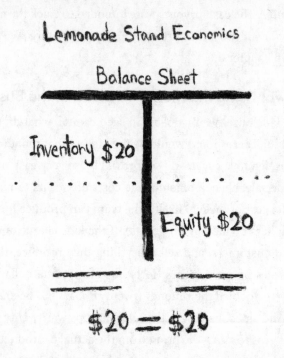

Lemonade Stand Economics

Balance Sheet

Inventory $20

Equity $20

$20 = $20

Of course, things are different in the adult world. Rent adds up, businesses last longer than a day, there's not enough foot traffic to sustain daily sales (hence, the need for marketing expenses), and not everyone employed by the company is an owner (resulting in labor expenses). This is a long way of saying that in adult companies, *gross profit* does not equal *net profit*. For any given level of gross profit, then, maximizing net profit, from an equity owner's perspective, means trying to minimize labor, marketing, rent, and other costs. Because labor is just another expense recorded alongside payments to people like advertisers and landlords, it can be tempting for leaders to succumb to a visual stimulus that primes them to forget that "labor" represents their colleagues.

Lemonade Stand Economics

Income Statement

Sales	$40
Minus: cost of goods Sold	20
Gross Profit	$20
Minus: Labor	0
Minus: Marketing	0
Minus: Rent	0
Minus: Other costs	0
*Net Profit	$20

*Assumes No Taxes!

It's worth emphasizing that a key takeaway reinforced by lemonade stand economics is the primary importance of the balance sheet. You cannot sell what you do not own. Meaning, the assets on your balance sheet drive your income statement, not the other way around. Whatever price you may set, you can only sell as much lemonade as you have.

The lemonade stand also reminds us that it's the quality of the assets, not the quantity, that matters. At some point lemonade begins to taste bad. The cups themselves get limp and soggy, the lemonade warm and watery. Having too many cups on the table also increases the risk of spilling, so they sometimes get stored beneath the table. With the passage of time, these sad little cups often get sold at a much lower level of gross profit, if not a loss.

Again, remember the camis? Are camis all that different from cups of lemonade? Not at all. Remember how our store managers had trouble selling them? In lemonade terms, they "tasted" bad. The store managers had never asked for those camis, but they were stuck figuring out what to do with them. So who *was* accountable for deciding to invest all that cash into those camis? The home office, which, consistent with accounting rules, recorded those camis on the balance sheet as an *asset.* Recall that I mentally recategorized the camis as toxic *liabilities.* And what do you want to do with liabilities? Get rid of them, ASAP! It's amazing how a simple change in mental classification can give rise to a different behavior. Calling something an "asset" makes us strangely complacent and resistant to getting rid of that thing. (Think about what is in your house or stashed in your garage or basement. Are those things assets, or actually liabilities? Hmmm—sounds like it might be time for that garage sale, after which you might find to your surprise that you need less space in your life, which could lead to a lower cost of living.)

It's a cardinal rule in business and in life: very few assets have the potential to be worth more *after* you buy them. Those that do are more properly called *investments.* Anything else—even if the accountants call them assets—is never again quite as financially valuable, period. Remember, then, not all assets are investments. In fact, many "assets," especially ones you acquired late at night while watching a catchy infomercial or clicking on a digital ad on your phone, could actually be better described as liabilities. Investors generally own assets that have the potential to appreciate in value over time. Consumers generally own "assets" that depreciate in value over time. Be an investor.

I taught the lessons of the lemonade stand to as many people at Ashley as possible. Not surprisingly, people really got it. Intuitively, they knew the answers. Especially the part about who was, or *should be*, truly accountable for making decisions about which assets we should buy with the money we had raised, which led, inevitably, to rethinking *how* and *who* got bonuses based on *which* decisions.

Let me explain. By now, it was crystal clear to everyone that the corporate office was responsible for the cups of lemonade—the design and quantity of the cups, the lemons and sugar, you name it. This did *not* mean that the store managers were let off the hook. Some days you come to work, and power through, and sell too-warm lemonade as best you can. As it relates to those cups, where store managers *were* held strictly accountable was in their live-time communication with the corporate office about what was working and what wasn't. Do you remember the feedback loop between Ashley store managers and the corporate office that was discontinued by the former executive team? Let's just say that the feedback loop was reinstated with gusto.

This balance sheet–first mindset creates operational agility, too. The only way to have fewer stale cups on the table is to fine-tune operations in such a way that accelerates the cups-in, cups-out process. The faster and more efficiently you do this (without spilling or knocking over cups), the fresher the lemonade is, and the more cups you will sell at a higher price, with fewer storage costs. The ice has less time to melt, for one thing. Does this make sense? And yes, technology helped us, along with some nifty mathematical equations and improvements in our logistics system. But it all began with our collective insistence on never repeating the cami debacle. And to do this, we knew that we had to talk about what we owned (balance sheet) before we could talk about sales (income statement).

Following this line of reasoning, you can now probably understand better why I had a desk for an office, drove the aging Nissan company car, and didn't use company money to buy frivolous items. Technically, per the rules of business accounting, any cash spent on those items would be recorded as an *asset*. Would driving a cooler company car make me a better member of the team? By forgoing those status symbols, we were able to both buy more saleable cups *and* make long-term investments in the people or technologies that could help us make and sell more cups, which would generate more gross profit, which could then fund things like higher salaries.

I increasingly applied this same logic to the business of *me*, which required using slightly different terms. On my personal income statement, sales are called *salary*, and the cost of my "cup" is the time, health (physical and mental), commuting costs, and other opportunity costs, like giving up spending time with my family and children or choosing not to pursue my dreams, that are directly related to the time it takes to earn my salary.

I became vigilant about minimizing the "cost" of my own "sales," and I encouraged my colleagues to do the same. This issue became quite stark at my twenty-fifth college reunion, where I met many people who were income rich but balance sheet poor. What does that mean? Well, first, remember that real balance sheets, absent fraud, rarely lie. They are the ultimate truth-tellers. They serve as historical documents that chronicle *how* you decided to spend the money you earned. They reflect your values, as well as *what* you value.

For instance, say that you make an unwise decision on an ego-driven, long-term asset. For illustrative purposes, let's say it is an expensive luxury car (though it could be any number of things or habits). You don't really want it, but everyone else has one. Sure, accountants tell you what you bought is an asset. But is it? Isn't it a liability? And don't you now have to give up harder-to-see long-term intangible assets like time spent with your children, your health, your relationships, and freedom to pay for it? If something does not produce *true* value, why spend the money on it? Why not invest that money instead in something that *does* create future value?

This is where the limitations of business accounting, and our own bias toward prizing tangible items, help conceal the true cost of a decision like this. Those harder-to-see life assets are considered immeasurable. As a result, they appear nowhere on the typical balance sheet. Because of this, fluctuations in these human assets do not affect our income statement (or bank statements), so we don't track them.

Let's imagine that the luxury car costs $100,000. Factoring in income taxes, let's just say you have to earn an incremental $150,000 to pay for it over time. This "asset" now quietly drives a whole new set of behaviors. You take on a new, higher paying job that requires you to work nonstop, and also on weekends. You're more stressed, you have no time to exercise, and your family never sees you. What's the cost of all of this? Well, if these life assets were actually booked on the balance sheet, they would compel you to be honest and *depreciate* the value of these assets—and that cost would hit your income statement. Meaning, the incremental $150,000 you think you are earning is much less than you think because of the silent cost of these life assets declining in value.

Wait, it gets worse. Though they might not cost you actual cash in the short term, the long-term deterioration in these life assets typically ends up also costing you cash in a big way. What's the cash cost of a divorce or triple bypass surgery down the road? So think about it: If your goal is to earn an incremental $150,000 to pay for the car you only sort of want, but that increase causes you to gain fifty pounds and estranges you from your spouse and children, were you, in fact, better off making less and not buying that luxury car in the first place?

Step Three: Leverage

When we hear the word *leverage*, most of us think of its financial meaning. A mortgage to buy a house, credit card debt to fund Christmas gifts, national debt to fund the government's widening federal deficits. Now, there is nothing wrong with financial leverage. Used smartly, it can be an amazing tool. Like a tire jack, or a wheelbarrow, leverage makes it possible for us to amplify our efforts. Debt lets us *bend time* by fast-forwarding the future into the present. Who doesn't want to live in a better house or replace an old car with a newer one (or buy something better than Carrier Strike for their children on Christmas morning)?

But make no mistake: that debt is now on your balance sheet. You have to pay it back. If you don't, as we saw with Ashley Stewart, there are costs. Among them is loss of trust. Cash on delivery (that is, no credit) is no fun. Neither is hiring an armed police officer to patrol your lobby.

During my lemonade stand simulations, executive teams are encouraged to focus on other forms of leverage because, as we noted, lemonade stands generally use 100 percent equity. For instance, what about marketing, which is a form of leveraging your voice? When discussing their marketing strategy, teams invariably say they will

call on their friends to spread the message. Word-of-mouth marketing is true leverage—it's free, too!—that only works if you have a
network that trusts you. A cross-functionally trained team working
in an environment where each member has an ownership mindset
also creates tremendous operating leverage. Dan needs a bathroom
break, and Rachel is due at home to walk the dog. No problem. The
key to both these forms of leverage is that their availability depends
on the presence of intangible assets (namely, trust, slack, and redundancy) on your balance sheet. Whether or not you record it, your
past trustworthiness and your reputation are written in indelible
ink on your balance sheet.

In Ashley's case, even though the accounting rules decreed that
we were starting with a clean slate, the company's negative business
reputation was still dragging on our otherwise pristine balance
sheet. Only time, and good behavior, would ultimately erase that
smudge, that liability, on our balance sheet.

Like a lemonade stand, we had no financial leverage. Period.
Given our unillustrious history, what bank would have offered us a
loan? I wasn't able to get us a new line of credit until another six
months had gone by—and even *that* was based on Ashley's old, in-
the-box, asset-based loan formula. The bank was lending to our inventory, not our operations. From chapter 4, you now understand
what that implied—they still didn't really *trust* us or believe we had
any assets beyond the tangible. But, as it turned out, our results
were so good that we never came close to borrowing on that line of
credit, a fact I got a kick out of underscoring at least once a month
in our financial reporting packages.

So, instead, we focused on lemonade stand–type leverage out of
the gates. The kind of leverage money cannot buy. The team was

composed of well-informed, incredibly motivated individuals all pulling together in the same direction. The picture of the Brooklyn YWCA holiday party served as a poignant reminder and amplifier of our value system, our resilience, and our resolve. And fairly quickly, we accessed a different form of financial leverage that most business schools gloss over. Not surprisingly, it's one tied more closely to the social capital found in a lemonade stand on Main Street than it is to the financial capital of Wall Street.

During the first six months after bankruptcy, I spoke to every one of our vendors, whether they supplied clothes or technology. I laid out the same business plan and vision that the world's financial markets had rejected. I also added the following: *I'm sorry for the old company's past behavior. This is a new company, legally and in practice. This is the only time I will apologize for the past. Going forward, we will operate in a manner consistent with what I just explained to you. Our expectation is that you will do the same. If you don't, we're going to take our business elsewhere.* I then told them we would *not* be paying cash on delivery. I showed them our clean balance sheet. As a starting point, I asked for one to two days of payment terms. Over the course of my tenure, that one- to two-day period expanded to forty-five to seventy-five days of payment terms. In business accounting terms, even though these amounts outstanding are classified on a T-account as "short-term liabilities" under the header "accounts payable," I always looked at them as proof of the biggest *asset* we had created. Our vendors learned to *trust* us. Not to mention that this "float," as it's known, funded our growth without our having to raise additional equity capital, which would have meant giving up ownership and having a potentially distracting voice in the boardroom.

On a personal basis, I was aware that Meg was providing me, and everyone else associated with Ashley, a different form of leverage through social capital. I was away from home from Monday to Thursday every week. I wasn't there to drive our kids around, help clean the house, prepare meals, or respond to emergency calls from the school nurse. Meg did all of this while also managing the science portfolio of a leading nonprofit funding research to cure Alzheimer's disease. I remember Gina was always keenly sensitive to my last-minute airport scramble and was forever expressing grave remorse about my being separated from my family. Meg is hardly the only woman out there who provides uncompensated leverage for her family, while also earning less than market rates for their compensated positions. If I put on my finance hat, it doesn't add up, and every woman *and* man should know this.

Step Four: Defining Success

At the end of the lemonade stand simulation, I generally pose two final questions to all the competing teams. Assuming all else is equal, which team of ten-year-olds *wins*? And what does *winning* mean to a ten-year-old? After deliberating, most of the teams offer up a combined answer: *Whichever team had more friends and fun and began and ended the day with a better reputation in the neighborhood.* Has a truer statement ever been uttered?

No one buys lemonade from a neighborhood stand on the basis of the quality of the product. *No one.* Embedded in that dollar bill is a link to the past, and a nod to the future. Something of lasting value is created above and beyond the transaction. The familiarity and intimacy created by a neighborhood lemonade stand create a real and incremental asset. It's on the neighborhood's collective T-account.

Everyone in the neighborhood is the better for that lemonade stand. Everyone wins. Social capital combines with financial capital to create what's called a *positive externality,* like the crisp envelopes my mom used for *yongdon.*

What about *how* to define success? In theory, we can all agree that forty dollars in revenue from the cups of lemonade is an excellent result. We've maximized revenues. Everyone's happy.

Advanced Lesson

By the way, that number, forty dollars, could go even higher if, say, the kids were able to secure the lemonade ingredients up front, at no charge, with a promise to repay the vendor at the end of the day . . . and then proceeded to invest the twenty dollars in a hot stock over a twenty-four-hour period. But for the purposes of this discussion, let's stick with our original (and excellent) forty dollars in revenue.

But the winning team often does not end up with forty dollars in revenues. We drank some lemonade ourselves, and our goal was also to hang out and have fun. We wanted to balance having a good time with making money. It was really important for us to end the day with positive relationships, so we gave some lemonade away. Fair enough. How, then, would the people who financed this operation (the moms and dads of the world, that is) agree with this definition of success?

At the funding level (in this example, your parents are the real shareholders in many ways), social norms and expectations are no joke. Take that collective twenty dollars and spend it on video games? Maximize revenue at forty dollars but curse at your elderly neighbor, bully your friends, and leave a mess of napkins and cups on the lawn? You're in trouble. There will be consequences, unseen on an accountant's balance sheet, ones that aren't reflected in your gross or net profits. Things have a way of rearing their ugly heads, perhaps at the next neighborhood get-together. So watch yourself! Economists even have a term for this: *negative externality*—meaning when the consumption or production of something results in a cost to another party, but it isn't reflected on the guilty party's financial statements. Think pollution, for example. Because a lemonade stand operates in a world somewhere in between social norms and market norms, the business owners (the four ten-year-old kids) who create negative externalities end up paying for them one way or another in the form of extra chores, revoked privileges, or a flat "no" to the next great idea in need of parental funding.

At Ashley, we took to heart these final lessons of the lemonade stand. We committed to building a financially sustainable business model whose success was interwoven with its commitment to creating positive externalities for our store communities. This meant that *how* we went about it was just as important as the *what* and the *why*, maybe more so. Otherwise, what was the point of all this? It wasn't a burning desire to sell clothes that compelled me to overrule my more egotistical inclinations to reassume my position behind a desk in Boston. Instead, I forced myself to learn about the p-product (shark-bites, Marilyns, and peplums) to create a mathematically sustainable foundation for the P-Product that I genuinely cared about. It wasn't a concern about a clothing store that prompted one of our customers to offer to return her clothes hangers in order to help us stay afloat. We all co-created and co-owned a positive externality grounded in connectedness, self-confidence, friendship, and community—all the words I had said at the first town hall meeting, all the intangible qualities that I saw and heard in our stores. None of which was on the balance sheet, consistent with the rules of business accounting.

Remember, from what I observed at their best, the stores also served as a safe haven that gave Chary the opportunity to visit lonely, elderly customers in the hospital, and Shelley the space to serve healthy, daily doses of affirmation, whether customers left the store with a blouse or not. So Wall Street didn't like what Ashley's lemonade stand looked like? Well, maybe Wall Street didn't know everything after all. Its accounting rules fundamentally failed to capture all that was magnificent about this business and what it said about us all. The business had survived thanks to the strength of women like Chary who refused to allow the worst of corporate behavioral norms, which were in turn primed by the arbitrary rules of business accounting, to affect her relationships with her customers. We had to work to live, not the other way around. To do so, we had to unleash ourselves from the rules of business accounting and make our life assets more easily visible, trackable, and measurable.

Deep down, I guess, I had underestimated my own T-account. There was Steve. He had trusted me, in part because he knew the backstory behind my resignation from the elite private equity firm many years before. It turns out that as painful as it had been, that short-term liability was actually a long-term asset. The same could be said for some of my more painful or bittersweet memories growing up, like the story about my parents buying a menorah. Without my having had those experiences, this company would have been long since liquidated. When I focused on transforming Ashley's perceived liabilities into assets, many of my own perceived liabilities underwent the same metamorphosis. In that context, it was hard not to remember that day in Maine when I hugged Meg and said, *Why not me? Granted, no one is offering this face a modeling contract. I used to be a high school teacher. I have a growing mountain of school debt.*

Meg couldn't help laughing. *Really? That's your line?*

I didn't have the words for what I wanted to say. If I had, the future financier in me would have blown up that romantic moment by saying, *There are assets on my balance sheet that you can't see. It just might take time for them to emerge into something more tangible.* Fortunately, I kept my mouth shut long enough for her to say yes to my request for a first date.

I'm hardly alone. Remember, we all have a balance sheet. It's the sum total of our lives. Remember, too, that a life well lived generally has a balance sheet full of assets we cannot see, or touch. Our reputations, our friendships, our memories. The dynamic motion among these assets is what creates freedom and joy. None of these things can be bought. It's because of this that they cannot be reduced to a linear rule devised by a bunch of accountants. We accumulate them through our actions, not through our expenditures. They are investments of time, of energy, of heart.

Anyone who has lost a parent knows what it's like to go through their belongings. Most of these assets have no financial value. Dear as they are, and as emotional as they make us feel, they're just stuff, scratched and battered, with little resale value. That said, if those possessions also contain *jeong*, it's impossible to put a price tag on them or throw them out. Ultimately, I suppose the only real measurement for a life well lived is how missed you are when you die. And I know, from my years in private equity, that this is an asset that will never show up on your balance sheet if you use solely business accounting to track the T-account of your life.

Wrapping Things Up

Six months after our miraculous escape from the jaws of liquidation, which also roughly corresponded with the one-year anniversary of my first town hall, the balance sheet of our new company was clean. We had reset relationships. We had purged the company of people and contracts that no longer served our forward-looking collective purpose. We had created space for what was to come—new ideas, new colleagues, new customers.

Anyone still there knew unequivocally that far from being a "liability," being a plus-size Black woman was an asset at this company. Outside our office and stores, this may or may not have been true, and the world had delivered a verdict that indicated it had its doubts. But inside the company and its immediate surrounding ecosystem, we had successfully changed *the belief system*. Would the larger ecosystem agree and act in accordance with this belief? This was out of my immediate control, but I certainly knew that I was going to do everything in my power, as long as I was CEO, to ensure we would never, ever sacrifice *Product* for *product*.

That summer, our family took what would end up being our last family vacation with my dad. On one of those days, for a two-hour window, the Parkinson's symptoms miraculously abated, and my dad was 100 percent Dad. We even played a game of cards. I wanted to tell him everything that had happened, everything that I had learned. I wanted to tell him how much inspiration I had drawn from the way in which he ran his small business and lived his life. But it just didn't happen.

Living the life I did while respecting my parents' values as care-givers was, for a long time, hard for me to reconcile. But when I was put to the test, my parents' values, *caregiver* values, refused to bend. And *because* of it, not *in spite* of it, Ashley Stewart was absolutely *crushing* it financially.

Like the Ashley Stewart stores, my dad's modest pediatric practice was woven into the very fabric of the lives of the Long Island families he served. Tight-knit communities and local businesses hold each other accountable. During my lifetime, however, it seems to me that we've allowed the larger lemonade stands of the world to create negative externalities without demanding enough accountability from them. Instead, we marvel at their scale and "innovation," both of which have been fueled by the printing of paper money. And, for some reason, we just keep on buying cups of lemonade from them because some, like the social media platforms, charge us zero dollars and instead take our harder-to-define assets like privacy and data. We all know deep down there is a hidden cost, especially for our children. There is an enormous long-term liability building up on our collective T-account. Maybe that's the true cause of the gnawing feeling in our stomachs. We know we've all been complicit.

Over the course of a generation, just like the confusion over Monopoly's origin story, it seems we've convinced ourselves that financial and social capital have always been untethered and severed. That the *why* and the *how* have *always* been divorced from the profit motive. That making money was, and still is, all that matters.

That civic institutions serve the economy, and not the other way around. That the United States is a corporation, not a country.

How to move forward? Well, first, I knew we couldn't solve all of these societal problems on our own, so I made sure we focused on what we could control. I finally gave myself permission to trust my intuition, that childhood sense of right and wrong that, as I got older, I had allowed the world to smother under a tall stack of external validation. Not anymore. I felt free—while finally grasping the oxymoron that to be free you have to commit yourself to others. I felt strong, too.

It's one thing to clean out the proverbial closet or back room, and another to fundamentally alter behavior and engrain new habits. Bad habits die slowly. Talk is cheap. We had to remain vigilant. During those first six months of our rebirth, I doubled down on the word *kindness*. It was on, around, and infused in every part of our balance sheet.

I was now convinced beyond any doubt that the continued integration of kindness into our day-to-day operations and decision-making processes was key to our path forward.

chapter 6

integration

Without the tail rotor, or some other related mechanism, helicopters would just spin around and around.

Trust me when I say I fought hard to find another word for *kindness*. *Any* other word. At the same time, given everything we'd been through at Ashley Stewart, I felt reasonably confident that my colleagues, who had literally been through a battle for survival with me, understood what kindness was. They had lived it, immersed themselves in it. But could kindness *last*? Could kindness *scale*? Could kindness continue to help sustain and drive our bottom line? At some point, too, I needed to reconnect the company with the world beyond our immediate ecosystem of colleagues, customers, and vendors. What would kindness mean for future colleagues, and business relationships, who had not seen us in action, up close?

We all know that pop culture sentimentalizes kindness, while the business world dismisses it. Lemonade stands staffed by plucky kids in sneakers and overalls? No problem. But in the adult work-place? No. Armor on. Kindness is embarrassing, decidedly uncool. A curriculum centered around kindness isn't exactly dominating the world's business schools either. But why not? Kindness hasn't been shown *not* to work in business. Maybe it's because kindness, almost by definition, resists being reduced to a single number, which makes it difficult to run correlation and causality analyses. Or maybe it's because kindness is being improperly defined.

Try as I might, I couldn't come up with a better word. There *isn't* one, except maybe *love*, which is related to kindness, but not the same. Love is intimate, and personal, whereas kindness can be ex-changed by complete strangers. Meaning, kindness is much more scalable than love.

So how *do* you define kindness? It's not easy. Kindness isn't meant to be put in a box. It's a noun that should also be a verb—*to kind. Kinding.* Maybe that's part of the problem.

First, let me point out that over the centuries, a handful of ex-traordinary leaders—think about it, you probably know whom I'm referring to—have created world-changing movements grounded in the philosophy of kindness. Kindness is transcendent. Some of the world's leading philosophers, like Jean-Jacques Rousseau and Adam Smith, whose thoughts inspired then-radical concepts like liberty and free markets, wrote openly about kindness during the Age of Enlightenment. Also, if Sun Tzu, in his book *The Art of War*—which today's global military and business leaders still dog-ear, de-spite it being written in roughly the fifth century BCE—can reference kindness and compassion as core ingredients of leadership, how weak or beside-the-point can kindness be? So why is kindness often marginalized and misunderstood today?

To answer, let's see if we can first agree on what kindness *isn't*. Kindness is not niceness. Kindness is not random, despite all those bumper stickers. Kindness is not accidental. It is not martyrdom. What, then, *is* kindness? Kindness is intentional. Kindness is both forceful and malleable. Kindness is relentless and steady like flowing water. It requires a person (or an organization) to operate and act in a certain way, beyond mere good intentions. By calling on us to behave in ways that might, on the surface at least, run counter to our self-interest, kindness also requires courage—and a leap of faith.

When you think about it, kindness fundamentally involves an exchange, or a series of exchanges, with one or more living beings. Maybe that's why game theorists write about kindness as a strategy. It's an *investment* in a person *and* in a system. Kindness implies the expectation of some form of "return," but in this case, the "return" is nontransactional. Kindness is therefore grounded in some degree of hope and optimism for the future. Over the course of one or more of these exchanges, value is created above and beyond the obvious exchange of, say, the dollar bill handed over for a cup of lemonade. I believe that the best word to describe this value, this nebulous *asset*, this positive externality, is *goodwill*.

How do you know when something of value has been created? By the way it's received. You can't create value by yourself. You need a partner, or a counterparty. It's those others who determine if your *how* and *what* actually created value. Again, *kindness is an exchange*.

That's the tricky thing, though, isn't it? The value created by kindness is intangible. You need to feel it. And sense it. You need to use all your human faculties, not just your eyes. You need to be receptive to that warm, good ache spreading in your chest. You need to be present. It naturally follows that the best way to create and receive kindness is to wear very little armor—to be *vulnerable*, in other words.

Maybe the best way to capture the nuance of kindness is through the metaphor of the upside-down hedgehog.

Allow me to explain. At one point when my kids were young, they got it into their heads that we should get a hedgehog as a pet. I dutifully did my dad-research and noted the animal's high risk of getting foot and mouth disease. I then proceeded to watch one short video after the next of hedgehogs floating on their backs in a sink or tub as their owners gently washed their extremely soft undersides.

"Hey, here's a good life lesson," I told my kids, sounding, I remember thinking, a lot like my dad. "Try to live life with your belly exposed, and your spines—spines are those prickly, hollow hairs on hedgehogs' backs—retracted."

"But won't people poke a sharp stick in your belly, Daddy?"

"Yes—sometimes. But you take it out and hand it back to those people who do, while looking them directly in the eye and calmly asking, 'Did you *intend* to stick that thing in my stomach?'" I might have also added, but didn't in fear of sounding too much like a game theorist (which I am not!), *Now that you've gauged their intent, adjust your next move, and surround yourself with people who don't mistake your kindness for weakness.*

In the end, we decided not to get a hedgehog. But it was hard to forget one of their biggest distinguishing features: hedgehogs have two distinct sides, one soft, the other forceful. Sort of like kindness.

There is one last—and crucial—element of kindness that became evident to me around this same time. Fundamentally, kindness involves helping other living beings embrace their *agency*. Think back to how your favorite childhood teacher or coach made you feel. Chances are they saw your potential in ways you couldn't. They pushed you to see it, too. In return, you did your best for them. You couldn't bear the idea of disappointing them, but more important—as they likely told you—was you not disappointing *yourself*. And when you fell short, they forgave you. There was grace.

To me, kindness was Chary stopping by the local hospital in Brick Church to visit her elderly customers if she hadn't seen them in a while. Kindness was Randy putting his life in Boston on hold to come support me in Secaucus. Kindness was Gina conducting one of her many unofficial therapy sessions with her co-workers. Were their actions also net positive for themselves in the long run? Yes—as well they should be. Kindness is never self-undermining or weakening. By helping others embrace their agency, more often than not, you find your own.

So where does math fit into all of this? Well, first, let's be clear about one thing. Math is a science. It's the study of structure, order, and relations. It's *not* money. It's *not* accounting. It's *not* the exclusive province of business. It's *not* made by humans. From my perspective, the principles and properties of math are discovered, not invented. To me, math resides in nature. In the phases of the moon, in the tides, in gravity, in hedgehogs, and yes, in kindness. It makes sense that those same Enlightenment philosophers who helped readers discover their agency, which was made possible by concepts like liberty and free markets, spent a lot of time reflecting on kindness as they gave birth to the study of representative democracy and economics. Human beings desire agency; kindness involves the exchange of agency; and math quantifies the portion of that exchange that can be quantified.

Maybe that's why I blurted out the words *kindness and math* during that first town hall meeting. Amid the chaos, when everyone in the company, including me, was about to be stripped of all surface credentials and civility, only the truth remained. Despite being stuck inside what was a dehumanizing corporate video game, the only—the best—solution was to reestablish some sort of natural order. The words *kindness* and *math* came from a deep place. An intuitive place. A human place.

Leading a business with kindness and math, then, is fundamentally about creating a more natural space for the exchange of goods and services among human beings, *for* human beings. An equilibrium with fewer artificial boxes and constraints, and more and better flow, balance, and thus agility. Because of this, I believe that *leading with kindness and math can generate greater value over the long term.* More value to stakeholders and more value to society. Along the way, you might also notice more joy, not just in yourself but in the energy of those around you. It might cause you to pause and remind yourself not to confuse business conventions for the more transcendent truths of life. *Accounting* is a helpful reporting tool to facilitate comparison between companies, but it is *not* a true, accurate measure of *accountability*, a statement about our obligations to others. A conventionally defined *balance sheet* can never hope to capture the value of the assets present among living, breathing human beings. *Compensation* does not mean just *salary*. Has it ever? Expenditures that promote wellness and learning are *investments* that produce positive returns, even if the accounting rules compel you to book them as *expenses*.

I get it. We are all under enormous pressure to deliver financial results, especially with regard to income statement metrics. So let me give you some examples of how we integrated kindness and math into the operations, the very fabric, of Ashley Stewart. First, just as we did with the lemonade stand, I broke everything down into smaller, simpler pieces that everyone could relate to and understand. We were guided by the flow of more natural life behaviors (Home-You, not Work-You), as opposed to the boxy organizational charts that tend to mirror how accountants and financial statements organize expenditures. We then integrated those simple truths into a dynamic system whose goal was to reinforce, sometimes in unconscious ways, the type of long-term, value-creating behavior we desired. By weaving kindness into our operations, we were able to "monetize" those assets that can't be captured in typical corporate T-accounts, which made it necessary for us to create alternative measurement tools. Finally, we tracked the results and dutifully incorporated them into our financial systems, in accordance with the standard rules of business accounting. As we go through some of the examples below, it's important to remember that they are not linear, but are instead intended to reinforce one another.

Direct and Transparent

During the first town hall, do you remember what I told my colleagues? *If you lie, cheat, or steal from this company, you will be prosecuted to the fullest extent of the law.* Remember—kindness is not niceness. It is direct, forceful, vigilant, and does not suffer lightly those who create negative externalities or encumber the agency of others. Pointing to my Korean American male face and absurdly pleated khakis, I then added that I was probably the least qualified person on earth to lead Ashley Stewart. I concluded by telling everyone I needed help finding unproductive assets on our balance sheet that I could turn into cash to help fund payroll. Seriously—how much more direct or transparent can someone be?

In that same vein, I immediately set about getting rid of anything in the company that felt untruthful, indirect, obscure, mealymouthed, or sneaky. One of the first things we got rid of when we moved offices was the closed-circuit television and surveillance equipment installed in the old warehouse, whose primary purpose seemingly had been to spy on our stores. There is a fine but relatively obvious line between keeping an eye out for theft and snooping on people because you don't trust them. Jettisoned, too, were the expensive contracts enabling those systems. We implemented new security measures, but only in those stores whose managers requested them to ensure their *own* safety. *I trust you*, I told all our managers on my first conference call on the Starfish phone. I meant it. People rose to the occasion and embraced the accountability that only comes with true agency. Those who didn't, or couldn't, were shown the door. Just like that, we freed up millions of dollars that could then be invested more wisely and profitably, all while producing levels of shrink (a fancy industry term for theft) that were well below industry averages.

No one could hide, literally or metaphorically. Starting with me. Not only was my desk on naked public display, but it also had no drawers. Everyone always had access to me. Something you want to talk about? Do you have a complaint, or a great idea? Let's talk. I had zero intention of hiding out behind a moat of legal protections, handlers, questionnaires, or some inflated sense of self-regard. I wanted to be on the same plane as our customers and the women who served them day after day. The majority of the roughly fifty corporate workers who were not extended invitations to join us on our journey was comprised of managers who had mistaken seniority for superiority.

Another area of transparency was *data*. I couldn't expect colleagues armed with incomplete information to be 100 percent accountable for their decisions. That's why along with my own availability, my colleagues had access to all the data they needed about the overall operations of our company's lemonade stand, from the number of cups, to our lease and marketing expenses, to our aggregate payroll figures, and even to our electricity costs.

But there *was* a catch. People were expected to follow up by showing through their actions and behaviors that this data made their own performances *better*. If they didn't, then what was the point of investing the time and energy in making the data available?

You probably won't be surprised to learn, then, that performance feedback at Ashley was shared *daily*. Not every year, not twice a year, but every day. Good or bad and face-to-face. We always did our best to distinguish between a bad business decision and a bad *human* decision. Soft eyes balanced tough words when feedback was delivered around a bad business decision. Remember, though outcomes are not guaranteed, the thought processes behind making an assessment are more controllable. To be sure, this high volume of feedback didn't sit well with some people. Our environment of accountability and continuous learning made some uneasy. Those who couldn't work that way left—and that was *kind*. They exercised agency in opting out. I wished them well, knowing the collective would be better off, and they would be, too.

Why didn't I do what so many other CEOs do and "administer" only annual performance reviews? Because an overly ritualized performance review is a corporate construct. It's not real. Nor is it always direct, or useful. It lets problems fester and grow, discourages collaboration, and is usually a way for companies to build a file for people they want to get rid of. No thanks. I was intent on nourishing a culture that attracted and retained people who wanted to make an impact and to grow. We needed to be better every day for one another, and for Ashley, not because an annual report card told us to, but because we *wanted* to be. Some experts might call this a *performance culture*, one based on intrinsic motivation. That may not be the first thing that comes into your mind when you think of scaling kindness, but that's what made our counterintuitive approach so powerful.

There's plenty of brain science research about oxytocin, dopamine, and serotonin and their positive impact on employee and customer experience and loyalty. The interaction of creativity, empathy, and generosity involves many different parts of the brain. If the brain has only a limited amount of calories at its disposal, doesn't it stand to reason that fear, which triggers fight-or-flight reflexes, might steal calories away from higher value-add brain functions? At work *and* in life? Kindness, which promotes a direct and open cul-

ture that rewards process, and acknowledges the uncertainty of outcomes, is the antidote to fear and all the waste that comes with it.
Doesn't this make intuitive sense?

Humanity, Inc.

I never forgot the generosity and welcome I received in our stores
from women like Chary and Shelley when *I* was at my most vulnerable. I also still wince when I remember having to hire an armed security guard to assuage the concerns of colleagues who feared for their
physical safety because of a few irate vendors. Naturally, I thought
back to the boat incident with my dad, and other teenage scuffles of
my own, but none had ever left me fearing for my literal survival.

Many people are probably familiar with Abraham Maslow's
hierarchy of needs. Created in 1943, it's one of many different
frameworks for understanding human motivations, but it has
become a staple in management textbooks in part because its complexity has been neatly summarized into a catchy, striated pyramid.
At the bottom of Maslow's pyramid are human physiological
needs—food, water, and sleep. Safety and security come next, and
one level above that are our human needs for love, companionship, and friendship. At the top, like a star on a Christmas tree,
one layer above self-esteem, is *self-actualization*, or achieving our
full human potential. The popularized interpretation of this hierarchy is that people can't begin to address their higher-level needs
until they feel assured of the lower ones. Meaning, like a journey
on some game show, the climb up the pyramid is linear, with each
tier lighting up and emitting a chime when you have met the qual-
ifications to pursue your next phase of personal development.

I've always found this pyramid dated, classist, and patronizing. It also communicates a dangerous message cloaked in the legitimacy of behavioral science. Should individuals who need food, water, sleep, safety, and security be denied friendship or love? For someone working an entry-level job at a distribution center, should they be content that their basic needs are being met even if the conditions in which they work strip them of basic dignity? At Ashley Stewart, relative to my private equity life, I had a significant number of colleagues who lived lives with less certainty at the "bottom of the pyramid." But that didn't mean that their desire for agency was any less important to them *or* to me.

So, instead of abandoning the whole framework, we *bent* it and made it nonlinear. Just like we did with the T-account. Could everyone at Ashley come as close as they could to realizing their full potential, even if, like most people, they were also struggling to pay their bills, to keep their children safe, and to save what little money they could for retirement? A good and obvious first step was helping people identify the various systems affecting their personal lives and explaining how they worked. Even if those systems had no direct relevance to the job at hand, people work to live, not the other way around.

Our ongoing town halls became part of our solution. When Gina proposed that my town hall become a regular event, I was all over it. These town halls soon became part of our everyday workplace cadence, a combination freewheeling classroom and improvised TV show. We spoke about the many components of life, money, and joy. Many of my colleagues responded enthusiastically. *It feels like we're coming to work and getting paid to come to school!*

Sure, I know—work is work. We all put up with deadlines and go through periods of stress and misery. But work does not have to be awful, fraught, and an eternal source of apprehension and worry. Can we agree that ideally work should and could be more like a fizzy, idea-filled classroom where everyone can teach, learn, explore, be curious, and, not least, have fun? Learning should not stop after we get handed a diploma. At Ashley, the investment we made in general education was for our colleagues as people, which meant they were free to capitalize on it and secure employment at a better company in a better industry as they saw fit. You should not need to rely on an academic study to feel confident that this sort of environment would directly contribute to higher retention and thus lower friction costs associated with recruiting and hiring.

There is one more thing. It turns out that Maslow never intended for his theories to be presented in pyramidical form. Not surprisingly, his writings described a more holistic, multidirectional journey. Would it surprise you that recent efforts to clarify this misperception have shed light on the fact that the author of the famous pyramid was a business consultant? Does this strike you as oddly similar to the origin story of Monopoly?

Lighting the Way

Another example of the virtuous feedback loop that occurs when honesty and transparency intersect with humanity revolved around light bulbs. Yes, light bulbs. Trivial and boring as this may sound, it wasn't.

The light bulbs in our Brick Church, New Jersey, store—with their dark, dirty, intermittently flickering yellow color—drove me nuts. The ambience they created couldn't have been more at odds with the steady and glowing warmth created by Chary and Shelley. Along with making the clothes and store look tired and uninviting, those fragile fluorescent bulbs were also a major cause of workplace injury in our stores. But they were cheaper than higher-tech light bulbs, and for that reason, the company kept buying them. Previous management saw lighting as an income statement *expense.* I saw it as a balance sheet *investment.*

Think about all the mishaps that can happen in a dimly lit store. Customers tripping over taped-down rugs. Managers lugging heavy stepladders from the back room when the bulbs regularly burned out. Managers then *climbing* those rickety stepladders. Women wearing fashionable high heels on ladders. Get the picture? Investing in new, efficient LED light bulbs in all our stores cost us more up front, but it snuffed out a major safety issue, and they paid for themselves in eighteen months.

But here's where things start to get interesting. In the children's book *If You Give a Mouse a Cookie* by Laura Numeroff, a little boy gives a mouse a cookie and spends the next few hours suffering through the consequences. The mouse gets thirsty and asks for a glass of milk, and on and on it goes, a sequence of cause-and-effect disasters involving spills, nail scissors, and brooms. The moral of the story is that the boy should have anticipated the mouse's desire for milk. But, in our case, those new bulbs created a series of unintended *positive* effects.

First, the stronger, better light bulbs led to an increase in sales. (You can imagine how much better the clothes looked under good lighting.) More sales meant more cash. More cash meant more bonuses. More bonuses meant happier colleagues. Higher net profits meant we could accelerate the upgrading of our tech, which meant we finally added Wi-Fi to our stores, which led to our supply-ing every store manager with her own iPad. *So what?* You might ask. *A lot of people have iPads.*

Well, one of the best features of the iPad is its high-end camera. Our managers now had at their disposal a tool that not only liber-ated them from standing behind their ancient cash registers, but let them photograph and record special moments in the stores. Ac-cordingly, the next thing we did was test, and then ship out, a *step and repeat* to as many of our locations as possible.

A step and repeat is a retractable backdrop, or banner, the kind celebrities pose in front of for pictures before and after awards ceremonies. We had our managers position them beside the dress-ing rooms. The new step and repeats invited customers to snap a selfie, which our store managers also invariably captured with their iPads. A customer would model the new blouse she was con-sidering buying in a photo that she would share with her social media followers. Free advertising, in other words. Why spend money on marketing when your customers are willing to celebrate what's best about your company for free? The marketing dollars we then *didn't* have to spend allowed us to invest in other things that addressed my colleagues' needs outside work, such as a better healthcare plan. If you give a mouse a cookie *indeed.*

On the corporate T-account, you would have noticed the ap-pearance of step and repeats and LED light bulbs in the *long-term asset* category. Without understanding the intention behind those investments, the many ways in which their returns manifested themselves would not have been apparent to the casual observer. In this case, kindness and math converged to unleash profits where few thought to look.

Innovation for People's Sakes

Our relentless focus on protecting colleagues from the worst aspects of capitalism led to our first major investment in software after our emergence from bankruptcy. Fittingly, that software was a human resource information system. For the first time in company history, everyone was given visibility and a modicum of control over their schedules and lives. They could log in and log out and receive notices from the company. Paper schedules were now a thing of the past. The software enabled communication at scale to everyone, creating greater cohesion, synchronicity, and connectedness. But the real reason we chose the software package was less obvious. We could now pay people using a password-protected debit card.

Some of my colleagues were unbanked, making direct deposit impossible. It's not safe for anyone to walk around with a live check in their pocket. Our new debit cards also allowed our colleagues to bypass check-cashing stores, which take a usurious percentage of people's hard-earned money. Early on I told everyone, "I can't pay you a ton of money. We're not the biggest, 'richest' company. But at a minimum, what we pay you, you should be able to keep." With the technology upgrade, I focused on making sure that my unbanked colleagues were aware of and took advantage of this payment option. It was something I personally tracked and enforced with zeal. One other thing? It meant that our payroll expense accurately reflected the amounts that were actually going into the pockets of the people who worked for it.

I thought back to my childhood and the ways so many better-informed individuals and systems have their hands in people's pockets. One of the ugliest subsets of capitalism involves sophisticated people taking money from the country's most vulnerable and uninformed populations via overly punitive bad check fees, late fees, overdraft fees, and jacked-up interest rates. (Or those casinos that advertise on college campuses.) I thought about the story my dad had told us about his arrival in the United States. He had only four hundred dollars in his wallet. He parted with some of it at the airport to buy a camera to send photos of his new life in America back home to my mom, who, pregnant with my older brother, was still in Korea. Arriving in Pittsburgh for his medical residency, my dad hailed a taxi to go to his boarding house. The cab driver overcharged him by forty dollars. My dad always brought this story up during holidays, and he must have thought of it whenever he stayed late at work, unwilling to turn away patients who needed him. A cab driver taking advantage of a vulnerable young man, new to his country, who didn't speak any English? *Come on.* I think that we can all agree that taking money from those without full agency is borderline theft.

I tried to bring this general view about not pressing your advantage to how we treated our *customers*. During store visits, I would quietly ask managers not to push extra purchases if they knew customers were near their credit limits. *I know it's their money*, I would say, *but* . . .

A fine line, I'm aware. But that's balance for you. Down the road, for the same reasons, I also declined to implement Buy Now, Pay Later, which in my opinion makes it too easy to spend money unthinkingly. It just didn't feel right to me in the context of what we were trying to accomplish. That said, I was vigilant about protecting our company, particularly the store jobs, from customers looking to press *their* advantage. Bucking what was the trend in the broader industry, we said no to "free returns" or "unlimited free shipping," explaining to anyone who asked that the full cost of an e-commerce sale includes call center, fulfillment, shipping, return, and marketing costs. These "free" offers ended up costing *everyone*, and we weren't in the business of selling unprofitable cups of lemonade. What good are all these perks to you, I would ask the women shopping in our stores, if they end up driving this company out of business? After walking them through the math, I concluded by asking why they didn't just buy things here in the store, and support Chary and Shelley.

Much further down the road, one risk that no one could avoid was COVID-19. In the early days and weeks of the pandemic, my biggest priority continued to be the health and safety of my colleagues, especially when it became clear that COVID was having a disproportionate impact on the most vulnerable members of society: lower-income, plus-size, Black and Hispanic, frontline service workers, in all combinations. When the lockdowns happened, bigger companies with many more financial resources than ours immediately fired or furloughed a majority of part-time and full-time workers in their stores. But, with the approval of the board, I had squirreled away enough cash on our balance sheet to weather an unexpected shock to the system. (Ashley had come a long way, to put it mildly, to be in a position to have this cushion. The importance of rainy day funds is grounded in the truism that no one gives you money when you need it the most.) By allowing us to keep people employed and paid for much longer, this rainy day fund helped the company maintain critical continuity and connectedness until the stores reopened. I also told my executive team, all of whom voluntarily reduced their salaries, to give customer lists to our stores, so managers could check in with their regulars and spread actual information, not disinformation, about COVID. If this sounds shocking, think about the rules of the lemonade stand. Fair is fair.

In other words, commonsense decisions about humanity trumped any brittle or stagnant rules, including the notion that companies, and their officers, are supposed to prioritize the bottom line above everything else at all times. It won't surprise you to learn we had very few rules for the sake of rules. We streamlined the *War and Peace*–size operating manuals in our home office and stores into something that more resembled a weekly magazine. If a rule made no sense, or felt overly prescriptive, it was gone. Only those operating procedures that truly merited scaling were standardized. Investments in training and general education, grounded in a culture that emphasized trust, safety, and agency, created a more malleable form of agility and slack that software code simply cannot replicate. Investments in technology had to enhance our delivery of product *and* Product. We didn't fall into the trap of associating innovation with coolness, and instead insisted that innovation simply be kind (which the best sort of innovation often is).

One final observation on agility and slack: Given our demographic base, we had more deaths than we should have had during my time as CEO. Burying a family member is expensive, as I would later find out firsthand. If we heard about a death causing undue financial burden for one of our colleagues, we would make sure a modest check from Ashley would quietly show up to help pay for the funeral. If anyone told me this technically violated our rules, I would cock my head slightly, and say, *Really?*

The Collective We

Risk is one of life's constants. Absolute certainty is unobtainable, but we *can* all do our best to make better decisions about how we invest our time, money, and social capital by understanding the relationship between risk and return. Stock prices are theoretically random, and whether we like it or not, life is too. Sudden, unforeseeable things happen to people all the time. We could all respond by hiding out in our basements or attics, but most of us don't. Intuitively, we know the best way to reduce and dilute risk is by building strong teams—close friends, work colleagues, team members, you name it.

Biologists observe cooperative behavior everywhere in nature, including among ants, bees, bats, and trees. People cooperate, too. Yes, I know—humans are self-centered. Our inborn drive to survive and pass along our genes is relentless. But, if you pause for a second, you might realize that even the most basic organizational unit, the family, is a cooperative whose success depends on the dynamic interplay among the needs of the individual and the needs of the collective. It doesn't get a lot of mainstream airtime, but it's pretty well established in science that our ability to cooperate has been one of our species' most important mechanisms of survival. It turns out the phrase "survival of the fittest" has inadvertently cajoled us all to embrace yet another oversimplification and forget that there is always texture, like the essence of the oxymoron that is kindness.

This collective sharing of risk, which is sometimes referred to as *mutualism*, can be defined as you and me (or you and anyone else) depending on each other so we *both* benefit. In business, mutualism can be extremely tricky to get right, let alone balance. It's probably why companies send around annoying surveys about workplace happiness—do you want the free popcorn and meditation rooms in exchange for our monitoring your computer keyboard and mouse behaviors at home? Most "human capital" issues are typically handled by human resources departments, which, by the way, are under considerable pressure (much to the dismay of many HR professionals) to serve as corporate liability shields more than employee advocates.

From my perspective, the industry that most captures the intimate dynamics of mutualism is insurance. Yes, random things happen to us all, but the law of averages makes such incidents less costly and catastrophic to the affected lives when multiple lives are pooled. Take car insurance. Aggregating many, many lives means we all share in the risk, pay a lower premium, and protect ourselves against unexpected losses. I obsessed about insurance at Ashley Stewart, because it was where I could prove to myself mathematically that kindness was having an impact on *actual* behavior.

Remember the light bulbs, the stepladders, and the high heels? Many companies respond the same way to workplace injuries. An employee gets hurt. They go through an endless statutory process that takes place *outside* the company and then workers' compensation insurance pays their claim. Many companies treat their workers' compensation insurance premium and its annual increases as an inevitable cost of doing business. Problem solved.

But as CEO, I found the idea of someone getting hurt at work unacceptable. Revolting even. Imagine you're running a lemonade stand when one of your colleagues slips on an ice cube that you dropped or a spill you failed to clean up. Whose fault is it? Right— it's yours. Sure, accidents happen, but if we aren't doing everything in our power to prevent them, we shouldn't be allowed to pretend they're inevitable. Inspired by my dad's lecture the night he found me by the front door timing the pizza delivery driver, we used the same statutes and claims processes as everyone else, but viewed accidents through a root-cause lens. In effect, we nudged everyone to *behave* differently, and as the new set of behavior became the norm, we *then* memorialized it with a formal change in policy.

I made myself personally accountable for monitoring workers' compensation claims and levels. I reviewed every incident. My colleagues knew I needed to be the first or second person notified if someone got hurt. Injuries, I knew, generally result from bad processes. True accidents certainly happen, but bad processes are known and addressable liabilities. The rules of accounting do not require you to place these intangible future unknown liabilities on your company's balance sheet. But wouldn't workers' compensation incidents and claim levels serve as a meaningful proxy? In our case, we insisted that everyone, especially our store managers, prioritize our colleagues' safety. Workers' safety was a must-have, period—an asset, not a liability or an expense. People enthusiastically agreed and delivered.

And wouldn't you know it, but Ashley ended up shattering every actuarial table (these are the reams of historical data based on the collective behavior of tens of millions of people over many decades that are used to predict future outcomes), ultimately receiving one of our workers' compensation insurer's highest levels of recognition. Our claims and incidents went from far too high to *that* shockingly low. I remember a bunch of statisticians sitting at our round board table, their faces amazed. *How did you do this?* they asked.

How did we do this? Kindness and math, was my reply. (What I should have said was that we cared deeply about people—and great operations *integrate* kindness and math. And that they were looking at the past, whereas we were living in the future.) And yes, I know, winning an actuarial award isn't the same as winning an Oscar or a Grammy, but being recognized for our collective effort over an extended period made me incredibly proud. It was our social compact in action. It also created an additional financial benefit.

We were now lower risk, which meant we paid a lower annual premium. Using the savings from that premium, we were able to afford merit-based raises for deserving store managers even as the retail industry progressively became more challenging. After all, those managers were the ones who *drove* those savings. *They* were the rightful owners of this money.

Creating Real Value

In life, loud, flashy, mile-a-minute people tend to get all the attention. Sadly, it seems that work culture rewards this kind of behavior, too. But true value creators (and true value creation) are devilishly hard to find. It's why forward-thinking companies like Vanguard offer individuals the opportunity to invest their savings in broad index funds with minimal fees. Yes, it is *that* hard to beat the broader market. The financial community even has a fancy name—*alpha*— for investments that create truly value-add returns. Meaning, for a certain level of risk, an alpha investment has a higher return than its peer group. The older I get, the more I run away from people who claim they are smarter than the market.

Rare as they are, though, alpha opportunities *do* exist. I started FirePine in the belief that one cost-effective way to generate alpha is to turn perceived liabilities into assets. The only way to beat the law of averages is to fish in a different pond, so to speak, and in an informed and different way, too.

In our case, I was convinced Ashley's true value lay in our relationships, like the ones between Chary, Shelley, and their customers. Clothes are clothes. Fashion is fickle. That meant it was my job to design a system that recognized the people who made a true, quiet difference in our company, and to give them recognition and confidence, in the most graceful way possible. And then get out of their way, in much the same way as my friend's dad had done in my kindergarten class four decades earlier.

Whether I was in the office, or at home in Boston, I would regularly (and randomly) place calls to our store managers. *Hey, it's James, how's everything going?* On their end, in the beginning it could be flummoxing. Why was I calling? Were they in trouble? They would scramble to get me up-to-the-minute sales figures. But they soon grew used to my calling. They realized I *never* called asking for sales figures. I already knew those! By then, the managers were aware of my views on root-cause value creation. The ten-year-old inside each of us knows that sales are the result (but not the root cause) of a lot of foundational preparation. *Did you get the inventory you need?* I would ask. *Are you making sure you are hiring the right people and educating them about our principles?* And most important of all, *Are you good? Things okay?* In so many words, I was asking about the combined picture of their store's balance sheets and their own individual balance sheets.

Are you good? Things okay? Simple questions. But the treasure chests they opened always inspired me to do better. Our communications themselves changed. Take Chary. It didn't take long for her to start emailing *me*, not with sales figures, but to say hi or to tell me about a meaningful customer encounter or experience. One day, Chary even emailed me with a request. Was there any possibility that I could accompany her to the local city hall, where she had an appointment with officials to discuss a potential public-private partnership? "Of course," I said. On the day of the meeting, when the officials appeared, Chary was shocked when I introduced her and whispered, "You're on." For someone who hates public speaking, Chary did incredibly well. Afterward, she, Shelley, and I debriefed over lunch at a local restaurant, where I met Shelley's children for the first time.

It was Shelley, in fact, who inspired me to inaugurate a new award, which I called the CEO Citizenship Award. Everyone at Ashley was eligible to nominate a candidate, using three criteria: *Do they act like an owner? Are they a good friend? Are they a good mentor?* A manager may have shattered sales records that quarter, but if she didn't uphold balance sheet–oriented behavior around morale (team turnover), or safety (stepladders and high heels!), or agility (camis stored in the back room), she wasn't eligible to win. A manager with soft sales but whose actions created long-term intangible assets on the proverbial balance sheet would win instead. The cash bonus offered was the highest single dollar award offered to store workers, but equally if not more important was the prestige. The first winner of the CEO Citizenship Award was Shelley. The only person surprised about that was Shelley herself—which only confirmed she was the right choice.

It was Chary who insisted Shelley show up at our corporate offices the day we handed out the inaugural award. Chary and Shelley both took seats and began chatting and laughing. A few minutes later, I began describing to the room and those on the conference line (I was calling in from my home office in Boston) some of the traits of the winner. "It's *you!*" Shelley kept whispering to Chary. "I told you, baby, it's *you!*" It was clear that nothing would make Shelley happier than seeing her boss and close friend win. Then I called out Shelley's name. She burst into tears, covered her face with trembling hands, and was quickly smothered in hugs, the biggest, most affirming one coming from Chary.

I won't ever forget that night, how Shelley was rooting for her good friend and boss, Chary, convinced that no one else, least of all herself, deserved the CEO Citizenship Award. And how, when I said Shelley's name, no one was more excited for her than Chary. *All of us have done something right*, I thought. Our systems were encouraging and rewarding true value creators. The entire company, including our customers on social media, witnessed this exchange, and agreed. I was being true to my pledge regarding the *work* leg of the three-legged stool.

The Joys of Being an Upside-Down Hedgehog

In my experience, people tend to be scared at work. What could be worse than not being set up to succeed, or worse, being set up to fail? A bigger question is, Why would any boss, or company, intentionally set out to create a culture of fear?

Apart from a few sociopaths, most leaders don't do so on purpose. At the same time, few bosses slow down long enough to ask, *What is my intent here?* Instead, consciously or unconsciously, they mimic what they've been led to believe are the distinguishing features of effective leadership (picture the big-hatted cowboy astride the galloping horse or the designer-fleece-vest-wearing tech "genius" overseeing a mass termination over Zoom).

Look, I get it. Urgency and stress can create high performance in the short term—adrenaline can be a useful thing—but is a state of emergency sustainable over time? Can people do their best work, and keep their eyes on the future, when fear overcomes their bodies and triggers their fight-or-flight reflex? Brain science is very clear that the answer is no. I'm no shrinking violet myself. I expect high performance from my colleagues. I want to *win*, but in a way that balances the short term with the long term. This demands punctuated bursts of energy, along with a day-to-day meter that drives steady execution and yet also creates the time and space needed for wandering imagination. Fear and imagination aren't a good combo, as anyone who jerks awake at 2 a.m. from a nightmare can tell you.

For these reasons, my intent was to create a safe environment that unleashed creativity and innovation through a combination of slack and agility. Everyone was encouraged to be an upside-down hedgehog. Bristles down, soft bellies up. Every karaoke party, or nutty dance, or picnic game was another opportunity for all of us to play and have fun. So were the full circle moments when I took colleagues out to the Red Lobster in Secaucus—a popular graduation dinner spot for many of the women I served—where we would feast on the free cheddar biscuits. Tamara, I remember, would always insist on her biscuits being *piping hot*, as the rest of us doubled over in laughter. Gina's traditional potluck event around Thanksgiving became a near-legendary affair. It reached a point where business partners from Manhattan would clamor for an invitation and show up with homemade goodies.

But here's the important thing to remember. Just as safety must be embedded in the behavior of your home, it also needs to be embedded in the math. We came up with metrics that better measured "safety" within our company's numbers. We've already discussed how insurance is one place where the mutualism of kindness and math come together. But there is another complementary way they work.

A well-known term in finance is *portfolio diversification*, otherwise known as *spreading the risk*. Different stocks and bonds have different risk profiles based on maturity (when they pay out), volatility (how much their price changes), yields (how much cash they distribute to you on an annual basis), and their correlation to the larger financial market (the extent to which their value moves in tandem with the broader indices). Are camis, shark-bites, Marilyns, and peplums all that different from stocks and bonds? I didn't think so (maybe because I didn't know any better). So I wrote down a list of "equations" that created a diverse "portfolio" of clothes. Camis, for instance, are less volatile, safer investments whose yields are less correlated to the market. The required yield—or *gross margin*—on camis should be appreciably less than that of the fashion-forward miniskirt, which should deliver a high yield in a shorter amount of time, considering the fashion risk. In my mind, camis were the equivalent of low-risk bonds, whereas the fashion-forward miniskirts were the equivalent of a high-risk venture capital investment. More important, our portfolio, like kindness itself, did not demand perfection in each fashion selection. It *did*, however, insist on knowing how these various selections fit within the collective portfolio. Ultimately, this reduced the merchandising group's fear levels about making individual mistakes, which enhanced their excitement and creativity.

Then one day, it happened. I guess it was *bound* to happen. A fashion buyer bought a blue prom dress that the *entire world* rejected. She couldn't sell even one. No one wanted it. I could tell she was scared and self-conscious. Everyone looked on as I studied the blue prom dress. It didn't look all that ugly to me, but what did I, Mr. Pleated Khakis, know? "Is it really that awful?" I asked at last. Everyone laughed, the buyer the hardest. A one-off failure was just part of the equation. The blue prom dress was a venture investment with a high probability of being a complete wipeout. The math anticipated something like this happening. The math allowed for imperfection. The math allowed for humanity. More important was *learning* from that failure for the sake of future decision-making.

It was a turning point. Remember that I designed our system deliberately to ensure that no *one* person could ever make or break Ashley again. And sure, everyone wants excellence. Perfection is, of course, impossible. Chasing it just puts everyone on edge. And along with surveillance equipment, oversize employee manuals, and stacks of hidden camis, fear was no longer a part of our world.

Kindness, it's worth repeating, is an action, or a series of actions, that transcends any human-made set of rules, boxes, or systems. It lives at the same unfathomable level as the laws of math and the natural sciences. I believe strongly that organizations that mimic and embody these laws stand a significantly better chance of creating sustainable success.

At our holiday party that year, we celebrated. Seriously—who wouldn't? We had smashed every record possible around sales and profitability. We'd also done it with a clean and agile balance sheet, which meant that future performance would be unconstrained by bad inventory, or the past. *The best is yet to come*, I thought. I could see it in my colleagues' faces, noting their confidence as they ascended the karaoke stage and took to the dance floor. (Incidentally, not a single drop of alcohol was ever served at any of Gina's office holiday parties. Outside visitors used to remark on this and would nod knowingly when I told them we didn't need a stimulant to elicit joy, or drown out fear.) My investors were thrilled. Word had also trickled out to a few of the financiers who had summarily passed on us during my world tour of begging for money.

So it's working, huh, James? You got your team to do all that? How?

My answer? *Kindness and math.* I was no longer shy about speaking publicly about kindness. *Why*, I went on, *is it so hard to believe that investments in social capital—which cost nothing from a financial perspective—are not only worthwhile, but also lead to outsize financial returns?* The only cost—and maybe *cost* is the wrong word, the better word is *investment*—is time and humanity. These days, leaders eager to jump on the kindness bandwagon often fail to comprehend that the math, the accounting, and the operations have to align as well. There is no such thing as Kindness Day, in my mind at least. Kindness is a mindset. It is a state of operations that governs on a daily basis. It requires you to rethink T-accounts and embrace an expansive and longitudinal outlook on cause and effect.

Investors measure their performance on the basis of a metric known as IRR, or internal rate of return. The IRR tells investors how much money they made on an annualized basis, given the cash they put in and the cash that came out during a defined period of time. It is expressed as a percentage. For instance, if a lemonade stand turns a cash investment of twenty dollars into forty dollars over a five-year period, the IRR is roughly 15 percent.

Now, wouldn't it behoove these investors to replace some of that "cash in" with *social* capital? This is what start-up founders do all the time by bartering for things like website design and legal advice.

That's what we did when we earned our vendors' trust and they extended our payment terms, which allowed us to hold on to our cash longer. If you could relaunch your lemonade stand with fifteen dollars instead of twenty, and still return forty dollars to investors over a five-year period, the math would dictate that the IRR would be *much* higher (in fact, it is around 22 percent). Most of the operational examples in this chapter required very little financial investment while driving stronger returns. Going one step further, if kindness creates a system of operations that *also* increases the amount of cash coming out (resulting in lower insurance premiums, higher retention rates of colleagues and customers, fewer legal disputes, higher sales, more productive marketing spend), can you see how IRR would in fact be *much* higher? And, perhaps more important, how there also would be much less risk (more agility, slack, and redundancy) in achieving those returns? All of this does not even address the fact that creating social capital has a general, constructive impact beyond the company that a financial return can't capture, namely, *positive externalities*—and those positive externalities for employees, customers, and communities in turn create their *own* returns in a never-ending pattern of spirals.

And that's another magical feature to kindness that bears an uncanny resemblance to money: it operates as an open feedback loop. Allow me to explain.

Most systems, like most things in nature, seek equilibrium and homeostasis. Those are just fancy words for *balance*. To get there, there is a dynamic interaction between open feedback loops and closed feedback loops. Open feedback loops amplify change, whereas closed feedback loops bring the system back closer toward equilibrium. The goal of the human brain, for example, is self-regulation, and maintaining a steady state of survival by predicting the body's caloric and energy needs before they even happen, repeatedly. Childbirth, on the other hand, triggers a whole series of biological changes involving oxytocin and muscle contractions. The creation of new life, the ultimate example of *change*, is very painful (just ask Meg). Change requires open feedback loops. Knowing this might shed even more light on the meaning of the phrase "change can be painful." The brain, in order to protect us, works in an opposite way, sending us back to what we know. To make change, we need to break this cycle. One way of doing this is to embody our childhood selves, who were given permission to *not know* and were actively encouraged to experiment and evolve.

With compound interest, money can grow forever, at least if the interest rates stay positive. (Do you know what else can grow forever? Your credit card debt. It's the same math, just working in someone else's favor). The math of compounding means that wealth begets wealth. In this way, money is a rare asset that defies the equilibrium, or homeostasis, that we see in nature. Maybe that's why Albert Einstein referred to compound interest as the eighth wonder of the world. Can't the same be said of kindness? Like money—at least in my opinion—the impact of one or more acts of kindness can also compound forever. So why not try to live your life, and operate a business, in a way that aligns with *and* facilitates open feedback loops of kindness and money? The math would suggest you should.

These strategies revealed themselves during the first fifteen months after Ashley's rebirth. Mostly I thought about how different things were compared with the year before.

Things were working. Flowing. Green shoots were popping up in our financial metrics. Though I could see the exuberance at the many parties that Gina organized, some of the structural and profitable behavioral changes I've discussed in this chapter (like workers' compensation and the CEO Citizenship Award) would take a few more years to *really* come into full bloom. Kindness and math, you see, is a longitudinal strategy. Though there is some immediate gratification, it can take time for positive behavioral changes to compound and show up in financial statements. Lower insurance premiums, for example, are a future reward for past and present patterns of behavior. Remember that business accounting is generally a backward-looking framework. Try to live in the present with an eye to the future, in business *and* in life.

That said, as we all know, time bends to no one's will. Time is in control. And I had no idea that in short order, time would introduce tragedy into my life in such a way that my business and personal lives would unexpectedly converge—and that the hidden intangible assets on both Ashley's and my personal balance sheets would become painfully yet gratifyingly tangible in ways I never could have predicted or expected.

Bridge

chapter 7

goodwill

Dragonflies have been around for three hundred million years.

It had been nearly two years since the first town hall meeting. Twenty-three months of working almost nonstop. Fifteen months since Ashley Stewart's unlikely, unprecedented emergence from almost certain legal death. We had averted liquidation. Our company culture had changed in ways visible and invisible. And the financial results were staggering.

Ashley wasn't just working—we were *crushing it.* Against larger, traditional competitors with many more resources at their disposal. But we were also crushing it relative to our *own* expectations. That was even more important. In our first full calendar year of operations, we were on track to make more in pretax net profit than we paid the estate for all of the assets of the business. This is an unheard-of result. Trust me when I say those are results *any* investor would drool over, especially considering that the former incarnation of this brand hemorrhaged cash on an annual basis. And to this point, no one even knew what we had done, or how we had done it, beyond our immediate ecosystem of colleagues, vendors, landlords, and customers.

But word started trickling out. It's hard to bottle up the natural energy born of enthusiasm, communion, and success that comes from collective hard work. Talk of the *what* and *how* began spreading in the business community.

Still, we steered clear of the press. I didn't want us to get ahead of ourselves. To be sure, anyone glancing around our office and neighborhood stores could see how far we had come. Our stores all had new, snazzy overhead lights. Our store managers were now equipped with iPads. We began the process of replacing overly worn rugs, too, while also replacing the drab mud-brown brand logo with effervescent pink. Aside from these modest investments, we spent very little money on cosmetic changes. This wasn't some fancy corporate redesign that adds a layer of luster to an ugly underbelly; we were making *real* change. Good things come from within—*always.* The home office, where Gina continued to host celebrations and get-togethers, now radiated the spirit I had felt on my first visit to Brick Church. The potlucks and karaoke parties now had to make room for a spurt of baby showers. And, I admit, I broke down and approved the purchase of a miniature version of the industrial-size lunch warmer.

So why did my own three-legged stool feel so wobbly? The truth is, I was exhausted. Physically and mentally. Despite meting out some of my responsibilities to others, and compensating them accordingly, I was still doing way too much. For two years, I had worked insanely long hours without having any family members around. I adored my colleagues, but that did not replace my family. I'd surrendered to the worn grooves of my weekly round-trip routine from Boston to Newark, the day-to-day stresses of running a business, and the nightly trudge back to an unfamiliar bed, whose beaten-up mattress and stony pillow were intensifying the searing neck pain I woke up to every morning.

One Thursday night that summer, back in Boston after another action-packed week, I got a phone call that reminded me how life, as beautiful and exhilarating as it can be, is also cruel and unforgiving. My three-legged stool was already wobbly, but I couldn't foresee that all three legs were about to be kicked out from underneath me. I was at my kitchen table. The call was from my sister, Jennifer. She and my mom were driving my dad to hospice. As I headed toward my car, with a hastily packed bag, I saw my children crying. My face had told them all they needed to know.

Dad had been struggling of late, even more than usual. Parkinson's disease is merciless, and the trajectory is ever downward. Things had gotten so bad that he even spent a month or so in a skilled nursing facility. Quite simply, my mom had reached her breaking point and needed time off from the exhaustion of twenty-four-hour caregiving. Even though my dad couldn't communicate and was almost completely trapped inside his body, I knew that going into skilled nursing infuriated him—as his toppled-over IV stand testified. During our childhood, he used to tell us there was no way he would ever agree to go into such a facility. The unexpected pace of this last stage of his fight with Parkinson's made our options few, but I still harbor the sting of unresolved regrets that he had to spend even a single night there. When he returned home to the condo, his condition deteriorated so quickly my mom called hospice.

Hospice. It was a new word for me. Adult Koreans know it has traditionally been their responsibility to take care of their sick or elderly parents at home. My naiveté showed up in the stream of questions I asked the nurses. Have they considered *this* treatment, and couldn't *that* medication treat *those* symptoms? Their obliging expressions gave everything away, and I understood, finally. My dad was there to die.

Any son or daughter who has experienced hospice knows how beautiful and sad it is. Time slows and seems to congeal, but there is also a heightened sense of urgency to tie up loose ends. My dad's hospice room was a sacred space, a thin place, an everyday altar. The nurses were kind, attentive, and experienced. Still, it was my first time watching someone I loved die.

Don't ever let me fight against death, my dad used to say when we were kids. He was speaking as a medical physician. But even with a feeding tube in his stomach, and lacking all mobility, those words meant nothing. He probably surprised himself. Even when the body is broken and has no strength left, the will to live can be as relentless as the tides of an ocean.

I spent that first weekend in an adjustable recliner next to his bed. My dad was in terrible shape, his lips cracked and dry, his voice a whisper. But he knew I was by his side. I told him I loved him, and he told me he loved me. Like other fathers and sons, we hadn't said those words often enough while I was growing up. When he was dozing, my sister relayed a recent conversation about how my dad told her in private he wished he'd had more *fun* in his life. I always appreciated how Jennifer brought out my dad's warmth and love, the same love he showed his patients but had a harder time expressing with his sons. In fairness, his life hadn't been easy. He had done the best he could. I thought of his father's slap. Maybe, in the end, there was too much *han*. And I knew there were places in our relationship where I should have done better myself.

As I watched my dad sleep out of the corner of my eye, I started drafting an article about Ashley Stewart for *Harvard Business Review*. The editors had asked me for a business article to explain Ashley's meteoric success, but it became a eulogy for my dad, a way to tell him what I had been doing for the previous two years and how the company was a testament to what he had taught me. I read it to him. I didn't know whether he could hear it. It was even an apology of sorts.

A few days after I moved into my dad's hospice room, my cell phone rang. It was Meg. She sounded muted, scared, unlike herself. She was calling from the emergency department of Boston Children's Hospital. Aware of how bad things were with my dad, she had waited as long as she could before calling to tell me that Lila, our youngest daughter, who had just turned eight, had been in a serious accident at her summer camp. She was climbing some sort of apparatus during a camp-supervised activity when her strength gave out, and she fell and hit her head on her way down to the ground. She had been transferred by ambulance from our local hospital to Boston Children's emergency department, and Meg was waiting to find out her diagnosis.

The ER doctors and nurses were also having trouble comprehending the nature of the injury. What had happened exactly? How far had Lila fallen? Her injuries implied an impact whose severity could not possibly be consistent with a climbing exercise appropriate for an eight-year-old, and what the camp had reported on the phone was inconsistent with what Lila's siblings had seen. Meg couldn't get anyone at the camp to give her a straight answer. In hindsight, they were already circling the wagons and getting legal counsel involved, instead of answering vital queries for the physicians. The point is, I needed to come home as soon as possible.

I got in my car and drove the five-plus hours back to Boston, arriving at the hospital in the early morning. When I saw Lila's surgeon, I burst into tears. I couldn't hold it in any longer. I cried because my little girl's outlook was uncertain. I cried because my dad was dying. And I cried because Lila's surgeon, a first-generation Persian immigrant, reminded me of my dad—the same gentleness, and courtliness, and warmth.

Lila was entering the surgical suite. She was lucky, we were told. If she'd hit her head an inch to the right or the left, she would have died, or suffered permanent brain damage. Most of her teeth had been knocked loose, and her jaw was broken in two places. She couldn't speak. We didn't know if there was brain trauma from the severe concussion. A nurse told Meg and me that Lila was doubly lucky that the teeth she lost were her baby teeth. At the doctors' request, I pulled up a photo of my baby girl taken just two weeks earlier, smiling and toothy, so they could reset her jaw correctly.

The summer camp, a local, not-for-profit organization, wasn't providing any real—or credible—explanation for what had happened. When I went onto its website, I was surprised to see that the chairman of the camp's board of directors was a young managing director at a prominent private equity firm. He had applied for a job at my old firm, and I had interviewed him. I liked him. He carried himself with a natural humility. I had taken him out for a drink, as is customary for the industry, and I remember his calling me sheepishly to tell me he had forgotten his overnight bag in my car. We extended him an offer, but he declined. He called me afterward to apologize, noting the genuine connection that the two of us had.

While waiting for Lila to emerge from surgery, I thought of that night. The camp might be stonewalling us, but surely *he* would call me, right? Silence.

Meg and Lila stayed at the hospital. They would be there for about a week, with Lila beginning her recovery in utter silence, sipping on a liquid-only diet in the dark, to avoid aggravating her head injuries. The next morning, I drove with my two other children, Jared and Graylyn, and our dog, George, back to New Jersey. After dropping George off at my sister's, we spent that day helping the nurses moisten my dad's lips and tongue with mouth swabs. Jared and Graylyn read out loud to him the little notes they had written him. *You're strong, Harabeoji* (*harabeoji* means "grandfather" in Korean), and *You were always so good at playing Wii golf, Harabeoji!* They had never known him physically well enough to play real golf. We would end up tucking those notes inside his coffin.

My dad died at the end of the week. It was an ugly, unsettled death. My sister, my mom, and I were all by his bedside. My brother was on the phone, calling us when he was not performing surgery on his own patients in Milwaukee. My dad had so wanted to live more, and longer, but Parkinson's stole years and hopes and plans from him.

What needs to happen after someone dies? All my fancy degrees, and I didn't have a clue. Neither did my sister or my mom. We had no idea whom to call, or how to arrange for the removal of a body, or what funeral parlor to contact, or how to deal with any administrative requirements of the state. My mom, overwhelmed, broke down in tears. *My husband just died, and we're going down a to-do checklist?* At some point, Jennifer and I slipped out of the room to let her stand vigil. After years and years of nonstop care, our mom needed quiet time alone with her husband.

Along with dealing with practical logistics, we also had to decide what if any Korean rituals or traditions should play a part in my dad's funeral service. Fourteen years earlier, at our wedding rehearsal dinner, Meg and I dressed in the customary Korean wedding attire of resplendent silk *hanboks*. Meg looked so beautiful in her *hanbok*, and so did my mother-in-law in the *hanbok* my parents gifted her. My parents, along with my future in-laws, tossed dates at Meg, a Korean ritual grounded in the belief that the more dates a bride catches in the fabric of her *hanbok*, the more children she will be blessed with. (Out of a hundred or so dates, Meg caught around ninety, which was eventually distilled to three children.) Korean touches also played a role on our wedding day, a large Southern wedding that combined homemade grits with homemade *kimchi*. As the night went on, in what will always be a highlight of my life, Meg and I found ourselves sitting on chairs as our Jewish friends hoisted us through a spontaneous rendition of the hora.

My dad had been dead for less than an hour when my phone rang. It was Meg, calling from Lila's bedside. "Did your dad just die?"

"Yes," I said, unable to hide my surprise, "but how did you know that?"

"I just knew."

Meg is a lawyer, with a scientist's mind. She is brilliant, empirical, and analytical. "I just wanted to tell you that for the first time all week, Lila is calm," Meg said. "She's not in any pain, either. She even smiled." The doctors had assured her there would be no lasting cognitive damage. Meg paused. "I think it must have been your dad. I think he came here to be with Lila, that he wanted to check in on her."

I'm not a very superstitious person either. We were both silent, just *knowing* that my dad, finally freed from his body, had come up to tend to Lila. He was a pediatrician, after all, a lifelong caregiver. Even after death, he would be drawn to helping ease the suffering of a child, especially his youngest granddaughter.

Bear with me here, but there were other, hard-to-explain things going on, too. The room number of the hospice where my dad died was 202, the same apartment number in the Bronx building where my mom and dad had lived when I was first born. When my brother lived with our grandmother in Korea as a little boy, the tail number of his favorite playground toy airplane was 202. My mom's birthday was February 2—another 202—and my own birthday is February 20. Who knows, this could be pure coincidence. All I can tell you is that I derived great comfort from the fact that Lila's surgery room was number 2.

Lila kept improving and ultimately made a full recovery (emerging stronger and more confident than ever!)—that was the good news. The bad news, which infuriated Meg and me, was that the summer camp kept stonewalling us. Finally, toward the end of summer, a legal memo came in the mail, a formal step-by-step chronicling of all the facts related to our eight-year-old daughter's accident. In ways both subtle and accusatory, from our reading of it, the memo seemed to insinuate that Lila shared culpability, as did her older sister, Graylyn, for having inspired her sister by successfully completing the climb herself. The memo didn't bother to address why the camp hadn't followed head injury protocols, or immediately called an ambulance, or why they told Meg that Lila had suffered only a small cut.

For the first time, we learned that Lila and the other campers were "lead climbing" on a tall pole with metal staples for a ladder when the accident happened. What the memo didn't say, and what neither Meg nor I knew yet, is that lead climbing is a dangerous form of climbing reserved for experienced, well-trained climbers. It requires intricate coordination between a climber and a belayer (the person in charge of the safety rope), and any small failure can result in falls up to twenty feet. That explained the question surrounding the severity of trauma that our confused doctors had posed. What was an eight-year-old girl doing lead climbing in the first place at a local day camp, and on a course that was designed and inspected only for top-rope climbing? Good questions that we had to come up with ourselves, because the camp's memo addressed none of them.

Ultimately, we felt compelled to hire a team of consultants, who began each conversation saying, *There is no world in which any eight-year-old day camper should be lead climbing—everybody knows that.*

All this, and there was still no word from the private equity guy, the chairman of the camp's board. Meg and I were seething. Ultimately, Meg's father stepped in and placed a call to one of the most senior partners of that private equity firm, who has also served as a mentor to me over the years. It's not a widely publicized fact that for many titans of industry Meg's dad serves as unofficial consigliere. *Is that junior guy handling this correctly?* he asked rhetorically.

Within days, I received an email from the chastened board chairman. He and I met in the lobby of a local hotel. He was already sitting down when I walked in. I didn't say anything. I just stared at him. His eyes started welling up. In full view of the entire lobby. Those tears would later turn into uncontrolled sobs in front of the entire board of directors during a meeting that Meg and I effectively made happen.

I let him twist in the wind for a while without saying anything. Then I said: "*What happened to you?* What changed you? Was it the business world? Was it private equity? How could you *not* call me, like, the moment it happened? Lila is *eight* years old! Beyond comforting us, you couldn't bother to answer the doctors' questions? *What were you thinking?*"

He started crying. He was an empathic person, he said at last, someone who cared deeply about other people. He was an experienced climber himself, and he knew as soon as he found out about the lead climbing that the day camp was flat-out wrong. He should have pushed back more against the insurance company's and the CEO's handling of the situation. He grew up the son of a single mom—was I forgetting that? His values and ideals were exactly like mine. Did I remember that he, like me, even taught high school after college?

I just looked at him. I shook my head. "You better make this *right*," I said, and walked out.

He wasn't the only one. There was a second trustee on the camp's board of directors whom I vaguely knew, too. Another younger member of my Boston private equity community. When Meg and I met her, she couldn't even look us in the eye. "James, I have no pull here," she mumbled. "I'm just helping them with the numbers."

As it turns out, a third trustee was a trained attorney who happened to be the sister-in-law of our family dentist, who operates a private practice that has the same intimacy people felt in my dad's pediatric office. That dentist had diagnosed Lila's broken jaw over the phone when Meg called her from the first emergency room, telling her to get an immediate transfer to Boston Children's and its world-class oral surgeons. This third trustee, who obviously got an earful at home, also offered up a weak apology. *After reading it again, I can see why our legal response might have upset you.*

Meg and I breathed very deeply. There were many things we wanted to say and do, but in the end, we focused on doing our best to ensure that no other child or family would have to go through what Lila and we had gone through. Still, it was hard to shake my disbelief. I couldn't imagine a clearer illustration of how for-profit behavioral norms have come to dominate certain philanthropic organizations. Don't let form fool you—there are no lemonade stands there, either. It was a testament to the privileged world we live in that Meg and I could even dream of holding our daughter's summer camp accountable. We had every possible form of leverage, of financial *and* social capital, not to mention two degrees from Harvard Law School, to ensure that some sort of positive externality would come from this. If this had happened to me when I was growing up, or to any of the children of the women of Ashley Stewart, or to most people in this world, trust me when I say there would have been no justice whatsoever. In our case, we knew the camp was an important resource in the community, and we didn't want to sue it into oblivion. In the end, processes were changed regarding safety protocols across the entire camp, without our having to file a lawsuit.

My dad's wake was held the following Wednesday, in New Jersey. Lila wasn't cleared to travel yet, so she and Meg couldn't come, but Jared and Graylyn were with me. I took the whole week off, telling Gina in confidence about my dad and Lila, and instructing her not to tell anyone else. "Just say I'm taking a short vacation"—that sounded plausible, didn't it?—"and I'll be back before they know it."

I floated through my dad's wake in a dream state. Jennifer and I had compiled a mix of my dad's favorite songs, which serenaded the assembled guests. They included my dad's college friends, medical school classmates, golfing buddies, and fellow Korean immigrants who had come to the US around the same time my parents had. His former patients from Long Island sent a representative, who lived near the funeral home, to pay their respects. My childhood friend Joel was there, along with his mom, who had saved me from drowning, and his dad, who had taken my own dad under his wing and showed him the ropes of living in America. Also, there was Carol, the young nurse from my dad's office, who took such good care of us while my mom was in the hospital, now a mother to a teenage son. Knowing Meg and Lila couldn't be there, Meg's dad was generous enough to fly in from North Carolina to offer his shoulder and support. So did a few of my college roommates. Basically, my whole life was converging on this random funeral home in New Jersey.

What happened next is something I'll never forget. I was going around the room, thanking people for coming, when I looked up to see what appeared to be the entire Ashley Stewart corporate office. I guess Gina chose to disregard my explicit directive to stay quiet! They joined the other guests now leafing through the photo albums on the front table and reading the piles of handwritten cards and letters sent by patients after my dad retired.

Despite feeling unsteady, I gave a welcome speech. I was so flustered that I couldn't remember my niece's name even as I was staring directly at her. Afterward, flanked by my sister, brother, and mom, I took up my position in the receiving line. Person after person passed before us, expressing their condolences. I was barely holding it all together when I became aware of a burst and flourish of energy, a rustling commotion that signaled the arrival of new guests.

A small group of Black women dressed in fashionable attire had just come into the room and joined the tail end of the receiving line. In contrast to the confidence of their clothes, their expressions were apprehensive, uncertain, as if they weren't sure they had come to the right place or if they would be welcome.

The store managers. They showed up. They came directly from work. Led by *Chary*, who, after hugging my mom and exchanging a few words with her, now stood before me.

"Chary, what are you doing here?" I said.

"Well, James—where else would I be?" Chary explained that she and some other managers had carpooled the hour or so distance to the funeral parlor. They had come to honor my dad and to comfort *me.* Chary gripped my hand tightly.

"You didn't tell anyone about your dad? Or about your daughter? James—what's up with that? You don't think for one second that we wouldn't find out and be here for *you*?" Chary's words were enough to start me crying, and then she was crying, too. "I want you to know how proud your dad was of you, James—you know that, right?"

I couldn't stop crying. In front of everyone. *The whole world is here in this room*, I thought. *It wasn't just the five of us.* The present. The past. The ever-evolving future. All ages, races, ethnicities, and languages were there. It was like a human potluck. Two years earlier, I'd arrived in Secaucus to become the leader of a company I felt utterly unprepared to lead. I'd entered an unfamiliar world that at the same time felt familiar, and welcoming, and affirming. Now everything was reversed. My unlikely colleagues had now come inside *my* world.

Later, my mom told me about some of the conversations she had with Chary and other Ashley colleagues. "You did a good job, Mrs. Rhee," one said. Was it also true, my mom asked, that I talked about her at work all the time? That the character of the women reminded me of her?

Surrendering is a process. If I was keeping count—and you know that math matters to me—I had surrendered multiple times since that first town hall meeting two years before. Each surrender felt like the last, but none was. That day, I threw aside the last piece of armor.

I was forty-four years old. For the previous few years, I'd been asking myself, *What is real?* I pursued *real*, tracked it, thought about it day and night, aware only that it was vaguely linked to people and humanity. Vaguely linked to a childhood memory of a red helicopter. *Real*, I saw now, was in this room. *Real* was all around me.

The women of Ashley Stewart liked to say I was an iron man—relentless, a street fighter. But it wasn't that James they had shown up for. It was *me*.

The final surrender happened that day and in the weeks and months that followed. With my dad gone, I was finally able to shed all his ambitions for me, especially his long-standing desire that I, his son, lead an orderly, predictable, safe life. My dad's expectations made me sorrowful and resentful sometimes. *Dad, you took on even more risk. I can take on more because of you.* Without meaning to, I had been too cavalier in glossing over how important continuity and stability were to him, forgetting that he himself came from a long line of physicians, forgetting that he lived through a devastating war as a boy, forgetting that he effectively tore up the name-brand recognition of two prestigious degrees in Korea, leaving his homeland to start a new life in a strange country. I would forget that the things my dad wanted most for me were those things that he felt were missing from his own life. Security. Belonging.

The finance world, and private equity, was entirely alien to him.

And for the previous two years, I'd been selling clothes to plus-size Black women. Even when I explained to him a few times my true intentions and how much inspiration I took from mom's and his experience in America, he didn't understand. Or he chose not to. The language barrier made it hard to connect. We didn't have the shared framework to talk about some of these things. Why couldn't I agree to live inside a box? Wasn't the success and security of his children and grandchildren a big reason he had come to the US in the first place?

With his patients, my dad always did more than was absolutely necessary, even when they couldn't pay. *You never charge patients who can't afford care for their children*, he told us solemnly. His patients never forgot what he did for them, either. After he retired, and again after he died, the notes and letters our family received from his former patients all said the same thing. *We will never forget what your dad did for us.*

The most ironic part of all this? My dad *did* have security. And belonging. The wake bore testament to that. He also had a lot of courage. He ran his own small business and was his own boss. He created jobs and put three kids through college, all while saving and enriching so many lives. At his sixtieth birthday party, with his family and friends chiming in on the chorus, my dad sang "My Way," the Frank Sinatra song. In hospice, as he was dying, I played that song over and over, hoping he could hear it and understand he wasn't the only Rhee who insisted on doing life his own way.

As I sifted through his patients' letters, other memories danced in my mind, too. His baritone voice singing country songs. The strong smell of his aftershave. The big tips he left waitstaff at restaurants, and anyone unsung who provided a service. The image of him holding a baseball bat, his fingers clutching the wood a third of the way up. His love of *High Noon*, the 1952 film with Gary Cooper and Grace Kelly, in which the protagonists mete out justice as the townspeople whom they've sworn to protect cower in their homes. How he loved surprising us with Italian takeout from the restaurant next door to his small, shingled office after he saw the patients who needed him on Sundays.

Joining memories were colorful stories. How simple and rural Korea was when he was a boy. The air and ground, my dad told me, were alive with spiders, tigers, and dragonflies. The dragonflies, he even pursued. Whenever one landed, my dad would sneak up behind it while spinning his index finger slowly at first, then super fast. This, he said, hypnotized the insect, using their hyperacute eyesight against them. Taking advantage of the dragonfly's dizziness and pinching together its wings, he would take it home as a pet. I spent hours in our Long Island driveway and backyard, trying out this technique on one dragonfly after another, but it never worked. I could almost see my dad staring out the window, his eyes excited and affectionate, trying to keep from laughing.

Was the dragonfly story true? Do I even want to know? It's probably better off remaining a mystery, a joke even, between my dad and me. But Koreans from my dad's generation say the same thing. One or two told me that during the postwar years, when Koreans were poverty-stricken and life was impossibly difficult, they used to attach lengths of string to the hind legs of dragonflies and fly them in the air like little kites. There was also the story my dad told me about how clipping your fingernails and toenails at night attracts snakes. True? Half-true? Not true? I'm content with not knowing.

Along with the grace I allowed myself after my dad died, I allowed *him* as much, if not more. My understanding of who he was grew and deepened as time went on.

A few years after he died, I choreographed a last-minute trip to Disney World. Graylyn and Lila joined my mom and me, and together the four of us spent a few days at Epcot, sharing a roomy suite, eating huge breakfasts, and exchanging bites of Mexican street corn. But more than eating and having fun, it was something my mom said that stood out.

The four of us were making our way off the monorail at Epcot one morning when my mom stopped. Glancing at the huge parking lot, to my surprise she began to cry. "What's wrong?" I said, fearing she wasn't feeling well. But no, it was something else.

Did I remember the two trips we took as a family to Disney World when I was little? my mom asked. "Those trips were never easy," she went on. To save money on flights and motels, my dad drove twenty-four hours straight, hiding his fatigue from the rest of us. When we arrived and checked in at a motel an hour's drive from Epcot, usually he was so exhausted he could barely stand. The next day, he would drive us *back* to Epcot, and park in a huge, overcrowded lot, and we would make our way to the sites. We did not ride the monorail.

Tears were coming down her face. "And now, here we are. We're *right here*. *You* brought me here. We are staying at the actual resort, we can ride the monorail, and we're on the fanciest meal plan, and . . ."

It explained why she was crying. She was remembering how much my dad did for his family, and how he kept his fatigue, pain, and so much else, a private matter. This brought up another memory, another secret he kept in reserve.

Many Korean families, including ours, have their own dedicated burial site. My name, in fact, is etched on a stone in Korea, alongside generations of my ancestors. A year after our wedding, my parents took me and Meg, and Jennifer and her husband (a red-headed Irish American) on a trip to Seoul. In between seeing family members, and visiting local landmarks, the six of us paid a visit to the Rhee family burial site.

The Rhee family tomb is located an hour or so outside Seoul, in the Gwacheon district. It wasn't easy getting there. My dad, then in the early stages of Parkinson's, really struggled. We had to hike a low mountain, cross a series of streams, and bend and duck through brambles and under low-hanging branches. Finally, there it was. A dome of earth, resembling a four-foot-tall mound of rice covered in grass, inside of which were buried my grandparents.

We stood there for a while in silence before Meg and I broke off to walk around and read the names on the nearby stones. I soon rejoined my dad, who was standing where we had left him. I was shocked to see his body was racked with sobs. "I'm sorry," I heard him choke out. "I'm sorry. But I had to go."

He was apologizing to his parents. I think that he was speaking to his mother, in particular. He was saying he was sorry for leaving Korea. He was sorry he hadn't lived up to the expectations they had of him as the eldest son. The burden of his guilt—I had no idea. My dad must have carried it with him his whole life. Watching him sob in front of his parents' graves showed off the size and depth of his burden. Until then, I had little understanding of how difficult his decision to leave his family behind in Korea had been, and that, as the firstborn, he was supposed to take care of everyone. He spent the rest of his life quietly consumed with guilt.

I was grateful and glad that Meg was by my side that day to witness and understand this. Afterward, as we all rested atop a tree-protected hill, in wild grass thick with untrimmed weeds, I felt I understood my dad much better. That might have also been the day he let go of some of his own *han*.

That guilt, maybe, explained why during the biggest, boldest US holidays—Thanksgiving, Christmas, New Year's—his mood grew noticeably muted. He was probably thinking of his family in Korea, and how in their eyes he had never measured up, never fit inside a box. On his first and only visit to the United States, my grandfather criticized my dad's first house, my childhood home, because it was made of wood, not brick. *This is a poor man's house*, he told my dad coldly. It stands to reason that no amount of envelopes thick with cash, cartons of cigarettes, or bags of American candy airmailed home to Gwacheon could ever lessen the complexity of my dad's burden. But if he'd been able to see his own wake, my dad would have seen nothing but *jeong*. So much *jeong*.

A few days after the wake, my father-in-law and I drove down to North Carolina together. Meg, the children, and the dog drove alongside us in our beloved minivan. I thanked my father-in-law for coming and for always treating me like a son. We reminisced about the night when he first met my dad. They shook hands as two men who each had charted his own course. And here they were, two paths that could not have been more different, but whose guiding light of service and accountability was so very much the same.

Along the way, I also received word that the *Harvard Business Review* article that I had written by my dad's bedside was now online. "How I Brought Ashley Stewart Back from Bankruptcy" was the first major article about the company. I wrote every word of it, but the journal got to choose the title and graphic. I was unhappy with what they chose, and not just because the better word was *liquidation*, not bankruptcy. *I* should have been *We*. I was grateful, though, that the editors kept in my remarks about kindness.

What I'm about to say may sound impossibly strange, but I'll say it anyway. After the events surrounding my dad's death, I felt like a dragonfly myself. Transformed. No longer living under the surface of the water. I felt awake and alert, my senses buffed and almost metallically sharp. Never again would I let myself, or anyone, get jammed inside a box. Permission to live outside a box, to be free, and to feel secure in that freedom—that was my dad's final gift to me. Now it was my time to fly.

In Memoriam—
Notes from My Dad's Patients

I'm forty-two years old and three thousand miles away and I can still smell Dr. Rhee and feel his soft face while hugging me. As a little girl, I distinctly remember feeling like he was the gentlest, calmest man on the planet. He always made me feel at ease. He brought calm and grace into the room and I've never met his equal. I am truly sorry to learn he is gone. He was very loved.

* * *

No finer man was ever born and no finer doctor. I blessed the day I found him for my kids. He was remarkable. So sad to hear he is no longer with us. My kids are grown with children of their own. I don't think they will ever find a more concerned doctor, a warmer human being, and a hero to take care of my grand-children. I can only hope they come close. He was perfection.

* * *

To Mrs. Rhee and your children, thank you for sharing him with us. He made me feel that my children were as precious to him as they were to me. It is hard to write this while crying but I did not know he was ill so I am happy he is at peace. He joked when he was retiring (against many protests I am sure) that he would take turns living with each child to see who would put up with him. What a wonderful man, I feel blessed to have known him. My sincere condolences.

Act III

Joy

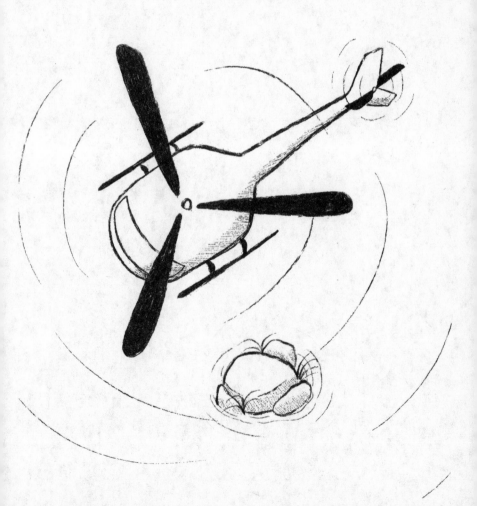

chapter 8

measurement

Helicopters are more costly to maintain than airplanes. Nor can they fly as high or as fast.

When I was growing up, there were times when my dad and I agreed on very little other than baseball. We could always bond over the New York Mets. My dad's face would beam as he recounted the story of the "hapless" 1969 Miracle Mets, who "shocked" the world by winning the World Series that year against incredible odds. My parents had moved to New York from Pittsburgh just the year before, so I can only imagine the positive impact that this underdog victory had on my dad's confidence.

A closer examination, however, would reveal that this team of "underdogs" had arguably one of the greatest sets of pitchers of all time, a group anchored by future Hall of Famers who were early in their careers. As "Miracle" also implies, the Mets relied on a bit of alchemy as well. It is well known in baseball lore that a black cat—a bringer of bad luck in many cultures—appeared out of nowhere and stared into their first-place opponent's dugout during a critical late-season game. The Mets ultimately went on to overtake the frontrunners, and the rest was history, so to speak.

As a little boy, I played baseball almost every day. I collected and traded baseball cards, while memorizing the statistics printed on their backsides. Like a lot of kids, I couldn't get enough of studying batting averages, home runs counts, and runs batted in. Today, if I close my eyes, I can still smell the dusty pink bubble gum enclosed inside the baseball card packets my mom bought me at the grocery store.

These days, my interest in baseball has waned. For a while, I was enthralled by how statisticians came up with new and better ways to predict a player's *future* performance. The importance of walks, or the ball's velocity as it leaves a hitter's bat—these were seriously cool additions to the more limited arsenal of measurements I grew up with. But over time baseball lost its fizz and fun for me. There was *too* much data. Too many statisticians. The art, warmth, and intrigue of baseball, of stolen bases and sacrifice bunts, took a backseat.

This new quantitative rigor also seems to focus almost exclusively on individual performance metrics rather than on team dynamics. Remember the plus-minus rating in ice hockey? The figure that measures an ice hockey player's holistic contribution to the team, versus their more obvious individual stats? There is still no baseball equivalent, at least that I'm aware of. It's too bad, because locker room cohesiveness and team chemistry are crucial to winning championships, especially in the long term. We all know this, so where are the measurements that could prove it?

As you can imagine, I also chafe at attempts to put baseball in a box. With the game declining in popularity, the powers-that-be have experimented with a number of "new" rules, their intention being to shorten the game for commercial reasons. *It's overlong*, was probably the thinking. *People don't have the attention span anymore.* Sadly, maybe they're right. But maybe the root cause of baseball's declining popularity is *also* its increasing tendency to collect statistics on seemingly every imaginable permutation on the field, and the resulting loss of alchemy.

Why is this important? Because baseball is one of the few sports historically unconstrained by traditional measurements of time, or points scored. A baseball game, in fact, has no time limit. The final score of baseball? The sky's the limit. In theory, a game of baseball can go on forever, clearing the way for more chance and randomness. I guess, in hindsight, like Jared playing Monopoly, I once watched and loved baseball because the system it created allowed space for magic to materialize. It was just so much *fun* and *real* in its unpredictability, which today's obsession with precise measurements seems hell-bent on squashing.

Sometime during the summer after my dad's wake, a red helicopter showed up on my desk. It was an unsolicited gift from a young woman who worked in our home office. She had heard me telling the story about my first red helicopter at one of the many team dinners I hosted at Red Lobster. It was this *second* red helicopter I held in my hand while delivering my TED Talk a year or so after my eventual departure from Ashley Stewart. Sitting there atop my desk, it got me thinking about a lot of things.

I always have been a stickler for measurement. It helps provide objectivity, establish benchmarks, and monitor progress. So, what was the right way to measure my dad's life? What was the right way to measure what I had just witnessed at the funeral home? Using math, I could give you an exact headcount of the guests at my dad's wake. The number of handshakes. The number of hugs. The duration of the words of condolence. I could also add up the number of notes and letters that my family received in the mail from three generations of patients (they *still* arrive today). Hey, I could use machine learning to gauge linguistic patterns and assess their sincerity. If pressed, I could even come up with a decent estimate of the amount of dollars spent on floral arrangements. (This last number would make a lot of modern-day economists especially excited.)

While I'm at it, what about the lemonade stand that was my dad's pediatric practice? Should its value be calculated solely on the basis of the number of patients (cups) my dad saw in a day? Its revenues, gross profit, and net profit (which you remember from chapter 5)? In keeping with what I see on the news these days, should his lemonade stand's success be measured by the number of prescriptions he wrote? Incentive compensation from these sales, funded by pharmaceutical companies, surely would have come in handy as his small business made less and less gross profit on a per-patient basis thanks to declining reimbursements, which when combined with the elevated cost of medical malpractice insurance, squeezed net profit further and further. As my dad and I watched the no-longer-Miracle Mets lose game after game, I still remember his baritone voice in our family room as he took calls from worried parents. *Mommy, your baby is going to be just fine; you don't need medicine.* He said this even though the malpractice insurance systems subtly *encourage* doctors to prescribe medication. It's harder to be sued if you prescribe something ineffective but safe than if you recommend a dose of tender loving care.

Would *financial metrics* be the best way to measure my dad's life and medical practice? Of course not! And you already *know* this. My dad's life, like yours, is best measured largely by intangible things. Things that are more difficult to quantify. In life, things whose value can be easily reduced to dollars are often the least important things to value. Fixation on quantification, on totals and sizes alone, can quickly turn into myopic obsession. Look, no doubt my dad had to keep watch over his gross and net profits, to ensure he could provide for his family. He needed to make *enough* money. But hasn't our society's focus on income, and money, tipped over into obsession? Do you really believe that minute-by-minute stock market price fluctuations matter in the long run? Short-term mania has taken our eyes off the real problems lurking on our collective balance sheet. There are too many people who do nothing *but* work, and yet *still* cannot climb out of the first rung of Maslow's hierarchy. My dad loved caring for children, but I'm fairly certain his pediatric practice would have been economically unviable in the United States of today.

Our lives, yours and mine, encompass the sum total of every interaction, good and bad, every moment of joy and suffering, that we experience over the years. Our actions, and the reactions they create, accumulate on *the balance sheet of our lives*. Income statements (the *what*) fade into history, but balance sheets (the *how*) remain forever. Remember, a person can be income rich and balance sheet poor. There's a big difference between someone's *net wealth*—referring to their financial wealth—and their net *worth*, which also encompasses all those intangible things that can't be measured through a single quantifiable figure—*love, loyalty, respect, caring, humor, generosity, character, family, friendship, legacy, reputation.* And whether you're an accounting whiz or not, you might know intuitively where these assets get recorded. On the T-account that is your life, they would be captured in the line item called *goodwill.* All that being said, however, your income *is* what pays the bills and puts food on the table. So, if a solid week's worth of work within the rules of our current system is not enough to give a person enough time and space to build *net wealth <u>and</u> net worth,* what are we collectively doing wrong?

The outpouring of love, affection, and sorrow present at my dad's wake was a measurement of the goodwill he helped create in his lifetime. The operational mechanism of goodwill is an open feedback loop, not a closed one. Money compounds through *interest.* Goodwill compounds through *time,* not to mention *feeling* and *memory.* But unlike money and interest rates, goodwill cannot be calculated precisely. It cannot be put inside a box. Like the Miracle Mets of old, there is an *alchemy* about it.

Why? Maybe it's because goodwill does not belong entirely to one person and, in fact, cannot exist without at least one additional person. The goodwill I saw and felt at the funeral home during my dad's wake was and is a collectively owned asset. It belongs to everybody. It's the ultimate positive externality. It comforted our family in our time of mourning, but it had *already* helped my dad's patients and their families, and I have to believe that remembering it was a positive for them again. Goodwill is the asset, like *jeong*, that records all of the positive externalities—all the "extras" on top of the literal one dollar lemonade stand payment, or my mom's ice-cold refreshments for the handymen, or my dad's hospital visits on his days off to sick babies and their worried parents—on the *balance sheet of our collective lives*. Goodwill is the asset created by the *investment* of kindness. And no, most modern-day economists do not measure it. But that does not make it unimportant.

Dr. Rhee, the world was a better place because you were in it. My dad died a man rich in what matters. A successful man. He died a net giver, an investor, in the collective balance sheet that is humanity. Not a net taker, or consumer. I just wish, as he noted to my sister, Jennifer, that he had been more able to see and enjoy the fruits of those investments. And I wish I could have done a better job helping him see them, too.

The ten-year-old lemonade stand owner inside you also knows this. It might even be the source of some of your concerns about "work-life balance." You wish that Home-You could show up in the office more, or, more poignantly, that Work-You would make fewer appearances in your living room and kitchen. But what are you to do when the rules of the game make this so difficult, when you realize that both the system and the norms generally absolve CEOs from having *any* fiduciary duty to you or any of the colleagues you exchange pleasantries with around the water cooler? Nope, according to the tenets of shareholder supremacy, for the most part CEOs are accountable *only* to the board of directors, which is accountable *only* to the shareholders, meaning accountable only for profit as it's calculated from that limited perspective.

What do you do for a living? How much money do you make?

Sadly, some consultants and investors today might honestly an-swer, *Oh, I advise and bankroll companies that reward doctors for selling excessive amounts of narcotics to patients when they are at their most vulnerable and have the least amount of agency. What about you?* I imagine I'm not alone in my worry about pri-vate equity investing in hospice care. It's difficult to reconcile these things when we read our children bedtime stories about what's important in life. Our cognitive dissonance deepens when we are reminded that many authoritative studies on well-being conclude that close relationships are the single most important predictor of a long, happy life. Not money, or intelligence, or DNA, but rela-tionships. So if work dominates most people's lives (and it does), thereby kicking out the other two legs of the three-legged stool (which it also does), does that mean most of our relationships will be work-related? Do we have time for anything else? Little wonder that reports show we are all lonelier than we've ever been. Men, especially.

But, just remember: We live in a world filled with human-made rules. They're not the laws of nature. You are a leader. You *own* your life. You were born with this agency. We've collectively made these rules. Some of these rules are more in your direct control, whereas others require you to vote for someone who will make choices that best represent your interests. My advice is to be very intentional about your understanding, and therefore your choice, of measure-ments. Ask yourself: Are those people you vote for, who are making those rules, truly looking out for your best interests? Or are they really looking out only for their own?

For instance, as I became more and more "educated" over the

years, I learned that the value of the red helicopter given to me when I was five years old should be measured by its contribution to the economy. Most economists today would measure the red helicopter solely by its dollar contribution to gross domestic product (GDP, that is, the total dollar value of goods produced and services provided in a country in a given year). So, what's that, five dollars in total? If you throw in the gasoline that my friend's dad burned through driving to our school, maybe it rises to six dollars total? News channels and higher learning have done a good job persuading us that GDP was intended to serve as the *sole* measurement of a country's overall productivity *and* well-being. But that was never its intention! Even Simon Kuzmets, the actual inventor of the GDP measurement itself, warned the US Congress about using it as a proxy for the welfare of a nation. GDP is a country's *income statement* measurement, not a *balance sheet* measurement. Solely measuring annual inflows and outflows does *not* reveal our long-term assets and liabilities! Any other interpretation is lazy and wrong. Instead, ask *how* did we grow GDP? (Huge amounts of government and consumer debt.) *How* are people doing? (Child and adolescent mental health issues are soaring, and teachers and primary care physicians are quitting in droves.) How well-equipped is the US to handle the future cost of progressive conditions like Alzheimer's disease? (Not.) We do not keep a balance sheet for our country that properly reflects the present and the future. We're not *measuring* properly, let alone being clear about what we're *not* measuring with our fellow citizens. When was the last time you drew out the balance sheet, the T-account, of your *own* life? Give it a try. It can be illuminating and surprising.

(Hidden Assets)	(Hidden Liabilities)
Relationships	Back pain
Hobbies	Ulcer
Family	Drinking Problem
Time to daydream	Insomnia
Freedom	Fear
Health	Anger
Sense of Humor	Jealousy
Agility	Feelings of Inadequacy
Wellness	⋮
⋮	

From the day I first set foot inside Ashley Stewart headquarters, I began the process of exercising more agency about which measurements we would use to gauge success. Remember how we built and relied on a simple cash model of inflows and outflows to track our early progress. Cash never lies, we said. Another example was our relentless focus on the balance sheet. *Our sales (income statement) are down <u>because</u> of our inventory of unsold camis (balance sheet).* But, most significant, using kindness and math as guiding lights, we changed the *vector*—the direction—of preexisting norms.

This means we exercised our agency to embed the best of humanity's norms into our work lives, while limiting the flow of work norms into our home lives. In many instances, we did this without any rule book or how-to manual. We had to use our best informed judgment, along with the inspiration we gleaned from the childhood lemonade stand. And then, as the examples in chapter 6 show, we loosened our grip on the reins and allowed the positive spirals of cause and effect to show us the way forward. To drive this point home further, perhaps think about what I mean when I say that I work hard to prevent my *home* from becoming a *house*. Consider the difference between owning a *house* and owning a *home*. They are different, no? Both would be technically classified as the same *asset* in business accounting terms, but a *home* brings with it other intangible assets—warmth, family, memories, meals, the passage of time itself. Think about all the difficult-to-quantify actions that are necessary to transform a *house* into a *home*. A *home* implies that you have created an incremental asset called *goodwill*. When a *home* transforms back into a *house*, an incremental liability called *bad will* has appeared, taking a huge bite out of your figurative equity account.

It may not sound that way, but I did not have the luxury of getting too philosophical about all this stuff that fall. I was thinking instead about my old friend Steve, who had been there at my time of need during the bankruptcy nearly two and a half years before. But that summer, I had just received word that Steve and his partners were parting ways. After a few awkward pleasantries, Steve's partners informed me they wanted to sell their majority ownership interest in Ashley Stewart. They wanted a clean break from Steve's investments, and we would have to go back on the market and entertain a new group of suitors.

I understood, and it made sense. Remember, I had witnessed my fair share of disagreement among private equity partners. I recognized the pattern. In retrospect, Steve's championing of me and his investment in Ashley Stewart were likely both symptoms and causes of a growing distance between his firm and him. When I hung up, I remember sighing, feeling a bit tired, and desiring even just a small respite from the circus that was my life.

But here's the important thing. I made a distinction between events and circumstances beyond my control and those firmly *within* my control. As I did with my friend Joel when we were kids, I chose my own adventure, so to speak. After all we at Ashley had been through, I wasn't about to allow an unexpected event to distract me from piloting this submarine away from the tentacles of a giant octopus and toward Atlantis. I was fully aware that Steve's partners were the majority shareholder of our newly thriving company. Because of this, they had the right to control the Ashley Stewart board of directors, which ultimately hires and fires CEOs and makes other critical decisions like raising financial capital through an IPO (initial public offering) or selling the company. That said, there was no mistaking who had de facto control. *Me.* Steve's firm was wise enough to recognize that it had *legal* control but I had what is called *negative control.* Through the combination of my ownership interest through FirePine Group, as well as the loyalty I enjoyed from leadership given (not taken), I knew that I didn't need legal control to influence the final outcome. We were both rational enough to know that our current strong operating performance kept all our economic interests firmly aligned.

Steve's former partners and I worked together smoothly and collaboratively. But Ashley's success meant there was little doubt about whose voice would be strongest regarding the final decision on the investment banking firm we hired, what the teaser and presentation materials (our dating site profile) would look like, and within a certain range of financial outcomes, who would be selected as the new majority owner. This time, the Misfit Toys were excited about the sales process. I didn't see any crumpled faces. They were seasoned veterans now. They were brimming with confidence because we had achieved everything—and more—we said we would the first time around. *This time*, the numbers spoke for themselves. Despite the overall pressure the retail industry was facing, I knew we would have no trouble getting *a lot* of first dates. But I wasn't about to let Ashley settle down with just anyone.

We started by selecting an investment banking firm with a female managing director who was still relatively early in her career. She got it right away. The process she ran was both standardized (so investors wouldn't be scared off) *and* customized (so that the right investors would show up). I knew we had chosen the right banker when she rolled her eyes after two New York City private equity women, leaning back in their chairs, cavalierly informed me that their firm specialized in collecting *assets* like Ashley. We just smiled at each other and then quietly eliminated them from the process, as they clearly wouldn't align with our perspective on value or worth.

The truth was, our numbers were so good that we could have scrawled them on a piece of scrap paper and gotten bites. Many of the firms that had laughed at us the first time around could not conceal their shock. Our digital growth rivaled that of digitally native start-ups. Even more impressive, we had done it while generating, not burning through, cash. Our cross-functionally trained team accomplished all the complex operational maneuvering we had promised in a seamless and orchestrated fashion, without any need for high-priced consultants. We had more *cash* sitting on our balance sheet than we had paid for all the assets of our business. This is an unheard-of result. It would be the equivalent of buying a house for $100,000, operating a lemonade stand out front that netted you $150,000 in after-tax savings, and still owning the house free and clear of debt. Do you think that house is *still* worth only $100,000?

But numbers were just one part. Any potential investor was going to be impressed by ours. No, this time around, we composed and presented the *storyline* we had wanted to tell from the start. We splashed the otherwise two-dimensional financial figures with candid photographs of all the different people, the *real* people, who played a role in our performance. In what might have been a first, the investment materials, which are generally dull and forgettable, led off with a quote from a store manager (you guessed it, it was Chary) expressing her amazement at what could happen when a group of people took off their armor and locked arms together.

As I said, I wasn't going to allow just any suitor to buy a majority ownership interest in Ashley Stewart. To ensure sustainability, it was important that the new majority owner be curious enough, and intellectually and emotionally agile enough, to understand and appreciate not just the *what*, but also the *why* and especially the *how* of what we had done. During the management presentations, we questioned prospective investors as much as they questioned us. We wanted to make sure they understood the root cause of our success, which was grounded at the intersection of fundamental behavioral change and intentional measurement. We wanted to be sure they aligned with our vision for the future, a world in which the principles of social and economic mutualism might help stem the tide of fracturing hyperindividualism.

What follows are a few of the principles we measured and acted upon, along with some of the illustrations we used to make it tangible to our prospective investors. The end result, as you will see, was a majestic home run.

Creating Leverage by Bending Space and Time

Our step and repeats didn't just serve the purpose of enticing our customers to become brand evangelists. They also served an operational purpose that allowed us to bend seemingly immutable metrics. If this sounds wacky, let me explain.

When my dad would take our family out fishing on Long Island Sound, there were days the fish just wouldn't bite, no matter how much chum we tossed in the water. Throwing chum can get tedious (and expensive), which is why it's a good idea sometimes to put down the fishing rod, sit back, and just enjoy the sun while eating *kimbap*.

Selling cups of lemonade is no different. They are unwise ten-year-olds who premise their future operations on buying a big table and assuming summer will never end. Not only does that table cost more up front and require more storage space during off-hours (not to mention insurance coverage), but its sheer size tempts the kids to buy and fill more lemonade cups than necessary during cooler autumn and spring days. It might also drive them to spend more on paper and markers to generate thirst that just might not exist.

Retail selling space is no different. There are times of the year when people just don't want to shop for new clothes. Most retail businesses, however, are required to pay the same rent for a fixed amount of square footage no matter what month it may be. As humans, we feel uncomfortable when we don't use something we've already paid for (remember the concept of *sunk cost*?). This leads to the very natural temptation for retailers to overbuy inventory just to fill up space. I was determined to avoid this trap.

During slower months, I worked with the operations teams to position the step and repeats to *cut off space*, effectively creating a visually appealing *wall*. At the same time, I asked our finance and technology teams to co-create a dynamic reporting system that altered the stated square footage of each of our stores on the basis of the season. During slow months, from the perspective of our inventory buyers and customers, stores magically "shrank," thereby creating a better balance between supply and demand. This *primed* us to buy fewer "cups," thus keeping the lemonade super-fresh, resulting in higher margins. Basically, we created the conditions necessary for our natural faculties to make the right decisions.

Very few numbers, contracts, and investments escaped this multidimensional lens. For instance, we were very careful about making long-term commitments that did not have the value of *optionality* embedded in their terms. We thought long and hard before entering into long-term commitments. Don't we all want to have time enough to assess as many different options as possible, instead of committing to a single path for the rest of our lives? We did not make decisions presuming the best (that is, buying the biggest table in anticipation of peak summertime demand or traffic). We did not give in to the temptation of overconfidence or blind optimism. This same mindset also meant we *never* overhired.

Similarly, in my personal life, I have not made long-term commitments or investments based on the assumption that my annual cash inflows will be steady or go up every year. Minimizing overly optimistic forecasts and expectations reduces risk and allows for greater agility during periods of peak and trough earnings. Reducing unnecessary consumption creates space on your balance sheet for assets that can be used to make higher returning investments. I've always wanted to be a producer and an investor, not a consumer. And I make it a point to treat others this way, too. Sadly, our economy relies on treating most people as consumers. Worsening this problem, unfortunately, is an educational system that fails to teach our children about the fundamental distinction between investment and consumption.

Risk Return Meets Fairness

Believe it or not, but those same step and repeats inspired yet another measurement we used in our commercial dealings. (Who would imagine they could come in handy this often?) During the holiday season, one of our major software partners invited us to attend a swanky Manhattan party. It was a big deal for some of my colleagues—their first time as prized guests at a corporate holiday party with all the eye-catching excesses such soirées typically entail.

When we arrived, the first thing I noticed was that Ashley Stewart was *not* included on the welcome wall step and repeat. A cluster of other brand logos were emblazoned on the shiny plastic, but our newly designed pink logo wasn't among them. I could tell from the disappointed faces of my colleagues that they saw this as proof we were unimportant. On my way home from the party, I thanked our hosts, adding how much I hoped we would be on the step and repeat next year.

Ultimately, I became quite close to the executives leading that global software company. While headlining some of their biggest tech conferences, I mentioned the disproportionate impact that our missing logo had on my colleagues. People are emotional! People have feelings! Don't let anyone tell you otherwise, even if most economists continue to build their models on the premise that people are rational, logical, and utility-driven. Down the road, this small conversation created the seeds of much bigger discussions around the pricing of the renewal of our subscription agreement with that company.

First, understand that it is industry practice for certain software companies to require their customers to pay annual subscription fees up front. Insurance companies do the same thing with your annual premium. Remember, we had succeeded in financing much of Ashley's growth through cash "lent" to us from our vendors, who trusted us enough to change our payment terms from cash-on-delivery to around sixty days. The same principle applied here. During a call, we asked this same global software company if they thought it reasonable for our much smaller company, operating with the burden of much riskier social constraints, to cede 365 days of "float" to *them*.

Again, with these contracts, *everyone* pays up front. No exceptions. And Ashley had been through bankruptcy not once but twice. But we were now extremely low-risk, and if the company execs had any doubts, we showed them our balance sheet. *Oh*, they said, *you're not risky*. At which point we doubled down on the fairness argument. There was silence. *We understand*, they said. *And no, that doesn't seem right*. Together, using some basic financial formulas rooted in the power of compound interest, we properly calculated the opportunity cost to Ashley Stewart for paying up front, and mutually agreed to reduce the up-front payment by the resulting dollar figure. In exchange for their getting our cash up front, we needed to be compensated for the money we would have made if we had invested that cash in profit-generating opportunities. In other words, they had to pay us for our opportunity costs.

During my years as CEO, I engaged in *many* matter-of-fact conversations along these same lines. Too many financial arrangements belong to the same distasteful family as payday loans, predatory credit card marketing efforts, and casino advertising on college campuses. In law school, I learned about contracts of adhesion, in which a party offering a critical product or service gets to dictate terms while the other party has no choice but to accept them. All too often, the deck is stacked against the same people over and over again. Winning is one thing. But repeatedly taking advantage of people who lack the information, optionality, or power to exercise true agency is plain cowardice. Mutual disclosure and mutual understanding of the underlying premise of an agreement is not only fair; it's entirely consistent with a well-functioning system of capitalism.

Balancing the Direction of the Flow of Money

By now, you know that many Ashley Stewart stores are in predominantly low- to moderate-income neighborhoods. As our e-commerce sales grew, we studied amalgamated purchase data coming from women residing in higher-income neighborhoods. And because we tracked to the last penny how much the true costs were to produce, sell, and ship our cups of lemonade, I could tell you fairly accurately how much true cash net profit was coming into our lemonade stands from *outside* our core neighborhoods and communities.

Why does this matter? I viewed this new pool of financial capital as an appropriate source of funding for investments in longer-term "assets" in our neighborhoods—new rugs, fixtures, and technology; higher wages; and more community-building activities. I tracked this pool separately. An economist might say that our core communities ran a capital surplus vis-à-vis the world, which, I might add, gave me a great deal of personal satisfaction, too.

During the run-up to bankruptcy, potential investors had expressed skepticism that our brand, which celebrated a certain segment of Black, plus-size women, could attract non-Black customers. I would just shake my head, suppressing the impulse to wax eloquent about the universality of the humanity of art, fashion, food, or music, or to provide a history lesson about the intellectual property contributions, largely undercompensated or uncompensated, of Black America to the world. For all these reasons, as our following among non-Black women ticked upward, the world somehow felt smaller to me. And that created joy for me, as well.

We continued to track store profitability like a hawk, making sure that online sales wouldn't undercut our physical stores. Our intention (the capital-*P* Product) had always been to preserve a safe place for a deserving group of women—so why would we want to design a system that endangered the very stores we had fought so hard to preserve? We also turned the table on commercial real estate landlords. *We think you should build out the stores for us, and bear the up-front investment risk*, we would say matter-of-factly. And yes, that took a fair bit of chutzpah. After all, Ashley Stewart was only three years removed from not being able to pay its monthly rents. Inside, I was chortling, but my financial brain told me we were entirely justified to insist on this arrangement. *We will bring traffic to your shopping center. You need to measure the positive externality that we create.* And, wouldn't you know it, the construction of two of the three new stores we opened was funded by the *landlords.*

Over the years, I have sometimes been asked about my views on the following acronyms: DEI (diversity, equity, and inclusion), CSR (corporate social responsibility), and ESG (environmental, social, and governance). Unless implemented wisely, I worry that these acronyms can take focus away from the root causes of the undeniable disparities in outcomes of things like net wealth and representation at the leadership and board levels. I worry that if these initiatives come up short, critics will give up trying to fix anything, without acknowledging that these programs mainly address symptoms, not root causes like inequitable access to a quality education. Businesses can make a dent in closing disparities, but there is also a clear need for thoughtful partnership with civic institutions. Home-Us needs to speak up. Home-Us needs to show up more. I raise an eyebrow, or both, when I see DEI functioning with a limited budget that is completely divorced from the money-making engine of the company, CSR reporting into marketing, and ESG being used merely as a convenient way for certain wealth management firms to attract client assets. At Ashley Stewart, we did not use these acronyms. Instead, as you saw with how we measured our e-commerce results, we strived to weave kindness and math into the very fabric of our business model. From our perspective, the ability to balance kindness and math was a sign of an agile mind.

Counting board members and new hires matters. But as trained systems thinkers will tell you, the rubber meets the road only after the initial euphoria dies down. It is a lot sexier to say you made new hires than it is to talk about retention and development, and to start a glitzy scholarship program that enrolls first-year students while ignoring them when they become financially strapped sophomores struggling to remain in school. Math is math. You can measure what's easy or popular to see, or you can measure what actually makes a difference. The key is your intention in selecting what you are measuring, isn't it?

We were highly imperfect at Ashley. I'm sure we failed on many standard metrics. I was never able to solve certain systemic issues plaguing the broader retail industry, including raising the minimum wage for our part-time sales associates. So I voluntarily cut my salary by 20 percent as time went on, and there were years most everyone earned a bonus while I did not take one. I also made sure that the total dollar value of wages paid to people was roughly equivalent to total dollar proceeds paid out to shareholders over my seven-year tenure. As an aside, we also asked our customers whether they would be willing to pay more for this blouse or that pair of pants if it were made in an environmentally sustainable way. The answer was always *no*. I understood. Why should this extra financial burden (which is the cost of offsetting systemic negative externalities) fall on *them*?

The Joy of Investing in People

In my experience, it's often difficult to measure a direct "return on investment" in people. There are plenty of high-priced consultants who analyze incremental "productivity" gains, but in truth, many of those "gains" take time, are intangible, and stem from people's ability to learn and then *invest* in those around them. Have you ever seen the video of singer/songwriter Adele's reaction when she was surprised mid-concert by the appearance of her eighth-grade English teacher? They had been together for only one year, but it took about two decades for that feedback loop to make itself tangible, with Adele telling her teacher that she had changed the trajectory of her life. I still feel the same way about Mrs. Griffith, my kindergarten teacher.

A seeming exception to this statement involves investments in salespeople. The return on sales training can appear to be more easily quantifiable. You sold more cups of lemonade because you attended a seminar? Great—you're the best! Never mind the mess you made for everyone else to clean up, or the fact that great operations and product design made it all possible in the first place. We've already talked about the CEO Citizenship Award, which intentionally excluded sales performance, the granddaddy of all "income statement" measurements. But our search for true value creators, true *alpha*, extended further than that.

To be a member of the senior executive team, you had to prove daily that you understood the entire flow of operations and the marginal *profitability* of the business at each stage of the product cycle. We mapped out decision flows and studied multivariable causes and effects. This exercise helped us identify and promote those colleagues, most of whom happened to be women, who were linked, directly *and* indirectly, to positive outcomes. I called these colleagues *dotted line people* . . . since so many steps in the operational flow passed through their hands. One woman stood out so much I nicknamed her WD-40, because she made everything run that much more smoothly. While I was at Ashley, she went from part-time employee to full-time equity owner, whom we trusted to work from home when she saw fit, given the length of her commute and her family commitments.

We measured other things, too. I've already talked about smashing the actuarial tables and winning a prestigious workers' compensation award. But how about the fact that I can tell you in no uncertain terms that sexual harassment incidents virtually disappeared? Yes, I know that sexual harassment cases are massively underreported, so I hesitate to brag about this. But I do think it's fair to say that it was incredibly clear to everyone that there was zero tolerance for it. The culture change eliminated the need for bulky legal teams and legal costs, which of course freed up millions of dollars to reinvest in lemonade cups, marketing, and salaries.

Incidentally, there was *no* finite measurement for the pride I felt seeing Chary earn a promotion to area manager, Gina manage her own formal budget for all things home office, Tamara flex her media prowess on CBS Radio, Randy act on his itch to leave and become a professional comedian, and Donna graduate from the school of Ashley Stewart to attend business school at MIT Sloan School of Management. We celebrated each of them and others for their accomplishments and contributions both at and beyond Ashley Stewart.

That leaves us with one final metric. I recently was asked to speak at JPMorgan Chase's Global Leadership Conference. At one point, I asked, "How many people in the audience like babies?" My question was met with puzzled laughter. What a strange thing to ask.

"Because if we're all being honest," I went on, "babies aren't always 100 percent easy to love. They're unpredictable. They're messy. They cry a lot. They don't do what we tell them to do. We can't put them in a box. But we love them anyway. And—as a small aside, as we stare down pockets of declining birth rates—babies are also rather central to the future of humanity, no?"

One statistic that had caught my attention when I arrived at Ashley was the surprisingly low number of pregnancies in our workforce. There was, I surmised, a correlation between women getting pregnant and their overall confidence about where the company was going, or not going, including the future of their jobs and healthcare coverage. This made sense. I wrote a note to myself.

As the years went by, these numbers reversed themselves. Pregnancies rose significantly. How did I know that? I *measured* them. As a statistic, it was significant, a reflection of confidence, an expression of hope. The rise in pregnancies told me that Ashley was on a positive, upward trajectory, and that this left-for-dead company was also attracting younger women just beginning their families and careers. All of this was good for business, good for the world.

"So why wouldn't we want to run businesses in a manner that encourages families to form?" I went on at the conference. "Why wouldn't you take a long, hard look at your policies on leave, and benefits, and emotional safety, to ensure they encourage families, especially women, to feel proud, and happy, and confident about being pregnant and having babies? Dads, too. All parents. Do we live to work, or work to live?"

Other than the potluck, my favorite home office celebrations were Gina's surprise baby showers. They brought everyone so much joy. Yes, we counted the number of those showers. But do you think we bothered to count, or *not* count, the number of times those new moms brought their new babies into the office to introduce them around? No—to me *that* belonged to the world of alchemy.

Unleashed from the Rules of Business Accounting

Standardized measurements are useful. As we've noted, accounting rules and financial statements enable comparison. That said, it is always useful to have a standard up until the point it stifles creativity or adaptation. Trouble arises when standards like accounting, which are meant to accurately reflect past performance, distort *forward-looking* operations in unintended ways.

No set of standardized measurements could have predicted what we accomplished at Ashley. (For that matter, I'm not sure any form of artificial intelligence will ever be able to predict what the convergence of this collective accomplished.) In truth, some of the numbers, tangible and intangible, were already there when the world slammed the door in our face. Investors were unwilling or unable to expand their definition of assets beyond the business accounting perspective of a proper T-account. For some reason, in the business context, these standardized measurements (sales growth, earnings growth) encourage an overly simplistic and linear dialogue around growth.

Wall Street demands predictability and rationality, so executives come up with all sorts of ways to spit out the numbers they are being asked to report to. But the truth is, because companies are made up of *people*, sometimes a company's income statement does not grow—even when its balance sheet is improving. On the other hand, sometimes a company's (or country's) income statement grows, but on the back of a deteriorating balance sheet. The same goes for the business of *you*. Your income may fluctuate from year to year, especially if you work freelance or are a start-up founder, but beyond your financial returns, you should try to generate annual improvement on your *balance sheet*. Even in those years when your *net wealth* declines, it's hard, but try to improve agility by focusing on doing things that enhance your *net worth*. Instead of growth being a straight line, up and to the right, perhaps we should aspire to a more sustainable growth pattern that looks more like an expanding circle.

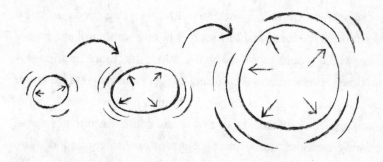

Let me give you two examples of unintended behavioral consequences that often get ignored but are squarely attributable to the linearity of business accounting. Imagine that one ten-year-old kid's cups of lemonade are, in fact, software, and Wall Street wants to see a really high gross profit on those software cups. The thing is, accounting rules dictate that some of that kid's software engineers' salaries have to be reflected in the cost of the cup. But, if you hire consultants instead, their fees *don't* have to be allocated to that cup. What would savvy you do? Well, you just might decide to replace your employees with independent contractors (thereby saving on healthcare costs, too). Will those independent contractors care as much about writing code that doesn't break, given they will be long gone by the time it gets heavy use? Maybe not, but it may still feel like the right answer to you if Wall Street values your equity on the basis of short-term gross margin profitability metrics.

Here's another example as it relates to Ashley. I made the decision to purchase more of our inventory from domestic US sources, which meant our cups were more expensive. Why would I do that? I thought it more important to design and procure product closer to delivery dates because of the accelerating fashion cycles. Meaning, I was willing to pay more per cup in return for getting back four to six weeks of the extra *time* associated with importing goods on ships. Presumably, the more fashion-correct blouse would sell at a higher price, which would offset its higher cost. And, more important— and this is another thing accounting *doesn't* measure—I felt that our operations and supply chain would be much more agile . . . all of which proved to be true. Does this sound counterintuitive? Maybe, but only because human-made conventions have nudged us to think so.

There was perhaps no clearer example of the importance of understanding and then choosing the correct measurement than the night I sat alone in the New York offices of Ashley's law firm. Just me, a half-eaten sandwich, and a stack of legal documents. My job was to sign my name fifty or so times. The result would be a wire transfer of cold hard cash that would net the company's shareholders proceeds well into the nine figures.

In my capacity as chairman and CEO, and the general partner of FirePine Group, I was the company's single largest individual shareholder. After signing my name those fifty or so times, the reward would be a life-changing amount of money for me and many of the original Misfit Toys. It's hard to explain, but I wasn't running up and down the hallways whooping it up. I didn't feel like grabbing a microphone and belting out a Springsteen anthem. That's not to say I wasn't enormously pleased, grateful, and excited. I definitely clenched my fists and pumped them a few times. But the feeling was muted. Less Bruce Springsteen, more Leonard Cohen.

Part of it might have been because I was comparing that moment to what I had seen and felt at my dad's wake. Part of it might have been because I did not need the external validation at that point to confirm the true value of what we had created. To really understand the complexity of the emotions I experienced, you need to understand the way the financial world defines goodwill.

Believe it or not—I opened my TED Talk by providing the accounting definition of goodwill. Way to jazz up an audience, huh? According to the generally accepted accounting principles (GAAP), goodwill is an intangible asset that shows up as a line entry on a balance sheet. It's duly recorded only when there is a transaction whereby some outside entity pays a purchase price for a business that's higher than the fair value of its identifiable tangible and intangible assets, net of liabilities. The difference between the purchase price and that documented net fair value is deemed *goodwill*.

Let me explain this again, in simpler language. Say that we negotiate with a buyer to pay one hundred dollars for our lemonade stand. We won't sell for less, and the buyer won't pay more. How do we record the purchase price such that the T-account is in balance? Our accountants place a value on every cup, sugar cube, chair, and the table, and subtract amounts owed to the grocery store, but the result is only eighty-three dollars of net fair value. The difference ($100 minus $83) is deemed *goodwill*. In that way, and only that way, can the balance sheet actually *balance*. Meaning, the phantom seventeen dollars has to be accounted for somehow, some way— otherwise the right-hand side of the T-account would add up to $100, while the left-hand side would only add up to $83. I might also add that the word *goodwill* is generally tossed out when it's getting late, and the accountants and investment bankers on both sides just want to agree on the balance sheet and call it a day. *Can we just attribute the differential to goodwill, and all go home?*

Wait—it gets better. Goodwill is dutifully recorded as a long-term intangible asset. According to the rules of accounting, once it's been recorded, goodwill can never be increased by the company on its own. It either stays the same or, if the prospects of the business's future stream of cash flow decreases, gets marked down accordingly. Only a change in ownership, a recognition of value by a new purchaser with money, can increase goodwill on a corporate balance sheet.

Is there any better way to show how different the rules of work are from the rules of life? In business accounting, goodwill can be created only by *money*, from an outside source. But in our personal lives, goodwill refers to communal assets created by the connectedness we share with other people. In fact, the interjection of money into the equation can actually *ruin* the asset created by humanity. As my dad's wake shows, goodwill in our personal lives *can* appreciate upward. In fact, in life, the longer you live, the more opportunities you have to grow that goodwill asset on your personal balance sheet. It's *your* choice to behave in a prosocial way. It's *your* choice to guard against the T-account of business taking over the T-account of your life.

Because of the way business accounting works, if you want to in-crease the amount of goodwill on a corporate balance sheet, you should buy a company and overpay for it. Wearing my investor hat for a moment, I've always gotten a kick out of screening for companies with bloated goodwill numbers on their balance sheets. Those figures are sometimes indicators of companies that are saddled with unreal-istic growth expectations. Maybe they are overpaying for acquisitions in order to show income statement growth, or maybe they are justi-fying inflated valuations because they have access to cheap debt fi-nancing. Or both. And, unfortunately, it is often the workers who get hurt the most because of this. *Can I have a raise? Can we invest in new technology to stay relevant?* Nope, we have to pay the interest on our debt. Sorry about that. Employees who do not own stock do not benefit from the potentially higher equity returns that come with the higher risk of a company carrying debt. They only get the risk.

Look, there is a good reason why GAAP and accountants will not allow a company to write up its goodwill account. Without going into the gory details, I'll merely say that because of the way accounting works, that would give companies too much incentive and leeway to report higher income statement earnings. What I *am* saying, how-ever, is that this does not preclude company leadership from tracking the *other* goodwill on their *internal* earnings reports. What makes a company actually worth more than its tangible assets? Its people, and the ingenuity they create *together.* Once real goodwill is on that inter-nal report, its fluctuation will hit net profit, and thus someone will have to track it on a day-in and day-out basis. And if someone tracks it, then it's more likely to be measured, and the company will have incentive to manage its activities and improve performance on those measurements. That's just the way human nature works.

These were some of the things I contemplated as I signed my way to financial freedom. I thought at length about these two definitions of goodwill, about my life as a high school teacher and as a private equity guy. I thought about my dad's modest pediatric practice that he built from scratch with his own hands. I thought about the good-will I had seen at the Brooklyn YWCA and the New Jersey funeral home. I thought about my friend in kindergarten, his dad, and the five-dollar red helicopter whose value I cannot even begin to measure. And it all made sense to me. It goes without saying that I was crystal clear about which definition of goodwill measured a good life, while also being grateful that I knew the intricacies of how to calculate, generate, and measure the *other* definition of goodwill. I also know what a privileged position I was in to be able to understand *both* definitions of goodwill. And now you are, too.

And, given that this is a chapter on measurement, I can't help but end it by saying that, for the record, if you had been an investor in FirePine Group, if you had taken a chance on Chary, Shelley, Gina, the Misfit Toys, and *Ashley*, and my relationship with them, and our operating model, your IRR (internal rate of return) on this invest-ment would have been a staggering 160 percent per annum for those three years. And we didn't use one dollar of financial leverage, or debt, to achieve those returns.

I did the best I could to explain all of this when I delivered my fifteen-minute TED Talk. It took me the better part of these pages to really do it justice. Below are some modified excerpts from the portion of the TED Talk that gets the most questions and attention. I've italicized certain words in order to convey or underscore their texture, from both an emotional and financial perspective. I hope it helps crystallize in your mind the dynamics of agency, distributed decision-making, agility, and open feedback loops, as well as the importance of a narrative that ties present with past and future. Visualizing the movement of liabilities from the right-hand side to the left-hand side, and the resulting upward adjustment in equity to the T-account, helps show how you might record the effects of turning liabilities into assets.

Kindness distributes the *joy* of problem-solving to everyone. It creates a *safe* environment that *unleashes innovation*, especially the unselfish kind. And it turns *perceived liabilities* into *assets*, which, as any financial accountant will tell you, *mathematically* has to result in the *creation of real equity value* in every meaning of the word . . .

And I know that none of this would have been possible without the lessons that I learned from my friend's father way back in kindergarten. He *invested* dollars, but *also* his *time* and his *heart*, into a little toy red helicopter. And in the *way* that he did it, it created a *real asset* called *goodwill*. And that goodwill *compounded quietly* for decades and then ultimately helped save a company, around a thousand jobs, and a safe place for a really deserving group of women. And in doing so, he taught an enduring lesson that helped this grown man *regain his balance*, a *true balance*, by remembering to *slow down* and to see the world through the eyes of a five-year-old child, who knows unequivocally that there is one and only one definition of goodwill that creates *real value* in life and, yeah, in business, too.

chapter 9

connectedness

*Helicopters are used
by medics. They lift
off vertically.*

F ive years into my tenure at Ashley Stewart, I had dinner with
Charisse Jones, a friend, author, and business reporter for a
national newspaper. Charisse was part of a team that won a
Pulitzer Prize for its coverage of the 1992 Los Angeles riots. Half-
way through our meal, Charisse hesitated. Her expression was difficult to read. I prodded. *"What?"* I asked. She looked me straight in
the eye and told me to brace myself, because she was about to give
me the highest compliment that she, as a Black woman, could give
another person. Did I know—or had anyone ever told me—that I
had "the heart of a Black woman"? And, did I understand the *meaning* of that?

I paused, fidgeted in my chair, and looked down to collect my
thoughts. A few years before, an article had appeared on the front
page of the print edition of the *Boston Globe* at the time of the an-

nouncement of Ashley Stewart's sale. Its headline had conveyed a similar sentiment. These were weighty words. After another pause, I exhaled, reestablished eye contact, and told Charisse what I *thought* those words meant. "Do you mean someone who cares deeply, and who often gives her heart without getting much in return? Someone who perseveres, who holds out hope, even when there seems little reason to have it? Someone who feels the burden of responsibility not just for her family but also for a broadly defined set of *Others*? Someone who just wants better for her children?" *Is that close?* my eyes asked. Across the table, she quietly nodded. I am quite sure that we were both thinking about our moms.

I am the son of two immigrants. I watched my mother's life in the United States be filled with immense hardship, and I grew up hearing stories about my grandmother raising four children as a single mother in the devastation that was postwar Korea. On a daily basis working alongside the women of Ashley Stewart, I had borne witness to the same resoluteness, entrepreneurship, and optimism that had propelled my mom and grandmother through their own challenges. They could have given up, but they chose not to. And they never let what they faced—the impersonal struggles or the personal indignities—embitter them.

I told Charisse that she was being overly generous. But she and I did agree on one thing: there is no higher compliment to be paid.

Over the years as CEO, I had countless conversations in the back rooms of stores in neighborhoods across America similar to the one I had with Charisse. In mahogany-paneled conference rooms in Manhattan. In faraway cities like Amsterdam, London, and São Paolo, to name just a few. And how similar, too, was the arc of those conversations to my first exchange with Chary and Shelley in the back room of their store. Do you remember how Shelley playfully fiddled with my phone as we bonded over Tom Brady, shredded overly prescriptive operating manuals, and realized both our mothers were nurses? We found common ground, and with the passage of time and the building of trust based on good intention, and *action* that backed up that good intention, I eventually met her children in a local restaurant and reminded them to treasure their mom.

Kindness, you'll remember, is a sequence of reciprocity, of reciprocated choices, of actions communicated in multisensory ways. Chary, Shelley, and I never rushed those initial conversations. Eye contact was steady, laughter was plentiful, and transparency was at a premium. We needed one another, but we never treated one another as a means to an end. Instead, we *invested* in our relationship, which ultimately empowered us to tackle much more difficult topics freely and honestly, all of which *reinforced* our mutual trust, another open and virtuous feedback loop.

In my visits to stores across the country, against the backdrop of a lot of increasingly charged rhetoric roiling society, we found refuge in the back rooms. There we shared meals and talked about anything and everything. *How is Lila? What, she dominated the ropes course at school, while beaming at Meg and you when she made it to the very top?* In this safe setting, I once admitted that I sometimes had a hard time recognizing colleagues because of the frequency with which their hairstyles changed. They would laugh, and then *teach me*, using a tone I imagine matched that of the older Jewish woman who had taught my parents about the religious significance of the menorah. I learned about the multitude of hair-straightening chemicals for Black hair, some of which can cause permanent hair loss, and about wigs, weaves, and extensions. I grew to appreciate the debate that exists among Black women who wear their hair naturally and those who don't. And I felt a pit in my stomach when they explained how external norms, biases, and even policies sometimes made their natural hair a source of pain, a reminder that they didn't fit the "mold." I'm sure they saw the gathering storm clouds in my eyes—similar to the look I had given the salesclerk at the hardware store decades earlier, or anyone who satiated their own smallness by making my *mom* feel small.

It's worth emphasizing that we could talk about these deeper conversations because of countless "smaller" conversations that established a foundation of trust and care. There was no ulterior motive, aside from our getting to know one another better. These exchanges always took place in settings that felt safe to each of us, in moments when we gave each other permission to be ourselves, in sometimes imperceptible ways. What I learned, I filed away quietly in my head, knowing it would make me a better friend to the company, to all the people of Ashley, down the road.

You might think it goes without saying that my colleagues were free to wear their hair at work however they wanted. But, in fact, it *does* need to be said, given how many private and public sector companies and institutions historically haven't officially or unofficially allowed it—and still don't.

I had to pause and ask myself how it would feel if my natural hair was arbitrarily deemed unacceptable. Now let me put on my private equity and finance hat for a second. If I had explicitly or implicitly compelled my colleagues to spend their hard-earned wages on hair products with sometimes-toxic side effects, then would I have been

any different from the payday lenders I fought so hard to make ob-
solete? Most of us know about the "pink tax," which refers to the fact
that many equivalent products and services (dry cleaning, moistur-
izers) that are marketed to women cost more than those marketed
to men. It *costs* more to be female. Now consider how the pink tax
might be higher if you're *female* and *Black*.

Trust gave rise to other learning opportunities. Turnabout was
fair play, and so *they* asked *me* their fair share of questions. One was,
How is it you have so much soul? The implication was that most
Asian people don't have this quality. I chuckled, knowing that for
some I was one of the few Asian men they had come to know this
intimately, and I explained that Asians *did* have soul, *lots* of it, but
sometimes found it hard to express it publicly. Or perhaps society,
whose narrative is controlled by very few groups, doesn't give Asians
permission (or, in the case of traditional media, *airtime*) to show off
that soul in public settings. Maybe the "success box" designed for
Asians does not afford *space* for any deviation from the image that
shapes an overly simplistic and misguided perspective.

There was lots of head-nodding. The media is incentivized by
profit to generalize and sensationalize. We consume carefully cu-
rated storylines about monolithic groups—storylines that focus
on people's skin color while glossing over their *character*. Left out
are the truth and complexity of most people's lives and relationships across all races, ethnicities, and backgrounds. The end result, sadly, is that *most of us don't really know one another.* Which
is a shame.

But that wasn't true at Ashley. Beginning with the very first
conference call on that antiquated Starfish phone, the field group
and I established a special connection. When it seemed like the

entire world turned its back on me, women like Chary and Shelley had my back. I knew it. They gave me permission to be *me*. Despite what I *didn't* have in common with them (race, gender, and, yes, my pleated khaki fashion sense), and my lack of retail operating experience, they accepted me. I was *enough*. The skillset and knowledge that I kept in my Batman utility belt, they joked, were no doubt a nice bonus. But as to why they trusted me so willingly? Well, the women used to say that they could "feel" my heart, or my soul, from day one. If they had known Korean, they might have said *jeong*.

Word got around. Some of the titans of industry, and my Wall Street contacts, would even needle me, asking why I was still there with Ashley. *James, now that you've shown everyone what you can do, don't you think that you are playing too small? What's next? Dude, take the money and run! It's time to buy another few companies and do some deals.* I would smile, and generally demur, and ponder the words Joseph Heller had said to his friend Kurt Vonnegut about knowing that he had enough. More than money, I was serenely at peace with my self-worth and self-identity, which were grounded in the honesty of my relationships. As you've read, my "financial freedom" came only after I had achieved emotional freedom. I was crystal clear in my understanding that the balance sheet of my life was, and is, chock-full of the assets I chose with intentionality. I was also more realistic about the fact that goodwill can only come from joy and sadness, accountability to one's self and to others.

Still, there were those who pressed the issue. *There will be time to raise a private equity fund, if I want, in the future,* was my reply to the standard inquiry. *At present, the best investment of my time is staying put.* Meg, my children, and I were in agreement on this. Others kept asking, *What about your <u>identity</u>, James? You're a private equity guy!* I am embarrassed to say that there are a few occasions when my eyes can bore holes into the oblivious. *Do <u>you</u> really believe I came here and then stayed to sell <u>clothes</u>? Do you <u>really</u> believe that blouses and pants are responsible for this company's unprecedented transformation?*

And no, maybe those weren't fair answers, but I hadn't exactly invited the questions. My interrogators hadn't been through what we at Ashley had been through. But maybe that's why they kept asking. Maybe they were genuinely curious. Maybe they were unhappy in *their* boxes. Maybe *they* were looking for a *polynya*, a way out. Realizing this, I tried to exhibit more patience and grace. So I described what it was like in the Secaucus warehouse, in that windowless cafeteria with the old-fashioned lunch warmer. What it felt like to be left for dead by the entire world, only to emerge triumphant in a tough, competitive environment without the benefit of piles of money supplied by overly indulgent venture capitalists. How good "Here Comes the Sun" sounded, even coming out of my cheap computer speakers. And how intense my tears were when virtually the entire company ignored orders to stay away and came to hug my mom while walking the receiving line at my dad's wake.

From these conversations, I found my answer. *I'm staying here because I'm not done yet.* There was still more to accomplish. Trust me, there were easier things to do than continue to commute every week from Boston to New Jersey and run an undersized retail company in an age of power, consolidation, and online dominance.

Truth be told, I did miss aspects of my private equity career and life. But during that time, one of the most venerable lemonade stands of them all, Toys "R" Us, literally vanished under the weight of debt, private equity ownership, and technological obsolescence. No doubt this also influenced my decision to stay on.

Not least, I needed to make sure Ashley Stewart could survive without me. The team was not quite ready yet. To ensure sustainability, I also had to reintroduce the company to a broader ecosystem, in the hopes that one day, in its time of need (should that ever arise), it could rely on a reservoir of goodwill, a different perspective on its value, and a winning storyline. Despite making some progress on those fronts, we still needed to explore and change how the bigger culture saw, heard, and experienced us. To do this, we had to sing as a chorus and see whether the world heard our story differently this time around. What did I use to convey this connectedness to the broader world? I drew inspiration from nature and music.

Fractal **is a word with which some of you might be familiar. If** not, go outside. Walk along the beach or look up into the sky. Go and look anywhere that is not human-made. Fractals are found in trees, plants—have you ever looked closely at a fern or a pine cone?—coastlines, snowflakes, clouds, the clustering of galaxies, and even seashells. Close your eyes and try to picture what you learned in school. Try to recall the way your capillaries, your smallest blood vessels, spread out inside you to connect your arteries to your veins. Do you also remember thinking that the way in which they spread out and expand inside your body is similar to how rivers branch out to transport rainfall from the land to the ocean?

What about trees? Did you ever notice that each branch is sort of a mini-tree?

So what *is* a fractal? It's an infinite set of self-similar patterns that repeat indefinitely and at multiple scales. Whether you look from up high or up close, the same intricate shapes perfectly repeat and build on themselves. In other words, despite appearing complex, they're made from repeating the same simple process over and over again in a, yup, you guessed it, open feedback loop. Simple is hard, yes, but simple, once achieved, can *scale*. Put another way, fractals are about the relationship that exists between the large and the small. Because they can repeat forever, fractals cannot be put in a box. For this reason, their underlying mathematics are used to study chaos theory and other complex, irregular, difficult-to-measure things like weather patterns and stock market prices.

Did you know that your brain couldn't function without fractal geometry? There are approximately eighty-six billion neurons in an average brain, but an average of one hundred trillion synapses, or connections, *among* those neurons. If you picture the branching pattern of the neurons' axons and dendrites, which create those synaptic connections, they look an awful lot like the branching pattern of capillaries and rivers. It should come as no surprise, then, that fractal patterns attract us to nature as our eyes and brains are wired to find comfort in the soothing patterns hidden there in plain sight. *Unless you pause, and hover for just a bit, you might miss the positive things right in front of you.*

So what does all this talk about fractals have to do with how I planned to accomplish my last goal of making myself unnecessary? Well, you'll have to allow me some creative license. Throughout this book, we have talked about patterns, connections, simplicity, *and* scale. We learned some basic business accounting and organizational theory through a lemonade stand. As I tell global executives, if you can't get that right, what chance do you have with much larger-scale enterprises?

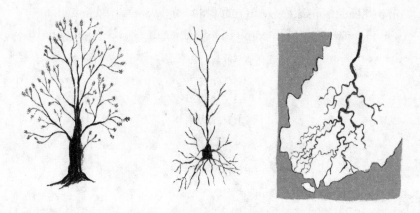

On a personal level, patterns from my own past helped me navigate what seemed at first glance to be an impossible set of future tasks. My first conversation with Chary and Shelley played out over and over again in neighborhoods across the country, while their friendship reflected and inspired the broader success of the CEO Citizenship Award. Those conversations and encounters were small and seemingly insignificant in the grand scheme of things, but I knew that getting them right mattered most. Digging deeper, they had their roots, in turn, in exchanges I had with my dad and especially my mom, in a different place and time. Gradually, because they were real, and genuine, those conversations and encounters grew. Because organizations are nothing more than a series of exchanges between and among people, they spread, organically. The recurring theme was *act first, talk second. Change behavior first, codify the behavioral change second.* Money was not the initial, nor the dominant, input. We didn't thump our chests, even after busting actuarial tables, which implicitly meant that we had turned history on its head. Consistent with that philosophy, we stayed patient and waited for the world to come to *us*, rather than us reaching out to the world.

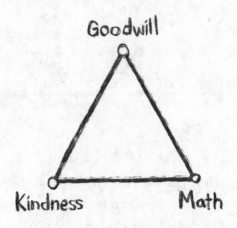

The core fractal at the center of all that was the triangle created by kindness, math, and goodwill. Kindness and math at the base of the triangle, with the resulting goodwill at the apex. My kindergarten friend and me at the base, my friend's dad at the apex. Chary and Shelley at the base, the CEO Citizenship Award at the apex.

Simple is hard. But doable. Especially if you do it bit by bit, piece by piece. After several years of quiet, deliberate choices, we had fundamentally changed Ashley's internal culture and our own perspective by weaving simple fractals into the operational tapestry. We had *already* created a genuinely new organization. But it went beyond that. Fractals repeat and *spread*, by definition. They had led to the creation of a *new ecosystem*. Everyone saw it. Everyone felt it. Even our long-term vendors and landlords, who once held the company in disdain, became our fiercest advocates. I knew the tide had turned when Alan, one of our most skeptical vendors, began asking me for advice about his *own* business, while showing up at our potlucks with homemade gestures of gratitude. I was insistent that no one describe what we had done as a *turnaround*. That didn't feel big enough. Ashley Stewart was a whole-cloth *creation*, a *reinvention*, that identified and then scaled, very profitably, its best core fractals.

My memories of the world rejecting us, of doors getting slammed in my face, of eye rolls, and smirks, of firm after firm saying *Ashley Stewart isn't exactly a lived experience for us, James*, still stung somewhat. But those memories were fading, replaced by feelings of immense pride and satisfaction. All we could do was slide open the curtains and show everyone our story. How would the world react?

We had no need for market research to tell us who we were or slick advertising and marketing consultants to invent campaigns to make us seem special. No—we knew our story cold. The lead actress was Ashley. Like the characters in a musical, we all knew the storyline, and our lines, by heart, too. Now we needed to figure out the best way for the world to weave *its* story within ours. Meaning, we were not going to bend or compromise our story to fit someone else's narrative.

So, in true fractal style, we focused on the core base of the triangle relationship between us and our friend (the customer). The apex of this triangle was Ashley Stewart, the company. In much the same way we had reframed our internal finances by bringing in Randy and Donna, we proceeded to build a media production company within the four walls of our company. I recruited younger filmmakers with no retail experience or, frankly, much interest in selling clothes, and entrusted them to capture the essence of what had happened not just for our customers or our other external stakeholders, but for *us*. We had a great story that I wanted to make sure everybody *within* Ashley got to experience first, especially since our narrative was based on *their* contributions. Ours was a musical of the real lives of our colleagues inside and outside work. This let us convey important but somewhat dry information in an engaging format. Would it surprise you to hear that Tamara became an influential spokesperson on topics like worker safety? *Ladies, mind your step on those stepladders . . .*

For years, I had listened, paying close attention to the words and actions I heard and observed in the stores. What words and phrases kept recurring? How did they correlate with behavior? Which ones seemed to connect people at the most transcendent level? Which ones established safety and belonging while also inspiring courage and growth? Those words found their way into our internal communications, which we approached with scientific rigor.

What does that mean in practice? Well, for one, the operational manuals got leaner and leaner with each passing year. Well-timed, multisensory media kept everyone well choreographed and punctuated key learnings or initiatives with fun, memorable, and oftentimes emotional vignettes that featured their fellow colleagues. And voilà, Ashley TV was born. Once we got into the rhythm of operating an in-house production company, we simply turned everything *inside out.* Soon, customers and other "friends of the firm" started to appear on Ashley TV.

Remember those iPads and strategically situated step and repeats? As any ten-year-old lemonade stand owner knows, and as we've discovered, word-of-mouth advertising is free. It's the ultimate form of leverage. Did a colleague or a customer have a strong opinion about her experience with us? (I might add that this strategy works only for companies that practice what they preach. If you say one thing and do another, you can be sure your customers and employees will report exactly *that*.) We were confident enough to let the world see exactly who we were—imperfect but trying, with the right intentions and pretty decent execution. We would often use internal content for external customer-facing purposes. Authentic, check. Economical, check.

This strategy set us apart further. During this time, self-proclaimed "innovative" companies were busy raising expensive venture capital to fund contrived customer acquisition campaigns in the hope of goosing their sales. Not us. We maintained our discipline and focused on ensuring that the gross margins on the core cup of lemonade, after any and all expenses, remained *profitable.* We did not have the luxury of being frivolous, and we knew what mattered. We continued keeping a close eye on the balance sheet and focused on growing our stockpile of cash so that we could make wise investments for the future. By maintaining our focus on these basics, we put ourselves in a position to benefit from the inherent leverage of fractals.

Ripple Effect and Earned Media

The truth spreads. The truth is free. *The truth is a fractal.* While other businesses *bought* media coverage, or outsourced their storytelling, we just spoke the truth. I knew we would garner all sorts of earned media, instead of our spraying dollars at paid media. All we needed was an invitation. The *right* invitation. When that happened, I knew the flywheels would start spinning left and right.

Around the time I wrote my signature fifty or so times in that law firm conference room, two articles made their way onto the front pages of two prestigious newspapers within twenty-four hours of each other. I already mentioned the first one in the *Boston Globe*, my hometown newspaper. Though the newspaper originally assigned a simple article describing Ashley's sale, as it was being written, it morphed into something different. My friend Steve's attorney—a partner at a powerful Los Angeles law firm—noted how my disarming honesty swayed a roomful of "cutthroat investors," while a leading fashion blogger testified that I might be a plus-size Black woman inside. A day later, the *Washington Post* published an article that focused more on the prescient bets we were making on the zeitgeist, namely, that *this woman's time has come.*

But probably nothing had a bigger impact than the meticulously researched profile of Ashley that appeared in the print edition of the year-end, highly anticipated, "good business" issue of *Bloomberg Businessweek.* The CEO of Microsoft graced the cover. The journalist, who ultimately became a friend, concluded her article by saying that our story made her want to *cry.* She had immersed herself in our company. I'm guessing she felt vindicated in her beliefs not only that humanity had a place in business, but that work was capable of helping individuals live fuller lives.

Soon, other reports appeared from CNN, ABC News, the US Chamber of Commerce, and elsewhere. People, and news organizations, *wanted* to tell our story, *wanted* to write about us, *wanted* to celebrate what we had done. Our story made them feel good, and they wanted their readers or viewers to feel good, too. We had tapped into that delicate but meaningful fractal in all of us—*humanity*. The red helicopter lying in wait, and eager to lift off.

Along with swelling media attention, the powers-that-be within the traditional retail industry were also taking notice. With the tech giants swallowing up market share, department stores and specialty retail companies were in increasing peril. I was invited to help kick off the world's biggest annual retail extravaganza, hosted by the National Retail Federation and known as the Big Show, at the Javits Center in Manhattan. A year earlier, its foundation had awarded me its highest recognition for CEO excellence alongside some of the industry's longest tenured and most successful executives. That day, I took part in the opening session of the Big Show, alongside the CEOs of Walmart USA and Macy's. The event was moderated by the president of Home Shopping Network, who was filling in for the CEO, whose first grandchild had just been born. At the time, I remember thinking that the CEO was making an important statement by prioritizing her family over the panel discussion.

As I looked out over the five-thousand-plus people packed in the Javits Center's primary amphitheater, I couldn't help but laugh. *People's memories are short! How quickly things can change!* For more than two decades, Ashley Stewart had been a corporate pariah, a punch line, a joke. And I was a "private equity guy" who, up until a little less than four years before, had zero retail operating experience other than my stints as a busboy and dishwasher back in high school. Now there I was on a panel alongside the leaders of three of the world's best-known retail companies.

I almost never wore a tie anymore (I was trying to make a clean break from the private equity dress code), but in deference to an event peppered with fashionistas, I had stopped by Macy's flagship store in Herald Square the night before. To help with my selection, the two sales associates asked for details. *Where was I going? What was I doing?* I explained that I'd be sitting next to their CEO on a big stage, though I couldn't help noticing that one of the sales associates was much more focused on my role as Ashley's "Chief Best Friend." The changes at her Ashley store were tangible, she said, and she could feel them, too. Before I left, the three of us posed for a selfie.

My goal onstage at the Javits Center was to convey a sense of hope—and even to try to change minds by changing hearts first. Instructions on how to leverage bond duration math to maximize inventory productivity could wait another day. With an audience programmed to seek packaged solutions from any number of tech companies showcasing their services upstairs, I focused instead on two simple—and free—human qualities: connectedness and transparency. During our session, at my request, the moderator displayed the selfie from Herald Square on the huge digital screen behind us. Against that backdrop, I explained to everyone, while pointedly looking at the CEOs of Macy's and Walmart USA as I spoke, that we were all mutually dependent on one another. I was rooting for them, I went on, because *they* employed some of my customers—and I worked alongside some of *theirs*. They gave me a funny look in response . . . but the audience got it *immediately*.

During the wrap-up, each of us was asked to dispense advice on the single most important area of focus going forward. The first two responses regarding operations and product were accurate. No argument from me there. But when I said, in no uncertain terms, *transparency*, you could hear everyone in the theater inhale together.

In my mind, transparency transcends operations and product. Transparency is the upside-down hedgehog. It means you show your intent to any and all who care to look. There is no subterfuge. No hidden meaning. With clarity of intent, teams share data, mistakes, and credit for great ideas. I don't care what industry it is.

That day, social media went crazy. I don't think it is an overstatement to say that the mindset of an entire industry shifted somewhat that day, too. *Find your soul*, beseeched one article by a top industry analyst. *Minnow swallows whale*, read another subsequent post. Over time, I leveraged my seat on the National Retail Federation board of directors to help bridge relationships between the many professional and social worlds of which I was and am a part—finance, technology, academia, and consumer retail. Convergence often requires a facilitator, and only four years removed from being a full-time private equity guy, I was happy to play that role, and grateful for their trust.

From there, Ashley's story and influence continued spreading in concentric circles, rippling outward across a variety of industries. I won an award from the EY Entrepreneur of the Year program and found myself being rushed off for a keynote panel at the Dreamforce summit while sitting at a table with Yo-Yo Ma, watching Leslie Odom Jr., who played the original Aaron Burr in Lin-Manuel Miranda's *Hamilton*, sing fewer than ten feet away. Sure, I was more than a little starstruck. But of all those recognitions and memorable moments, there are two that struck a particularly deep emotional chord for me.

One day, I received an email from the CEO of JPMorgan Chase, inviting me to join the charter advisory board for a new initiative, Advancing Black Pathways. Somewhere on the internet is a portrait of me, wearing a goofy smile, positioned between the smiles of Condoleezza Rice and the late Colin Powell, two former US secretaries of state. At our first board meeting, I casually mentioned to General Powell that he had been my commencement day speaker at Harvard College. He paused, smiled wryly, and thanked me, while squeezing my shoulder, for making him feel old. Later, on the literal four-year anniversary of my dad's passing, I delivered remarks to McKinsey & Company's global retail and consumer group in the gothic halls of one of Europe's oldest universities. The presentation started off with pictures of Chary, Shelley, my grandmother, and my mom. I wonder how many times over the centuries faces like theirs had graced those hallowed halls.

The Longest Feedback Loop

Once a teacher, always a teacher. Is there any other profession whose fruits are more beneficial to our broader national and global communities? But the returns on their investments, as the interaction between Adele and her favorite teacher demonstrated, often take a generation to reveal themselves. Thanks to Gina's foresight, our little town halls devoted to crazy concepts like three-legged stools, lemonade stands, and controlled chaos became naturally engrained in the ebbs and flows of our "operational tides." Today, every time I think about someone remarking *It feels like we are getting paid to come to school,* I can't help but smile. It doesn't get any better than that.

Over sandwiches, during my visits to the neighborhood stores across the country, a few of my colleagues started to make remarks along these lines: *James—we appreciate your investing in us. But it's also a little late. I wish we had learned this when we were younger. Do you think you could spend time with our <u>children</u>? Teach them what you know, and teach them what we did.*

They didn't have to ask twice. I had been teaching a winter-session course at Duke Law School called "How the World Works." The course focuses on balancing the systems of life, money, and joy and represents an attempt to teach the basics of finance, accounting, behavioral psychology, law, and philosophy in a truly interdisciplinary and practical way. I took this same curriculum and taught it at historically Black colleges and universities (HBCUs) and at institutions focused on first-generation college students. The numbers varied, but I generally visited around six campuses each year, and showed up with more than a syllabus. Every time I taught, I announced one or two new merit scholarship winners selected from among those students who took the time to watch a man going on and on about the lemonade stand of life. Once a year, we flew those students to Brooklyn and handed them checks in front of a three-thousand-plus audience at the Kings Theatre. Not just to dazzle and celebrate them, but because we knew the audience was packed with industry leaders interested in hiring proactive young people, and maybe we could help jump-start their careers.

I am still in touch with many of those students. I tease them sometimes that we made an *investment*, and in return, many of them keep me abreast of what's going on in their lives. I treasure those notes and conversations deeply. I think back to the day when my dad, who hated shopping, took me to buy that blue spring jacket. I can still picture him putting it on me, smoothing out the wrinkles. *Sorry we don't have any of those types of connections in this country, James.* Now, years later, I *have* those connections, and I'll continue to share them with those children and their parents who do not.

The Bittersweet Brooklyn YWCA Holiday Party Revisited

Do you remember the holiday party at the Brooklyn YWCA when Tamara and the others cried as I offered up a veiled apology for failing to secure funding for the company? As sad as that night was, joy was also present. In the collective suffering, in rhythm with the dance tunes coming from the little boom box, there was a celebration of our four months together and the fellowship we had created and shared. In that moment, it felt like we had lost but also somehow won. We had fought and given our all, *together.* It's often in the unlikeliest of places, with the unlikeliest of friends, where we find the spirit of hope and resolve. That little nudge from Meg (*That doesn't sound like you, James*) was all I needed to tap into the strength and multisensory beauty that moment encapsulated. From despair comes triumph. Alchemy at its finest.

During that same time, when the Misfit Toys were getting their crash course in Bankruptcy 101, I showed them a short clip that I had found from *Britain's Got Talent*. It featured Beyoncé Knowles—who of course needs no introduction—appearing on a reality show in *support* of an enormously talented but nervous contestant singing the song "Listen."

If you don't know the song, it's about a woman finding her voice after struggling through years of self-doubt caused by people holding her down. In the clip, the two women are dressed to the nines, but what made the performance so emotional was how gracious Beyoncé was to not overshadow or overpower a clearly starstruck up-and-comer. She even held her hand. Amid the mouse-gray filing cabinets and mud-brown carpeting at Ashley's headquarters, I had nothing else to show a browbeaten team what I knew was the true spirit of Ashley. That spirit, created only through connectedness between and among people, was what was worth preserving.

I had seen Chary and Shelley, and many others like them, playing the role of Beyoncé. They did it without any fanfare, and without seeking credit. It was around that spirit, that goodwill, that I composed an entirely new set of mathematical algorithms, legal structures, and operating protocols. The whole world had once rejected Ashley Stewart. It was now incumbent on us to have the courage and grace to forgive and invite the whole world in. To make what we had done, what we stood for—the *how*—tangible to everyone.

To help do that, we created and produced something we called Finding Ashley Stewart. Its underlying mission was simple. During the course of the year, we encouraged our colleagues and customers to identify and celebrate unsung female leaders in our neighborhoods and communities. We used our stores as launching points to galvanize, to crystallize, to make tangible the intangible. Selection criteria were based on the pillars of confidence, leadership, public service, and kindness—in short, women who created positive externalities in their communities. National voting was made possible by our enhanced digital capabilities, and our finalists gathered at the Kings Theatre in Brooklyn in September. A panel of celebrity judges and leaders who understood the depth of what we had done selected the winners with the help of three-thousand-plus foot-stomping audience members. And, oh yeah, interspersed within all of that, the night featured rocking performances from legendary groups like En Vogue and Salt-N-Pepa (who had collaborated on the song "Whatta Man").

Sound complicated? Yes and no. Focusing on the simple, and showing the world our real-life day-in and day-out, made it possible for many hands to make light work. Let's start with the space and time.

It was no coincidence that the Kings Theatre is only a few miles away from the Brooklyn YWCA. Nor was it a coincidence that the event took place in the autumn, the anniversary of the initial forging of our Ashley fellowship. The Kings Theatre is located in the same neighborhood where the first-ever Ashley Stewart store opened its doors in 1991. Where did my creative inspiration for Finding Ashley Stewart come from? Well, it was the love child of the unscripted portions of the Beyoncé video and the organic movements of the women at our bittersweet Brooklyn YWCA holiday party. The audience activation stations in the foyer were simply larger versions of Gina's holiday parties and summer picnics. As for the music acts? Well, they were nothing more than our karaoke performances, with Grammy Award–winning professionals standing in for a bunch of well-intended amateurs. And who do you think opened the entire show? If you guessed Tamara, you guessed right! People were amazed at what we pulled off. We weren't. We'd done all of it already, just on a smaller scale.

Remember, the feedback loop of kindness requires an action *and* a reaction. Done right, the resulting asset is *goodwill*. And what was the reaction? Imagine, if you will, an exhilarating victory dance, a three-hour-long extravaganza that encapsulated the best, most positive, most joyful, and human *feeling* possible. I think Abraham Maslow would have agreed that we achieved transcendence during those three hours. Attendees described the night using words often reserved for church or the awe you feel in the presence of a spectacular sunset. Finding Ashley Stewart was a convening. A ministry almost. A fellowship. A celebration of a shared humanity. A revival. A *movement* come to life. Those weren't my words. They were written all over the internet, and uttered and repeated in conversations as people danced out of the theater.

A movement can't be planned, mandated, or forced into existence. It springs from truth, the kind that is deep down inside all of us. The truth that's taught in a childhood fable, the kind that sings from the page even though on the surface, it's just a bunch of animals talking to one another. The difference was that what we did, in that space and in that time, was real. It *happened*. Yes, the Getty Images from that night are indelible (go look—they're still online!). But the feeling—boy, that *feeling*!—will live forever in the hearts and minds of anyone who was fortunate enough to be in the audience. That fractal was, and will be, never-ending.

We ended up hosting three of those finales, all of them at the Kings Theatre. If you check the internet, you will find borderline fantastical photos of the women of Ashley and me surrounded by celebrities, influencers, dignitaries, and performers. The photos of Emmy Award–winning comedienne Loni Love (who emceed two of our three shows) and me never fail to cheer me up when I feel down. My friends know that glitz and showbiz are not generally my thing, but once a year, it seemed okay (and really fun).

Another thing I appreciated about those nights? The celebrities who were there felt the *realness* of the evening, along with a degree of relief, of permission, to take off *their* armor and be themselves. Just like us, they're regular people.

I'm not one to pick favorites, but in this case I will. The *first* Finding Ashley Stewart. It was rough, scrappy, and imperfect. And those liabilities became assets. Boris Kodjoe, the actor, served as emcee. Iyanla Vanzant, the renowned spiritual life coach, unexpectedly joined us to help hand out scholarships to two young women from her alma mater, Medgar Evers College, encouraging them to stand for what they believed in. The president of the Borough of Brooklyn, who ultimately became the mayor of New York, issued a proclamation declaring it to be Ashley Stewart Day. En Vogue crushed their performance, making intense eye contact with me while singing a few of their greatest hits, and later posted a picture of me with them, along with words of encouragement, on social media. I sat between the president of the National Urban League and Nicole Ari Parker, the actress who played Denzel Washington's wife in *Remember the Titans*. Crazy, yes—but somehow it all made sense. So did the invitation from Whoopi Goldberg to meet for tea at her home, after which she gave me a tour and insisted that I hold her Oscar. And wouldn't you know it, but Meg and I attended the Oscars a few years later as guests of the US chairman of PricewaterhouseCoopers, the global accounting firm. As much as I hate to admit, it was ridiculously fun wearing black tie and rubbing elbows with the Hollywood glitterati.

But what I remember most from that first Finding Ashley Stewart was seeing my colleagues and Ashley vendors, most of whom had suffered greatly during those times, dancing, applauding, and crying. Some of those vendors had been angry enough for me to hire the armed security guard in that depressing warehouse we called an office. Now they were here in person, funding the scholarships awarded to our customers' children. Also helping finance our cause, and delivering for us, was Carolyn, my first-ever quote-unquote girlfriend from sixth grade. ("Do you remember how you drove me to the SATs in high school because I was so nervous?" Carolyn, now a global advertising executive, asked after we were reunited by the CEO of Home Shopping Network. "I do," I said. "We listened to Mozart together on the beach that morning.") Carolyn, like so many other executives in our extended ecosystem, cut through the red tape within her company and provided the sponsorship dollars necessary for us to afford an event like this. Right before I entered stage left, a video appeared of our store managers recounting the true story of our transformation from each of their perspectives. *This is the story of you . . . and me*, it began. *I finally felt safe*, said one manager. Then Chary appeared. *He did everything he said he was going to do*, she said.

The theme song from the movie "Rocky" filled the theater as I made my way onstage. A real stage, not a makeshift stage like the one in Mrs. Griffith's kindergarten classroom. *We're only a few years removed from having nothing*, I thought again. No Wi-Fi. No money. No hope. No corporate goodwill. The audience may not have known what they were feeling, but I knew. It was palpable to me. *Inspiration. Permission. Affirmation. If you can do this, we can, too.* Then a hush fell over the theater.

In front of an audience that was a fractal of what was best in America, I told everyone that the spirit of what we had done deserved a setting as beautiful and boundary-less as the Kings Theatre. It was always there, I explained. Ashley, like all of us, just needed friends to believe in her. Through kindness and math, in that order, we had unleashed what was already there.

They gave me—us!—a standing ovation. I punched the air with my fist, as a boxer would. I felt that warm, good ache in my chest. And I gave myself permission to bask in a job well done, for that moment in time, in that particular space. It felt triumphant.

When you do something special, people will corner and quiz you. They're often looking for an elixir, a potion to deliver supernatural results. But by now, you know there is no one elixir, or magic shortcut. It begins with your own lemonade stand. It requires good intentions, the will to *persevere*, and disciplined execution. It requires you to *not* second-guess your intuition about human behavior (the good and the bad), *and* it requires a systemic understanding of the foundational tenets of subjects like history, math, finance, accounting, economics, cognitive science, behavioral psychology, and corporate law. (What's in this book is a solid start.) It *ends* with the willingness to pause and free yourself from artificially drawn constructs, from boxes, and to embrace oxymorons. To realize that true freedom paradoxically emerges only through your *connectedness with others* and with nature. To understand the past without being imprisoned by it. To know that the future is in the ever-evolving present. That kindness is the ultimate form of courage. That kindness is quite profitable. And that simple can scale.

But simple is hard.

That said, I want to take this time to answer the one question I most frequently get asked. *What was the single most important thing you did?* My answer is simple: *I heard Ashley's song clearly.*

First, I listened intently. Then, I created a space where Ashley could sing her song.

Her *song*. I heard the song being sung by Chary, Shelley, Gina, Tamara, and our other colleagues and customers. They trusted me enough to sing it unfiltered, in places where they felt uncomfortable or not entirely welcome. Each individual song was unique, but collectively they reminded me of the songs my mom sang at our kitchen table or inside her red Volvo.

But something funny happened along the way. By listening and giving permission, *I* received something in return. I understood *my* song better. *My song*. My new friends gave *me* permission. They listened to *me*, too. Music was—*is*—a huge part of my life. Remember, I'm a classically trained violinist, who in high school sang in the jazz ensemble. But anyone who knows me *well* also knows I can sing a mean rock anthem. I don't just mumble along to "Born to Run"—I can flat out *sing* it. *That* James, the one who belts out rock anthems, had become buried under the weight of cubicles, spreadsheets, legal documents, and external expectations. But like my own dormant leadership instincts, my love of music was always there. *That* ear had always guided my investments in consumer brands, my judgment in reading the dynamics of a boardroom, and my intuition regarding the pitch and timbre of an executive's answers to my due diligence inquiries.

I've always loved Leonardo da Vinci's famous quote about developing a complete mind. *Study the science of art. Study the art of science. Learn how to see. Realize that everything connects to everything else.* Now, finally, I understood. All I needed was a nudge. All I needed was permission. I'm hoping that this book has given you permission to do the same.

There is a technical term in music called counterpoint. In counterpoint, two standalone melodies are played together. Neither is dominant. Neither is harmony. Each one sounds beautiful played alone. But when played together, a new, third melody emerges, one more beautiful than the two melodies played separately.

So what was the one thing I think I did well? Well, I once heard Yo-Yo Ma describe music as an expression of ideas, thoughts, feelings, and spatial structure conveyed in sound. I think that I listened and then sang Ashley's song with feeling. And when I sang *her* song, I found *my* song. The two songs together created a third song, which was consciously and unconsciously embedded in the day-to-day flows of the human exchanges that comprised a business named Ashley Stewart. And the world could hear the truth in that song and enthusiastically decided to sing along.

Korea's unofficial national anthem is "Arirang." It is estimated that the song is more than six hundred years old. Like many folk songs, fables, and truths, "Arirang" has no known composer or author. The origin story is obscure, rooted in alchemy. Some believe "Arirang" came from farmers toiling in the fields during times of struggle and suffering. Even the meaning of what is a rather simple song is up for debate. One interpretation is that it is about two lovers, separated, the man dying as he is crossing a river to be with the woman he loves. Whichever meaning you ascribe to it, the haunting melody conveys what is important. It's a bittersweet song of paradox. Of separation *and* togetherness, of suffering *and* hope, of struggle *and* resolve.

During the Japanese occupation of Korea, when singing the actual national anthem meant punishment by death, Koreans sang

"Arirang" as a resolute protest song. Today, the song has become an anthem of hope for the reunification of North and South Korea, which remain divided by the same war that robbed my mom of her father.

When I was growing up, my parents would sometimes sing this song—my dad especially, with his college and medical school classmates, after a few glasses of *soju*, the clear Korean alcohol. He couldn't have been aware that the first known recording of "Arirang" happened not in Korea, but in Washington, DC. In 1896, an ethnologist named Alice Fletcher recorded a trio of Korean students singing "Arirang." The students were enrolled at Howard University, arguably the most prestigious historically Black university in the United States. From its founding via charter by the US Congress in 1867, Howard has been nonsectarian and open to all genders and races, from *day one*. When I found this out, I just smiled.

Toward the very beginning of this book, I wrote that I saw my mom and dad as being a beat or two behind, a half measure off. The Misfit Toys and the women of Ashley Stewart were, too. But a beat or two behind *what*? A half measure off *what*? Maybe the real issue is that I was expecting their songs to match someone else's melody. Depends on your perspective, I guess. As for me, I learned to just listen and discover the beauty of those songs without comparison. All of them. All together.

chapter 10

reverberation

Hovering is the most difficult maneuver for helicopter pilots.

My childhood home was surrounded by trees. To this day, I associate the sound of crickets in the chilly night air with the end of summer and the start of a new school year. In Korea, another insect, the dragonfly, has a special connection with autumn. One culturally important dragonfly, nicknamed the *gochu* dragonfly (named for the Korean chili pepper), *turns red* in the fall.

Like other dragonflies, the *gochu* dragonfly's magnificent and dramatic appearance is short-lived. It dies within months of emerging from the water as a nymph and completing its metamorphosis. Understandably, mythology surrounds visits from red dragonflies. Some say they portend good and bad omens about loss, death, love, and change. Maybe that's why *many* global cultures associate red dragonflies with spiritual transformation, courage, and abundance. I sometimes wonder if any of the dragonflies my dad pursued as a little boy were a *gochu* dragonfly. I never got to ask him that question.

It's uncanny how meaningful each autumn was during my tenure at Ashley Stewart. When I first arrived in Secaucus, the city was just beginning to shiver under a stiff autumnal chill. The company almost died that fall. In observance of that time, we staged the annual finale of Finding Ashley Stewart at the tail end of hurricane season in September, always praying for one of those brisk fall evenings to come our way. And of course, my dad passed away just before being able to see the leaves turn for his seventy-fifth time. Autumn always served as a steady reminder of the change that both I and the company had undergone.

I had just started my seventh year of leading Ashley Stewart. Summer was ending, and it felt like my unexpected tenure at the company might be, too. It was time. I knew that the company was ready to move on without me. Over the long Labor Day weekend, signaling the end of summer for most Americans, I sat in the backyard of my sister Jennifer's house, watching her golden retriever paddle around her swimming pool with my niece and nephew. Along with keeping an eye on the kids, I also kept a close watch on my mom. She half sat, half reclined on a chaise on the elevated patio, occasionally dozing off, her hands now and again reaching down to cradle her abdomen. She was clearly in pain but didn't want anyone to know or make a fuss.

We had been worried about her all summer. Her appetite was off, and she was having bothersome digestion issues. Still, her doctors and she didn't seem all that concerned. It was probably something harmless, they agreed—the change to her blood pressure medication, or her diet, or maybe even lactose intolerance. Though there were a few concerning markers, the lab tests were still inconclusive. But for everyone's peace of mind, my mom had agreed to fly out to Milwaukee, where my brother, John, lived, to undergo additional tests. None of us knew on that late summer day that she would be gone four weeks later.

I had learned a lesson from Lila's accident and my dad's final days. This time around, I asked for help and drew strength from my many friends and colleagues. That said, it was important to continue to keep Ashley at the front and center of the narrative and not make it about myself. As much as I had appreciated everyone showing up at my dad's wake four years before, I kept my family outside the narrative of the musical that was our company. I made an exception with the publication of the *Harvard Business Review* article, but even then, there was only one small reference to my dad and his influence on me.

But life has a way of intertwining the business and the personal. We live but one life, right? So now I was contemplating making another exception—or perhaps permanently undoing the separation of Home-James and Work-James. Assuming my mom would undergo her tests in Milwaukee, return to New Jersey, and resume her normal activities, I was considering including her in the third annual Finding Ashley Stewart finale, which was scheduled for a Saturday in two weeks' time. How amazing, and how much of a full circle would it be, if my mom made a surprise appearance onstage to hand out scholarships to that year's winners from colleges and universities across the country? I could picture her sitting next to me, in the same seat in which I had been sitting while being serenaded by En Vogue just two years earlier. I pictured the big warm smile on her face and the excitement expressed by her hands.

But none of that ended up happening.

In Milwaukee, my mom stayed for a week or so with John and his family. I was grateful that they had that time together, and that John had created so much goodwill in his medical community. My mom received top-notch care because of it. As the results came in from her progressively more invasive tests, the doctors were able to make the diagnosis: late-stage pancreatic cancer. They insisted that she be admitted to the hospital immediately. A day after the event at the Kings Theatre, I flew to Milwaukee.

As many people know, pancreatic cancer is fast, painful, and almost always fatal. The diagnosis usually comes after it's too late to do anything. My mom's case was advanced and her odds were poor. Yes, there were aggressive treatments that could extend her life anywhere from six months to a year, but they would be painful and undignified. My mom was a nurse. It took her no time to reach her decision.

No treatment. It's time. It's over. The resoluteness of her voice made it clear there was to be no debate. I won't ever forget the quiet, the stillness, of her hands as she spoke. The same hands that over the years had talked, and laughed, and disagreed, now lay motionless and small in her lap as she lay on her hospital bed. All she wanted was to fly home to New Jersey.

Even that presented risks. Her doctors warned my brother and me that they were concerned she wouldn't survive the flight because of the potential physical side effects caused by changes in altitude and air pressure. Before leaving the hospital, I was asked to sign a

Do Not Resuscitate form as a witness. It was my first time seeing one of these, let alone signing one. From her wheelchair, my mom consented to that same directive and allowed the nurses to affix a carefully worded band of paper around her wrist.

The details from the trip back to New Jersey will forever be seared into my memory. My mom and I were both very emotional. I won't ever forget the generosity of the driver who picked us up from the hospital and took us to the airport. Somehow, without anyone saying anything, she intuited it was my mom's last trip. She helped me get her comfortable in her seat, and fastened her seat-belt, before turning to offer me a sudden warm embrace. I must have looked in desperate need of a hug.

No available wheelchairs were to be found when we got to the airport. "Why didn't you reserve one in advance?" asked a staff member. "Because I didn't know my mom would be flying home in a wheelchair," I pleaded. The employees behind the counter were brisk, rule-bound, and hyperefficient. My mom was dying, but the rules were the rules, and the system was the system.

During that encounter, I became aware of someone intently watching her colleagues inform me there were no options. Then—like Gina before my dad's wake, or Chary appearing at the wake—this woman leaped into action. Instead of accepting the status quo, she *did* something. Soon a wheelchair was found, and five minutes later, I was pushing my mom through security and down the long hallway to the gate. Passing a kiosk, my mom pointed out a two-for-twenty-dollars sale on neck cushions, commenting on what a good deal it was. I bought a pair, blue for my mom, gray for me, and we sat in the waiting area, gazing at each other with cushions around our necks, until it was time to board.

It was a harrowing flight, given her doctors' warning. To my relief, my mom slept most of the way, but when we arrived in Newark, her feet were so swollen she couldn't get her shoes back on.

We waited a long time at the luggage carousel. Inside one of her two enormous rolling bags was the stuffed teddy bear she had picked out for me when I was four years old. I can *still* see her grabbing it by one ear off the shelf in the toy aisle, and asking in Korean, *This one, do you like it?* I never gave him a name—he was just Teddy Bear. Knowing my mom was undergoing tests in Milwaukee, I had shipped Teddy Bear to my brother's house. I know, it sounds absurd, right? But I didn't know what else to do. Upon receiving the package, my mom texted me these exact words: *Your bear? This bear recalls me, healthy, energetic, young mother. Thank for your thoughtful mind.* Teddy Bear would rest beside my mom in hospice for the next twelve days.

Jennifer met us outside the terminal in her big SUV. Together, we gently maneuvered our mom into the back seat, as short-tempered police officers shouted for us to move along, and traffic attendants in orange vests windmilled their arms and screamed through their whistles. My sister and I exchanged a look. No words were necessary. She and my mom exchanged the same look. Everyone knew what was being said. Everyone knew where this was going. We weren't taking my mom home. *Nunchi* is a real thing. My family, and no doubt many others, had years of practice allowing our eyes and our faces to take the place of words.

Geurae. **Before she entered the room at the hospice center, I** heard my mom utter this word in a low voice. She had noted the room number on the door, 202—the very same room where my dad had died. *Geurae*. Depending on the context, *geurae* can simply mean *agreed*. In this context, however, *geurae* meant something closer to *so be it*. It was my mom offering her surrender.

For the next twelve days, until she died, I left my mom's side only twice. Basically, I moved in, sleeping in a reclining chair, though the hospice nurses quietly prepared a bed for me when one opened up. If the closeness of our relationship had always been implicit, now it became explicit. I took charge of her daily calendar, scheduling drop-by visits from her friends, some of whom she hadn't seen in years. Many showed up bearing gifts—fancy cookies, flower bouquets, miniature fruit slices punctured by tiny forks, a Korean specialty. Some came holding containers of homemade *jjigae*, stew, or *guk*, soup. The aroma of *kimchi* and bean paste permeated the room. It smelled so good. Surely, they knew my mom wouldn't and couldn't eat what they brought, but they wanted her to feel cared for, and loved. They also knew *I* would eat it, a sight they knew would make *my mom* happy. *Jeong*, a connection from one person to another. Before leaving, some even reached out to stroke my cheek, the way my mom used to, saying *Aigoo, neomu mallatda*, which in totality means *Oh no, your face has thinned out way too much from worry*.

Newer friends appeared too. In the four years since my dad had died, my mom had retired from her lifelong roles as a wife and full-time mother. She stopped cooking, she said, only breaking out her arsenal of utensils, including her beloved kitchen scissors (which Meg now uses), when I came to visit. She had joined a walking group and picked up hobbies, rejoining the world that her devotion to her husband's care had kept her from. Her life was different now, and her friends were, too. It was obvious she was a matriarch, a respected older woman within her community. Jennifer and I would compare notes, marveling at her independence and willingness to enroll in classes like Beginner's Excel. It had taken her a while to find her footing after Dad passed away. She needed the space and the time to create a new balance. And she found that identity by reaching deep inside and finding Hwa Ja. Not Mom, not Phyllis, not Matilda. Her name was *Hwa Ja*.

In between old and new friends stopping by the room, we kept ourselves busy. Mostly we talked and looked at old photos, but I also hooked up an old DVD player to her small television so we could watch old movies we'd watched together as a family. We watched *High Noon*, *The King and I*, and, of course, *The Sound of Music*, which our family used to watch together every year at Thanksgiving. My mom and dad always loved the song "Edelweiss," its message of loving your homeland, and the image of a tiny, tough, beautiful mountaintop flower. While we watched and napped together, my mom startled me when she poked me in the shoulder, pointed to the television, and observed that Brigitta, the middle daughter, reminded her of my daughter Graylyn.

We also sat in silence for a fair bit, especially when her voice started to fail her. How ironic that the slightest movements of her hands, and eyes, and mouth always had more to say to me than the spoken conversations I'd had with just about everyone else in my life. Over those twelve days, words paled in comparison to the act of simply sharing presence. In that silence, my perspective on my own life came together for me in ways I never could have predicted. The scattered pieces of my identity began to coalesce and make sense. It had less to do with me than with my growing understanding of who my mom really was.

• • •

A few days into our hospice stay, the nurses told Jennifer and me we could take my mom to her condo to finalize plans and arrangements. We had a two-hour time limit, including the time it took to get there and back.

My mom was clear and matter-of-fact. She told us which of her *hanboks* she wanted to be buried in, and how to tie the front knot. She pointed Jennifer and me to passwords and keys that opened drawers, cabinets, and ornamental Korean chests where her keepsakes were stored. Were there things, we asked, any objects of value or meaning, that she wished to leave friends, or her surviving brother and sister? Forty minutes to make the final arrangements for a human life—that was all we had. Would it surprise you to know that we spent fewer than five minutes talking about any commercial, tangible assets? Even those handful of items could generally fit in the palm of one hand.

As we left the condo, I was aware of a door closing on time, on the past, my mom's, my own, and our family's. Our heritage wasn't at risk of dying, but that didn't mean that a direct, proximate connection to Korea, to my parents' generation, and my own childhood, wasn't being severed. I felt this same way watching my mom greet and say goodbye to friends visiting her room. Soon to be in the past was this entire group of first-generation Korean immigrants who served as surrogate aunts and uncles for the three Rhee children, whose parents had no family of their own in their adopted country. We would see many of my mom's friends again at her memorial service, and wanting to hold tight to our past, and do as our parents would have done, we promised to attend future funerals in their stead.

I was wheeling my mom back to the car when she asked me to stop. She wanted one last look at the view outside her condo, the huge human-made pond encircled by the asphalt road. Again, she said *geurae*, this time more firmly. I felt awe. My mom was surrendering with a conviction I admired and dreaded at the same time. She took in the vista, and then we were back inside the car.

On the way back to hospice, my sister made a thoughtful suggestion. Why not stop at McDonald's and grab lunch? In the drive-thru, I ordered a Filet-O-Fish sandwich for my mom and a cheeseburger for me. For old time's sake. Later, propped up in her bed, though she hadn't eaten much of anything for days, my mom ate about a third of her Filet-O-Fish. Her eyes were bright. Who knows whether her sandwich tasted good and brought back good memories, or whether she was eating it because she knew how happy it would make Jennifer and me. I don't know, but after all the years, I once again joked that I still didn't understand how she, or anyone else for that matter, would actually choose the Filet-O-Fish. We all laughed with tears in our eyes.

I remember that day for another reason, too. *Jennifer.* My perspective on my sister had changed. When we were growing up, Jennifer was squarely in the baby sister category. She was five years younger, and I always had a hard time *not* envisioning her with her Cabbage Patch Kid doll, even when she was earning accolades of her own as an adult. She *wasn't* just my baby sister, though. Jennifer was a force, a leader, someone to be admired, especially considering how much she was juggling. She had lost *her* person, my dad, only four years before, and now here she was juggling not only my mom's care, but her own life, her husband, two children, two dogs, and new professional pursuits in early education. *My sister would have given my grandmother a run for her money*, I thought. Without her, I wouldn't have made it through what we were now going through. Seeing Jennifer as she *was* planted a seed of change that led to a much larger perspective.

Earlier I mentioned that during those twelve days my mom was in hospice, I left the facility only twice. The first time was to participate in the opening fireside chat with New Jersey's lieutenant governor at the state's first-ever summit to connect businesses owned by women; members of minority groups, including the LGBTQ community; and veterans to roughly one billion dollars in public and private sector contracting opportunities. The lieutenant governor asked me what the public sector could do to help the private sector, half expecting, I imagine, that I would deliver the standard myopic anthem of *cutting taxes*. I think I shocked her, and the audience, when I politely asked whether the state of New Jersey could focus on the public education system. Was there any doubt that a better-informed citizenry, properly prepared to embrace agency, would power innovation in the private sector? Such a simple solution—too bad none of us seems to have the patience or willingness to make the one investment that would bear the most fruit for our country, not to mention for humanity.

The second time I left the hospice was for Jared's birthday.

Given my mom's condition, and my own scattered attention, I hadn't been all that present for Meg and my kids for almost a month. Jared was turning sixteen, a big birthday. Still, the prospect of leaving my mom's side pained me, and I knew it made her unhappy, too. I wouldn't have even considered going if the hospice nurses hadn't given me the go-ahead. My mom's oxygen levels were slightly depressed, but she wasn't at imminent risk of dying, they told me. As added insurance, my brother was flying in that evening, and Jennifer planned on stopping by mid-morning to spend time with her before school pickup. Her own daughter, my niece, was preparing my mom's favorite soup, *miyeokguk*, which is made of edible seaweed, that my mom had prepared for us, as is custom, on each and every one of our birthdays. Seaweed symbolizes long life.

Before sunrise, as I prepared to leave for what was supposed to be a twenty-four-hour excursion, my mom said two things that I won't ever forget.

The first was, "No matter what, I always knew you were 100 percent on my side." My mom's voice was hoarse, low. "You always had my back," she whispered. She had said similar words to my wife during her final visit: *I always trusted you, Meg*, while patting Meg on her shoulder.

Look, my relationship with my mom had its ups and downs. There were moments over the years when she had seen fit to thwack me on the back of my head and reel off every single one of my shortcomings. Pretty recently, too. It was a long list! Before she flew to Milwaukee for tests, as a precautionary measure, Jennifer and I took an unplanned detour to visit her priest to discuss last rites and funeral services. I was wearing an orange New York Mets T-shirt and shorts. Before and after talking to the priest, my mom eyed me up and down, embarrassed by and disapproving of my attire. She even apologized to the priest for her sloppily dressed big-shot son. It was classic Mom. And if you must know, it *annoyed* me, just like it did every time she overexercised agency around my choices. But you know what? She was usually right, especially about the important stuff.

She said the second thing while I was escorting her to her small bathroom. "It's sad," she said.

"What's sad?" I asked.

"When you leave, I will be nothing." There was an emphasis on the word *nothing*. Those words were daggers in my chest.

I will be nothing. There were so many innocuous ways for me to interpret those words. At first, I took them to mean that because I was around, the hospice nurses gave her lots of extra attention. Or maybe she was referring to the small gestures I made to make sure she was as comfortable as possible. A refill of her ginger ale. A short jaunt around the courtyard, with me behind her, pushing her chair. The curating of the movies that we were watching together. But those interpretations were overcome by a rising and familiar suffocation behind my ribcage. *Dabdabhae.* Chest-tightening frustration.

It triggered my biggest latent fear—that my mom had sacrificed her identity and the ownership of her life to benefit her husband and children. That she had lived her life primarily through her three children. Of course, parents are naturally proud of their kids, but immigrant parents can take that pride and investment to extraordinarily extreme levels. A traditional Korean mom will oftentimes refer to herself as, say, "James's *umma*," *umma* meaning *mother*, rather than using her own name.

With my mom, I sometimes worried it went beyond that. That absent an identity of her own, she *became* her children. *You are your own person*, I said to her over the years more than once.

I drove to Boston with a heavy heart. Upon my arrival after the five-hour drive, my daughter Graylyn and I wasted no time in heading out again to buy birthday party favors. We were at the cash register, arms overflowing with small knickknacks, when my cell phone rang. It was Jennifer. According to the nurses, our mom had become "nonresponsive." Dropping Graylyn at home, and asking Jared for his understanding and forgiveness, I drove back down to New Jersey in record time.

I arrived in the late evening to find my brother, John, sitting by my mom's bedside. I stood over her and said, in a loud voice, "Mom, I'm back. It's me, James. I'm here." My mom's eyes opened. We locked eyes for a few seconds. Then her eyes closed again. Later, the hospice nurses told me they couldn't believe she had responded— but at the same time they also *could*.

For the next few hours, my brother, sister, and I sat around my mom's bed, talking, holding her hands, telling old stories. As the hours wore on, John graciously told us he would sit vigil overnight, and we should go home to Jennifer's and get some real rest. Grateful for the offer, we headed back to my sister's house. Within a few minutes of our sitting down on her couch, her cell phone rang. It was John. It was over.

Hospice nurses will tell you that dying patients sometimes find the strength of will to plan their own departures. I have to believe this was true for my mom. She had waited for me to come back so that she, or her eyes, could say a final goodbye. Then, she bravely surrendered to the unknown.

When I say that my life came together during the twelve days I spent in the hospice, and that I was finally able to gather, join, and make sense of its scattered and shattered pieces, I am talking less about events than I am about *perspective*. As my mom and I talked, I realized how completely wrong I had been about so many things.

I wasn't the strong one in our relationship. *She* was. My mother didn't need her fancy finance son to protect her. She'd survived a war and the loss of her father. I laughed out loud realizing that I was just a small player in the game of chess that was *her* life, a game that her own mother, my grandmother, had started. *Without you I am nothing*, my mom had said. In truth, was it the other way around? Or maybe both statements were true.

A few days earlier, two of my older female cousins (in Korean, I would have called them *nuna*, a beautiful name a male calls his older female relatives or respected female friends) had come by my mom's room to pay their respects. As I was walking them out, I suddenly burst into tears. "I don't know what I'm going to do," I blurted out. Words that shocked me. Words I had *never* said before, or since. I've *always* been someone who knows instinctively what to do, regardless of how challenging the situation. I thrive on uncertainty. I've made a career leading and investing in change. But at that moment, I was at a complete loss, and inconsolable.

Amid everything, I realized I had overlooked hidden truths, seminal truths, truths that underlie whatever qualities of strength and power I bring to my own life.

The first recognition? My mom and my grandmother were *in* me. I was a direct beneficiary of their love, generosity, knowledge, character, strength, grace, perseverance, and *kindness*, all of which had compounded quietly for three generations spanning two continents. No different from the way money compounds, exponentially, and in an open feedback loop. But what was even more important was that their investment of kindness had created positive externalities whose benefit and reach extended far beyond me. I was just a mere vehicle of distribution for them. I amplified their investment at the Brooklyn YWCA four months after I arrived at Ashley Stewart, and I had done the same at the Kings Theatre just two weeks earlier when our latest scholarship winners took the stage. With every conversation and quiet meal my colleagues and I shared, their goodwill was deposited and comingled inside stores in neighborhoods across America. My mom made her last direct deposit vis-à-vis my children when Meg brought them to say goodbye to her a week before she died. They had just left the room when my mom called them back. She instructed them to take with them all the goodies her friends had brought. *Akkapda*, she said, the Korean word for not wanting good things, gifts of *jeong*, to go to waste. To this day, my children still marvel about her presence of mind.

Second, and more crucially, I realized I had severely underestimated my mom's strength and conviction about who she was and what mattered to her. My mom *never* wavered in her perseverance. Neither did my grandmother, who, after her husband went missing, sold candies and carried out a series of odd jobs just to put food on the table for her four children.

I thought back to the incident at the hardware store, the clerk yelling at my mom because she didn't know how to say *anti-rust spray*. Yes, my mom cried in the car, but mixed in with her sadness was frustration and even anger. I'm sure my mom appreciated that her son loved her enough to intervene on that occasion, but let's be real—she was more than capable of fighting her own battles.

Not once did she ever allow the small slights and indignities she put up with almost daily to define her. Yes, I am sure they stung in the moment, but in the long run she did not lose sight of who she was, or question her own strength, courage, and ability. I know that because in the last years of her life, she showed her identity and resoluteness again and again. Some, if not many, things I had mistaken for weakness were, in fact, feats of improbable strength. What I had perceived as liabilities were actually her greatest assets.

Before she passed away, I felt the need to sit down and remind my mom of all her many accomplishments. In partnership with my dad, she had given her three children the gift of graduating from college debt-free. As the lemonade stand that was my dad's small business buckled under increasingly cutthroat players in medicine, what did my mom do? She got recertified as a nurse after nearly twenty-five years of being a full-time mom, which meant having to relearn and memorize complex medical terminology in English, her second language (even I, a native speaker, couldn't understand half of what was in her textbooks). For more than a decade, she took great pride in quietly tending to the suffering of Korean War veterans, while working long enough so that she and Dad qualified for New York State pension and healthcare benefits. With insurance secured, she nursed my dad by herself, lovingly and without complaint, for *fifteen years* until the end of his life. All the while having the presence of mind to slip *yongdon* into her son's jacket pocket when he wasn't looking. A little extra money in case I needed it.

When I reminded her of all this, my mom glanced up, her gaze strong, steely almost, a faint smile playing on her lips. *Geurae?* There was a hint of sarcasm. Again, in the Korean language, context is everything. In this context, what she was really saying was, *Wow, you don't say. You actually doubted me?* I just looked down.

For me, it was one of many moments of awakening and clarity, of understanding that my mom had always measured life on her *own* terms. She didn't abandon certain core principles on the basis of how much money she made, on GDP, or on any of the other yardsticks that she and my dad sent me off to master in the Ivy League and later Wall Street. She never hid behind a legal entity or a non-sensical rule to justify behavior she knew to be hurtful. She never assumed wrongly that everyone around her was an economic being, a rational actor. She intuited what brain scientists already know, that human beings are innately *emotional*. And she measured her life in the way that all of us intuitively know we should. On the *how*. She never once stopped being the lady who handed tall glasses of icy water to the lawn crew and passed out full-size candy bars to the local kids on Halloween. Those gestures were small, but they added up over the years. In their consistency over a lifetime, they grew in weight. She didn't need to make a splashy monetary gift to create lasting value and secure her legacy. She didn't need fancy degrees in law and business to act like an owner, be a good friend, be a good mentor. Her life created so much value. I'm pretty sure that not one investment banking training manual or neoclassical economics textbook would agree with me on this. But they're wrong.

Look, do I wish that my mom had known more about money? Do I wish she had allowed me to "take over" her finances? Do I wish that she could have enrolled in my Duke Law School class in order to gain a greater understanding of how the systems worked? Of course I do. (In many ways, that's why I wrote this book.) After she died, when I was reviewing her papers, I discovered her brokerage firm had done some eyebrow-raising things. Nothing illegal, but disappointing nevertheless. *Churning* is a term that refers to an above-average flurry of transactions that generate brokers' fees. The level of fees can be particularly elevated for certain high-risk equity and real estate funds. I called the company up, noting the churning in my mother's account and wondering aloud how appropriate some of the higher risk funds had been for a person nearing eighty years old with little investment experience. *But James*, they said, *you of all people know how this business works*, as if somehow that made it okay.

Nowadays, whenever I speak on the topic of leadership in fancy lecture halls and corporate boardrooms, I often bring up my mom, and then the examples of women like Chary. Was my mom a great leader? What is a leader if not someone who gives other people space, and then allows them to *own* that space with intentional nudging when necessary? Leaders are conductors. They allow people to sing their song while also listening to see whether it enhances the broader chorus. Leaders create accountability not through fear, but by *inspiring* others to be their best selves. They don't hide behind acronyms and human resource departments. They know the difference between math and measurement. They wrestle with the disparity in compensation between them and their colleagues, knowing that some of it is entirely justified while also working in earnest to mitigate the problem of income and wealth inequality. Leadership is a story, a walk, a collective conversation where everyone takes part and no one is sidelined. And leaders know that their true value add, their true *alpha*, is judged not in quarters but in years, decades, even generations. Instead of seeking credit, leaders *get on with it*. They don't talk about it, they *do* it. Relentlessly, too. And in understanding all of this, leaders, great leaders, are *kind*.

And, finally, great leaders also know when it's okay to lose. My mom demonstrated this when she chose to accept death without fear. Little did I know that her decision was nothing more than a fractal of a decision she had made long ago.

Every year when I was growing up, my family attended an all-day picnic at a nearby state park with the families of their high school and college classmates who had also moved to the United States. We would all lug oversize food coolers to a communal barbecue pit, the sprawling late-day lunch always followed by a variety of field games.

One day, a dozen or so teams were lined up for a relay race. My mom somehow ended up running the anchor leg for our team. The whistle sounded, and everyone began running. When my mom received the baton, our team was in second place. But victory was guaranteed because the team out in front had a little boy running the last leg. As he advanced, the boy was buckling under the pressure of running a race he knew he could not win. So my mom slowed down, long enough to let him pull away and then ultimately win the race.

On the car ride home, I was angry. "Why did you have to ruin the race like that?" I demanded from the back seat.

She turned around. Her voice was firm. "James—*ya*—did you really want your grown mom to race ahead and beat that boy? Is *that* what you want me to do?"

Ya—a sharp word used by older Korean people to scold their juniors and put them in their place. "Kind of," I mumbled into the seat leather.

My mom wasn't implying that she or anyone *not* do their best. What she was saying was that she was better than "just" winning. My mom was focused on winning the long game. And she taught her son a valuable lesson that day, and on so many days—lessons that he ultimately put to work in assisting a group of really deserving women to show the world their full potential.

It was at my dad's wake when I came to realize that my mom understood—really *knew*—what I was doing at Ashley. *These women are me, huh?* Yes, mom. After that, she listened to every podcast and interview I did along the way. She told me that she would cry every time I mentioned her influence on me. She was proud of me for finally comprehending my dad's related piece of advice—that *you will never achieve real success unless others are truly happy for your success.*

Even now, I can still hear my parents recounting one of their favorite Korean fables. They would tell it to us when we were misbehaving. The fable is about a mother frog and her little frog son.

In the fable, the little frog never listened to the mom frog. Near the end of her life, knowing her son always did the opposite of what she asked, the mom frog told him that after she died, she wanted to be buried near the riverbank. In truth, she wanted to be buried high up in the mountains, as far away from the water as she could get. Little could she know that after she died, her son would resolve to change his ways. He honored her request by burying his beloved mom beside the riverbank, where her grave was washed away after a big storm.

And *that*, my parents concluded, is why you hear frogs croaking by the water's edge. They aren't celebrating. They're in mourning. The son is expressing remorse.

I've made a lot of mistakes in my life, but one thing is for sure: I said goodbye to my mom knowing full well she knew exactly how much she had influenced and inspired me to make the decisions I've made in my life, both at home and especially at work. Especially as it related to Ashley.

I couldn't stop sobbing at my mom's funeral, especially when the first notes of "Edelweiss" filled the church, which was filled with flowers, thanks to Ashley stores across the country that had pooled their money to invest in beautiful bouquets. One store manager, who has since passed away, later told me, *We died that day, too, James.* I arrived at the church to find my old friend, Carolyn, there, waiting for me. It was both a touching surprise, and yet another full circle moment. Carolyn had known me my whole life, and wouldn't *not* be there for my mom and me.

On the night before, at the wake, my mom lay in an open coffin, dressed in the *hanbok* she had selected during that last visit to her condo. Despite our mom's attempt to teach me and Jennifer how to do it, some guests kept whispering in my ear, "You didn't tie the knot right."

I remember leaning awkwardly over the coffin, tying and untying the *hanbok* bow, trying to get it just right. Then it was Jennifer's turn. Then mine again. Our eyes kept meeting. *I don't know how to do this and you don't either and it's just so sad we can't figure out how to do this one last thing for Mom.* Still, what matters more, *speaking* or *doing*? In the end, instead of chastising me, one of her friends simply stepped in and fixed it.

In my eulogy I spoke emotionally about choices, about agency. How it probably wasn't my mom's choice to follow my dad to America and leave her newborn son behind with her own mother. It certainly wasn't her choice to lose her dad to the brutality of the Korean War. Nor, as a new immigrant, did my mom choose to be barraged by one system after another, none of which was exactly designed to help her thrive or to facilitate her success. No one ever spelled out the implicit rules under which she found herself living. She endured misogyny, racism, and some of the worst cruelties of which all of us are capable. Many of her countless contributions to the world were not only measured incorrectly, but they were not measured *period*. Her twenty-five years as a stay-at-home mom, raising three children and managing the household so that my dad could start his business, will *never* show up in any calculation of GDP.

Still, throughout all that, she more than held her own. She didn't quit. She persevered quietly. My seven years at Ashley Stewart had helped those truths surface and crystallize in my mind and heart. Ultimately, it took some unlikely friends, who bore little physical likeness to my mom but resembled her nonetheless, to help me see my mom for *who* she was, and her life for *what* it was. I concluded my eulogy with a covenant that I would do my best to remind the world of what and where true examples of leadership can be found.

In the two weeks after my mom died, I made a few decisions. It was time for me to move on. There was to be no negotiation. The majority owners of Ashley Stewart could see it in my eyes. For years, I had advocated for my colleagues' agency, which, not surprisingly, had strengthened my *own* agency. Unless you first show kindness to yourself, it's impossible to show it to others. It was time to reinvest in the other two legs of *my* three-legged stool: my family and myself. Instead of owning Ashley Stewart without me as CEO, the majority owner exercised its agency and elected to begin a sales process.

Once, during one of my very first teaching town halls, a longtime employee, who had seen all the trials and tribulations in the two decades before my arrival, raised her hand and asked, "What will happen to the company if you aren't around to make decisions about money?" I told her I wasn't concerned about that. I would teach my colleagues more than they needed to know to operate the day-to-day business. I knew those lessons had taken root and taken flight.

Instead, I told her, I had another worry. *Who's going to take care of, and protect, the culture that we've built?* That was what concerned me—the loss of what was intangible. It was everyone's job to create positive externalities, I went on, to build up a healthy reserve of goodwill they could all draw upon in the future. When the intangible is there, you take it for granted. When it's gone, you notice. You feel it. Just like kindness itself.

After my mom's funeral, I asked Gina to cancel all the major appointments on my calendar. All except one, that is. I was determined to honor one engagement, at Macy's. The newly appointed CEO had asked me to address the entire company about transformation.

My heart was still broken on the day I arrived at the Macy's Herald Square store. I had spent most of that morning going through my mom's most prized possessions: restaurant matchbooks saved from meaningful dinners, a single sherry glass inscribed with her funny/sad American name Phyllis, and cooking bowls for serving curry rice and *soojaebee*, a Korean peasant dish I haven't eaten since I left home for college.

It was a full circle moment. Asked whether I could make tangible the *how of transformation*, I pulled out the private label Macy's credit card I'd found in my mom's wallet. It was dated the year before I was born, an era when a husband had to co-sign his wife's credit card application. My mom had come to this very same space, in a different time, to purchase items for my nursery and make a good home in America for her baby.

That same Macy's card from her wallet was used over the years to buy us clothing, I told the audience. The night before, I had opened one of my mom's dresser drawers to find stacks of impeccably folded cashmere sweaters from Charter Club, Macy's private label brand. These were my mom's quiet indulgences. This drawerful of cashmere sweaters bore testament to a first-generation immigrant woman from Korea making her way in America. Charter Club was accessible luxury for my mom, and those sweaters must have comforted her and reassured her that our family was going to make it. The essence of such stories *is* Macy's, I continued, not the physical buildings, website, and clothing racks, which are merely impermanent mechanisms of distribution.

As an aside, those cashmere sweaters now lie quietly inside my family's cedar closet. I can't stand to part with them, or with my mom's rice maker, or the portable broiler that she used to make sukiyaki. From a purely accounting standpoint, those items are fully depreciated and have zero economic value. What they give me, and how they make me feel, has nothing to do with money. And for that reason, those assets are among my most valued.

A Macy's employee raised her hand with one last question: "Where does your courage come from?" She wasn't just referring to Ashley Stewart, but in general. Why did I decide to teach high school after graduating from Harvard? Why did I graduate law school and then plunge into the highest levels of finance without knowing initially how to use Excel? Why, years later, did I decide to found my own impact investing platform when I did not quite understand what that even meant?

I think that my answer took her by surprise. "My connection with my mom," I said after a moment. "I always knew that I could come home, stretch out on the rug in our family room, share a slice of Entenmann's chocolate cake with her, and talk about anything I wanted. I knew my mom always had my best interests at heart. I knew that what I did in the world wasn't why she loved me. To be sure, she was always proud of me. But she loved me for *how* I did what I did. And she loved me most of all because I was her son. It was that simple."

I have all sorts of fancy degrees, connections, titles, and financial security. These are all of the things that my mom wanted so desperately for me. In one of the greatest examples of dramatic irony, it was my mom who gave me the most important form of security— her unconditional love. But it was *how* she loved me that mattered most. She didn't smother me. She allowed me the space to make my own choices and make mistakes. She gave feedback, tough feedback, but she always forgave me for my many shortcomings. *This* security, this gift of true agency, infused every asset on my personal T-account. And now it is gone.

Ashley had a successful sale. Not the oversize financial returns of three years earlier, but one that ensured continuity for the company. The new owners entreated me to stay and offered me various financial inducements if I would. I declined. Ashley Stewart was not the right place for me anymore. A clean break was best. I made sure that the remaining Misfits were taken care of economically while reminding them of their responsibility as leaders. After thanking them for their trust, I gave them the most important advice I could give. *You already know what is right. You already know what to do. You know what feels wrong, what you don't want to live with. So get to it.*

Then, no doubt inspired by my mom's farewell to the world, I left without any fanfare. There was no emotional goodbye party lasting deep into the night. No tearful hugs. It wouldn't have been good for the company, and I didn't need the ego boost. Of the many messages

I received, one that I treasure most is from the same manager who sadly passed away shortly after my mom did—*Thank you for believing in us when it was hard to believe in ourselves.* I felt the same way about their belief in me. I also knew that my leaving came nowhere close to a final farewell. My relationships with Gina, Chary, Shelley, and many other colleagues, like most authentic relationships, do not rely on any kind of legal or corporate entity. They transcend those things.

Those women and I are still good friends today. Some of them have left the company, some have stayed. Would it surprise you to know that many of them joined me and Charisse Jones, my journalist friend, as my guests when I was recognized with the Frederick Douglass Award, the New York Urban League's most prestigious award, almost two years to the day after my departure from Ashley Stewart? They joined Tamara and her sister, who still served as an executive at the Brooklyn YWCA, as well as Alan, the once-skeptical clothing vendor who had asked me for business advice, as we listened to my sister, Jennifer, describe my affinity for taking naps on large sectional sofas. Couch-James is a pretty mellow guy, Jennifer added with a laugh.

Following my last day, I had the luxury of making one of the most important investments a person can make. I gave myself six months to find my *present* again and connect it to the future I desired for my life. *The lemonade stand of James.* I went through the same process and applied it to myself all over again. I assessed assets and liabilities, commitments and contracts, and chose to prioritize those things that would maximize value, broadly defined, in the future. Anything and *anyone* else, I removed from my balance sheet. As part of that process, I *invested* time in my wife, my children, and my sister, whose husband suffered a near-fatal stroke during the summer after I left Ashley Stewart (he has since made a heroic recovery, and I am so proud of him).

I spent much of that time in nature, surrendering to the calming influence of the hidden laws and patterns governing our planet. I spent time with family fly-fishing in the mountains of North Carolina, and even tried surfing off the shores of the same barrier island where I had proposed to Meg and witnessed Jared's sad awakening about the rules of Monopoly. For the record, I am awful at both. My father-in-law tied my flies, and my children heckled me because I never managed to even get up on the surfboard. But that wasn't the point. Amid that seeming imbalance, I found my balance again.

I mentioned that after my dad's wake, and as strange as it probably sounded, I felt like a dragonfly that had metamorphosed. Reflecting on what we had accomplished at Ashley Stewart over those seven years, I now felt like I was soaring through the air. Sure, dragonflies are beautiful, and yes, their metamorphosis inspires thoughts of alchemy and magic. But, make no mistake, what makes the dragonfly one of nature's most agile and efficient insects is the neurological system powering its four wings and compound eyes. Dragonflies do not chase their prey; rather, they intuit where to fly, and they have the motor coordination and vision, not to mention the ability to fly in any one of six different directions, to achieve their goal. Together, these *integrated* attributes make the dragonfly quite the force to be reckoned with. In other words, they have *nunchi* and the skillset to back it up.

While watching the sun rise over the Atlantic Ocean, I had one final aha moment related to the red helicopter. It turns out that the movement of modern-day helicopters was *inspired* by the dragonfly. Yes, both can fly in six different directions. But perhaps more important, both can hover in midair. As any helicopter pilot will attest, hovering is the hardest maneuver. It turns out that thoughtfully "staying still" requires a complexity of coordinated motions. Balance requires motion, remember? Staying still means you are not staying still at all. Stated another way, balance requires agility. Flying a helicopter is, in the end, a really good metaphor for entrepreneurship, whether in the business of life, or the life of business. You might not fly as high or as fast, but you can land in difficult terrain, lift off without a runway, and change directions. You cannot carry too many passengers, which means that you have to help others fly, too. In that way, they discover their agency. Thoughtfully, and in balance.

After my self-imposed six-month hiatus, I slowly began to re-engage with the world. It would take an additional two years before I felt ready to put pen to paper in earnest and begin writing this book. It turns out that traditional Korean customs, many of which I am sadly unaware, mandate a three-year period to mourn your parents. Today, I know only that memories of my mom no longer create that tightness in my chest. Grief has become strength.

Since leaving Ashley Stewart, I've struggled watching what's been unfolding in the world, as so many of us have. It's hard not to draw analogies to how things felt in that depressing, windowless cafeteria so many autumns ago. Fear triggers the desire for control, especially in the face of chaos. So does loneliness, and self-centeredness. Sadly, today there are many forms of leadership, human or technological,

that are happy to comfort us with false promises of guaranteed outcomes. It's tempting to cede our agency to them, but before doing
that, I hope you will take a moment to pause, to hover. During inflection points and periods of change, the best solutions are almost
never found in "either/or" statements. They involve "and" statements, with few if any "buts." Instead of building dams, the best
solutions unleash flows.

And here's what they *don't* do: They don't cling to the proverbial old lunch warmers of the world, as comforting as those might
be. They don't rely on a sequence of zeroes and ones that, by definition, reflect data only from the past. Rather, they make space for
duality, for twos, while engaging with the unpredictable and the
random that always arise when new people and ideas converge.

I accepted only two invitations when my unofficial six-month
hiatus ended. Both felt symbolic—in their own way and, more important, together as a whole. The first was from Massachusetts
Institute of Technology. Would I be willing to spend some time at
MIT Sloan School of Management with future business leaders and
current global executives and help them fulfill the MIT credo of balancing *mens et manus* (mind and hand)? *Yes,* I said. Less than a
month later, I received a cryptic Zoom invitation in my inbox. It was
from Howard University, the very same historically Black university
(it's affectionately referred to as "The Mecca") where, if you recall,
the Korean students who sang "Arirang" for Alice Fletcher attended.

A half-dozen people, including Howard's president and a handful
of deans and senior administrators, were on the call. The president
was the first to speak. "James—please don't say no. What I'm about to

say is, I think, the best investment of your time and impact I can imagine." He hesitated. "Would you consider spending some of your time with us as the John H. Johnson Chair of Entrepreneurship here at Howard University?"

My breath froze for a few seconds. My eyes watered. I was so emotional, so stunned, that I forgot I was on camera. "Oh, my gosh," I said. "Really? Are you sure?" I didn't point to my face this time, but I definitely cocked my head to one side in disbelief. At Howard, I could focus exclusively on what I actually cared about all along. The *Product*, not the *product*.

They were sure. "Just think about it. We would really love to have you here."

I was speechless. Later, after accepting, I told one of the senior administrators on that Zoom call how shocked and honored I had been. "I didn't think anyone really saw what we did," I said.

"Oh, no," she said. "We saw what you did. We saw it in the faces of the women you served." She might as well have said, *We saw the how, not the what.*

Since then, spending time teaching at both Howard University and MIT has reignited my imagination in difficult-to-measure ways. Just the idea of those two institutions and communities working together collaboratively has been a catalyst for numerous projects and investments, and a source of motivation for me to finally complete this book. I've delivered lectures and worked with leaders across so many different industries, geographies, ethnicities, and age groups— all inspired by my knowing that unlikely convergence can create new possibilities. I've learned more from my students than I have taught them, and I hope that they will recognize their wisdom in the pages of this book.

Nor will I forget the day I flew to Washington, DC, and first made my way to the Howard campus. It was late summer, and I was among the new faculty members gathered for a makeshift orientation session and tour. "Welcome," a female voice called out. Standing, the woman introduced herself, adding, "Who are you?"

"I'm James," and we shook hands.

"So James, what brings you to Howard?"

I stuffed my hands back in my pockets before replying. "Um— well, how much *time* do you have? Because it's sort of a long story." I laughed. And the two of us started walking, side by side, across campus under the warmth of a late summer sun.

Autumn was coming.

Coda

Ten days after submitting the first draft of the manuscript of this book, I boarded a flight to Seoul. It was my first time visiting Korea since losing both my parents. I wasn't sure what to expect or what emotions might overcome me. I was grateful to have Meg and our three children beside me for those two weeks. In addition to the moral support they gave me, their unfamiliarity with the language, country, and our extended family in Korea allowed me to focus on them and stay present, rather than drowning in memories of what was or could have been.

The timing of the trip was, in the end, uncanny. It almost felt preordained. It was as if the entirety of this book played out in slow motion before me. Let me explain. As I was airborne, a major bank collapsed. What happened? Well, the executive team failed to balance their T-account. They owned long-term assets financed with short-term liabilities. As trust dissipated and nervous depositors withdrew their money, Silicon Valley Bank, an iconic symbol of tech innovation and disruption, had no choice but to liquidate long-term assets in a fire sale to raise cash. Remember: Your income statement can be rendered meaningless if your balance sheet is broken. I couldn't help thinking that the simple rules of the lemonade stand could have helped prevent the third-largest bank failure in US history.

Four days later, the release of ChatGPT-4 sent a separate but related set of shock waves across the world. Sadly, we all could have predicted the frenzied and extreme reaction it triggered. Will artificial intelligence solve all of the world's problems? Will it lead to humanity's extinction? From my vantage point, the fundamental question it poses centers around a topic we explored throughout this book. Namely, the question of *agency*. To what extent should technology be used to enhance, augment, or supplant human decision-making? With its reliance on binary inputs populated from the past, will AI strip from agency those things that make us most human—chance, error, randomness, and emotion? As simple as it may sound, maybe the answers lie somewhere in our intuitive understanding of the meaning of kindness.

Between the bank failure and the release of ChatGPT-4, I delivered remarks to a roomful of business and civic leaders at an art studio in Insadong, a historic neighborhood in Seoul. A few of my parents' old classmates were also in attendance. My host for the evening was Yvonne, my honorary *nuna*, a communications strategy executive who had organized the event without asking for anything in return. That night we talked about many of the themes, concerns, and reasons for hope that I've written about in this book, and discussed their application to the very real conundrums facing Korea today. Despite its unprecedented financial success and technological prowess, Korea is suffering from declining birth rates and an alarming uptick in suicide and mental health issues among younger people. It's hardly alone.

None of us had all the answers. But we all agreed that agency was something to be prized and cherished. And that we owed it to future generations to at least try to address an educational system, and a collective balance sheet, that was failing them in so many different ways.

I concluded my remarks by asking the audience for permission to sing the song "Moon River." It was a song beloved by my parents, and many members of their generation. My dad used to sing it around our house, and I could easily picture him singing it to my mom when they were first dating, dreaming of the possibilities that lay ahead. With the help of some old photos and a borrowed guitar, that night we all bent space and time, together. The art studio, it turns out, was less than half a mile from where my parents had gone to high school. In the same way my dad had been at Boston Children's Hospital to make sure my daughter was okay, my mom and dad were there with me that night. Not in a sad way, but in a full circle way. I took delight in the randomness of it all. Here I was, the proud son of Youchan and Hwa Ja Rhee, survivors of the Korean War and caregivers to so many, sitting in the exact place of his parents' youth after the passage of nearly seventy years.

I closed my eyes and smiled as I sang about two drifters, off to see the world. And I felt that warm, good ache spreading deeply inside my chest.

Please come find me at www.redhelicopter.com. You will discover additional ways in which to explore and immerse yourself in the journey that is this book. I look forward to hearing *your* red helicopter story. Maybe we can share it with the world, together.

James Rhee, April 2, 2024

acknowledgments

After I announced my departure from Ashley Stewart, a store manager in Chicago posted a message on social media: *James, you have taught us, believed in us, motivated us, and inspired us, we are going to use everything that you have shown us and be a reflection of who you were to us . . . again we love you.*

I didn't know how to respond. Many years have passed since then. I would now like to use these same words to express my gratitude to her and all my former colleagues, especially the women in the stores. You believed in me when few others did, including myself. For seven years, I worked hard to be a better version of me. This book, I hope, will forever bear testament to the connectedness, the *jeong*, we created together. Whether I am inside a classroom or a boardroom, I often replay in my mind the conversations and moments we shared. I can never repay you for the outpouring of support you showed me and my family when my dad and then my mom passed away. Ride or die. Together, we rode.

Over the course of a lifetime, we share space and time with so many people, most of whom never become more than casual acquaintances or briefly glimpsed faces, but are heroes nonetheless. The airport employee who found a wheelchair for my mom, the Bronx grandmother who taught my parents a lesson about their new country, and the dad who gifted me a toy red helicopter with such grace are just three of the many individuals who helped shape my life. The narrative in this book is full of everyday heroes. They picked me up when I was down, and inspired me to do better on the many occasions when I fell short. In this context, as I reflect, I am struck by the wisdom of my mom's insistence on serving refreshments to anyone who showed up on the front steps of our childhood home.

Childhood is where this story begins. I am grateful to the teachers and administrators of Three Village School District on Long Island, New York. The classrooms and playgrounds of Minnesauke Elementary School, Mount Elementary School, Gelinas Junior High School, and Ward Melville High School provided the foundation for the agency I developed and shared during my adult years. Today, it's a privilege to pass along your lessons to many. Thank you to all of my neighbors—your real estate tax dollars funded a high-quality public school education. I recently learned that Mrs. Griffith, my beloved kindergarten teacher, passed away. I am sorry that she never got to read this book.

The arc of this narrative encompasses several continents and four generations. By necessity, it could only include a finite number of named and unnamed people courageous enough to exercise agency, bend systems, and make a difference. To the many individuals and organizations who have positively impacted my life, please know how grateful I am. Thank you for all of your very real contributions to this parable of our times.

During my conversation with Brené Brown on her *Dare to Lead* podcast, I told listeners that my first few attempts to write this book resulted in abject failure. Though I had been forewarned, I found out the hard way how isolating it is to write a book. It requires imposing a relentless physical, emotional, and intellectual rigor on otherwise random memories and creative sparks. For this reason, and many others, this book almost remained locked up inside my head, a song without a name. But several catalysts ultimately motivated me to push through.

First was the outpouring and encouragement I received from the TED community and Brené's devotees, as well as from fellow CEOs and my students. They convinced me I had to write this book.

Second, I had the support of an exceptional group of experienced thinkers, doers, and artists. Judith Curr is a legend in the publishing industry. I felt her steady presence, support, and intuitive alchemy throughout this process. Gabriella Page-Fort effortlessly played the role of editor, critic, bandmate, and ultimately and crucially, supportive friend. Neither Judith nor Gabi flinched when this first-time author casually remarked that the proposed book wouldn't fit inside a prescribed category or box. They listened intently and politely as I mused about drawing inspiration from Leonard Bernstein, Edward Elgar, and Bruce Springsteen, and writing a fugue in the key of E-flat major. Judith and Gabi, thank you for giving me the *space* to create freely. In return, I made doubly sure to get this book in on *time*!

From editorial to design to publicity to sales and marketing, the HarperOne team has been exceptional. At the risk of leaving out a name or two, sincere thanks go to Laina Adler, Ryan Amato, Louise Braverman, Stephen Brayda, Yvonne Chan, Jessie Dolch, Ann Edwards, Janet Evans-Scanlon, Daphney Guillaume, Julia Kent, Crissie Johnson Molina, Madison Oxx, Janice Suguitan, and Shannon Welch.

The team at Fortier Public Relations understood this book immediately, and I am grateful for the contributions of Mark Fortier, Ashtin Ballard, and Mckayla Yoo.

I met the illustrator of this book, Heyon Cho, through Yvonne Park, my host at the event in Insadong. Heyon was effortlessly able to capture my words and emotions in brushstrokes that evoked feelings of tradition and modernity. My thought-partner, Peter Smith, was quick to edit, critique, and improve upon my writing. He was also so remarkably steadfast in encouraging me to write the book that I wanted to, no matter what anyone said. Thank you to Rachel Chou for introducing me to my agent, Jim Levine, who heard the song even on the basis of some squiggly lines, pencil scribblings, a lemonade stand case study, and assorted musical notes. I never would have even submitted a book proposal if Jim hadn't grabbed me by the ear and taken the initiative to stroke the computer keyboard with his own fingers. Before that, Jeremy Zimmer and Hilary Beard were among the first to encourage me to write a book of some shape or form, and I'm grateful for their early support.

Third, my extended family provided me with unconditional love (sometimes of the tougher variety) and support. Thank you Jennifer, Lanty, Abby, and Sarah S. for providing feedback on early drafts. Will and Sarah P.—we raised our children together, and I'm grateful to you both for everything. Meg, you married a red helicopter boy drowning in school debt and trying on different suits of armor. Thank you, as always, for seeing me for me and loving me despite my shortcomings. To our children, you now know for sure there are more than just the five of us (though I have to say that when it's just the five of us in our family room, it's sort of awesome). Your past is filled with people who love you. Let that be the fuel that helps propel you into the future. George, you sure do bark a lot, but you were steadfast in your companionship as I grappled with this book.

Mom and Dad, *saranghaeyo*. I love you. This book is for you. More than anything, it was my desire to tell your story that got me through this whole process. Turns out I was observing and listening the whole time, even when you didn't think I was! On behalf of all the lives you touched and saved, thank you for your tireless service to those in need of care. What I wouldn't give to hear you sing "You Light Up My Life" one more time in our tiny family room on Hansom Lane. One day we will be reunited, but in the meantime, I've got some work to do.

about the author

James Rhee is a former high school teacher and Harvard Law School graduate who became a private equity investor and unexpectedly an acclaimed CEO. He bridges math with emotions by marrying capital with purpose, while composing systems that bridge peoples, disciplines, and ideas. His transformational leadership has been recognized by leading civic and business organizations. In addition to his private sector activities, James teaches at Howard University (where he was appointed the John H. Johnson Chair of Entrepreneurship), the MIT Sloan School of Management, and Duke University School of Law. His TED Talk and *Dare to Lead* interview with Brené Brown have captured the imagination of millions. He lives outside of Boston, Massachusetts.

Learn with us, lift off, and fly:
redhelicopter.com